An excellent, honest, true documentary of the Force between 1966 and 1999. Informative, factual, gut-wrenching, humorous and sometimes sad, these stories run the gamut from everyday mundane duties to the extreme duties and adventures that the general public is not even aware that members of the Force perform.

—*S/Sgt. Thomas William Dunlop (Retired)*

FROM "DEPOT" TO DETACHMENT

FACES OF THE FORCE

BY HELEN METELLA & PAMELA COWAN

TRUE STORIES OF
C-1966/67 TROOP

ROYAL CANADIAN MOUNTED POLICE

Cataloguing data available from Library and Archives Canada.
ISBN: 978-1-988783-52-9

All photos © C-1966/67 Troop
Badge photos: Janet Volman
Editor: Brian Mlazgar
Proofreader: Donna Grant
Designer: Heather Nickel
Made possible through Creative Saskatchewan's Book Publishing Production Grant Program.

Printed and bound in Canada.
September 2020

YOUR NICKEL'S WORTH PUBLISHING

Regina, SK.

It would be easy to dedicate this book to our fallen comrades, our wives, RCMP veterans, or to currently serving RCMP members, but the reality is that this book should be dedicated to all law enforcement officers, first responders, and members of the military who work tirelessly to make our country and our world a safer place.

—C-1966/67 Troop
September 2020

CONTENTS

In Memoriam

Afterword

FOREWORD

It was November 1966. Canada was preparing for the 100th Anniversary of Confederation, just two months away. For 32 young men from across this great country who were graduating from "Depot" as members of C-1966/67 Troop it was the beginning of a new life. This event set into motion the destinies of these newly minted Mounties in ways none of them could

Senator Bev Busson

ever imagine. Some would serve their entire working lives in the Royal Canadian Mounted Police (RCMP). Others would leave very early and go on to make their mark in other ways. All of them would be forever changed by the experience of being sworn in as members of, arguably, the best and certainly the most famous police force in the world.

The iconic red uniform is known across the planet as a symbol, not only of Canada, but of courage and integrity. Throughout history and almost without exception, those choosing to join "The

Force" make a difficult decision. In almost every case, they know they will be transferred far away from home, and separated from any support system they had. Few know, however, the extent to which their lives will change, and how different their view of humanity and their place in it will be. The training to become a member of this illustrious police force is tough. Courage and integrity are non-negotiable qualities of these RCMP recruits, but few understand the level of self-sacrifice and bravery that will be required of each of them.

This was true for C Troop. This amazing book, describing their "innocence lost," is compiled from the heartfelt and self-searching memories of the members of C-1966/67 Troop. It offers a seldom seen insight into the real lives and the real memories of what these young men went through in their efforts to make a difference. We are fortunate to be afforded the privilege of hearing not only about their experiences, but about the agony and the ecstasy behind these memories. Their gritty stories, told in real life language and with brutal frankness, are sometimes hard to read but always gripping. It is important to remember that these members of C Troop, to a man, have offered their stories, not for profit, but instead to donate to the legacy of the next generations of Mounties through the Mounted Police Heritage Centre. Even more important, their legacy is magnified by shining a light on the day-to-day dangers that often go unnoticed in all segments of law enforcement. Many still bear the scars of what they have had to deal with in carrying out their duties. We owe a debt of gratitude to these unsung heroes. Fifty-plus years later, the endowment of C Troop continues, and stands as a chronicle not only to their successes and their struggles, but also to the dedication and gallantry that distinguishes the members of the Royal Canadian Mounted Police today.

To the members of C-1966/67 Troop, thank you for sharing your experiences and your memories. You make me very proud.

—Senator Bev Busson, Commissioner,
Royal Canadian Mounted Police (Retired)

THIS BOOK HAS it all, from international intrigue to courageous acts of heroism in rural Canada. It's an engaging compilation of stories detailing authentic events, as told by members of one RCMP troop, C-1966/67.

W.L. (Les) Holmes

Each chapter is unique and as diverse as the member featured. The stories evoke a range of emotions—chuckles for sure, awe, empathy, and enough personal tragedy to bring a tear to my eye.

There are many books on the careers of individual members and on interesting criminal cases, but this is a true treasure. It contains the life stories of an entire RCMP troop, including their accomplishments after policing.

I had the honour and pleasure of working with several members of this troop. I was aware of certain horrific dangers during Jerry Forst's career, but it was only on reading this manuscript that I realized the sheer magnitude of those events.

I am most impressed with the extensive research that was involved. It is no small task to locate all troop members after 50 years. The "In Memoriam" section is a brilliant way of including the entire troop. Congratulations, C-1966/67 Troop, for a job well done. I salute you all.

—W.L. (Les) Holmes, Assistant Commissioner,
Royal Canadian Mounted Police (Retired)

ACKNOWLEDGMENTS

As WITH MOST police work, this book was the collaborative effort of many contributors and supporters. It was begun after the 50-year reunion of C-1966/67 Troop (hereafter C Troop), in 2016. Like our 30-year reunion, the fiftieth took place in Regina at the Royal Canadian Mounted Police (hereafter RCMP) Training Academy, "Depot" Division. The reunion inspired Pamela Cowan of the *Regina Leader-Post* to write an article about our troop for her newspaper, entitled "Life after 'Depot.'" The piece featured a brief overview of several troop members and was accompanied by a short video. Members of the public and then-serving cadets at "Depot" liked it, and encouraged us to produce a more comprehensive collection of stories.

We compiled these from several sources: at our 30-year reunion, each member had contributed a small piece on where and why he had joined the RCMP and recorded some outstanding memories. Among other things, that gave us first-hand recollections from our troop mates Ernie Otway and John Seniuk, who passed away after the 30-year reunion. We are so grateful their voices are preserved.

Each member then jotted down details of his own story and was later interviewed by a professional writer. Although many of us were forced to write profusely in our careers, it was almost always a "stick to the facts" effort. Now, we were confronted by writing about how our careers affected us. We appreciate the writers' ability to bring out the best and most interesting parts of our stories.

We would like to make special acknowledgment of our profound respect for two of our key training instructors, Tony Antoniuk and Doug Farentholtz.

Tony inherited us as his first training troop, cared deeply about us, and tried his best to prepare us for the real-life adventures of being an RCMP officer. It was not an easy job to bring 32 civilians from across Canada and weave them into a cohesive group who would honour the traditions of the RCMP and have each member's back. We needed to act as one if required, but also to cultivate our individual strengths. That was his task and challenge. We also knew that if we reflected positively on him, he would be promoted from a Constable to a Corporal; he was promoted.

Doug was our Physical Training (PT) instructor and was responsible for making civilians with a questionable level of fitness into police officers able to handle physical confrontations with success. Boxing used to be a standard training tool but was no longer deemed adequate, so Doug worked with us and developed a system of isometric exercises that has evolved into the Physical Abilities Requirement (PARE) Program now employed by many police and fire units.

All of our training instructors and field personnel had a hand in elevating our abilities and confidence. They taught us how to contain a field operation, such as a domestic dispute or the scene of a crime, and also how to be prepared to impart our observations, investigations and evidence collection in a legally acceptable manner in a court of law. We thank them for having successfully developed these skills in us all.

We would also like to pay tribute to each member who contributed to this book and to those very few who, for personal reasons, declined to participate. We would have loved their contributions but we respect their decisions. We also express special gratitude to the family members of our deceased troop mates who added their memories. We recognize it could not have been easy and may have evoked some sadness, but we hope this book will act as a tribute to their family member's service and dedication to the RCMP and the citizens of Canada.

We also want to acknowledge the largely unrecognized role of our wives throughout our active service and during our post-service struggles. Since cell phones were non-existent for most of our service, and radio communications were sketchy, our wives were frequently left in the dark worrying, especially when extended shifts in remote areas were common. They also contributed their time and effort to this book by reading and critiquing our individual stories, contributing their own portions, and supporting us throughout. We also recognize the sacrifices of our children. We are fathers who missed school concerts and meet-the-teacher nights, sports games and dance classes because we were working. Christmas and other holidays were frequently disrupted by shift work. In small communities, our children were often the victims of bullying as the offspring of the town cop. Things were not always easy for them.

We owe a huge debt of gratitude to the RCMP Heritage Centre, especially Al Nicholson, its former CEO; Dan Topping, the

Executive Director; and Chari Jackson, the Manager of Human Resources and Finance, all of whom supported and pushed forward our idea for this book. We thank our publisher, Heather Nickel, of Your Nickel's Worth Publishing, who saw the potential and provided encouragement and ideas. Thank you to our two professional writers, Pamela Cowan and Helen Metella, and to our editor, Brian Mlazgar, who ably wove these stories into a cohesive whole.

The members of C Troop would also like to thank Janet Volman of Edmonton for her help in preparing troop badges and photographs for both our 50-year reunion and for this book. Without her help this would not have been possible. Janet goes out of her way to help others and spends many hours volunteering her time with Special Olympics.

Most importantly, we must acknowledge one of our own troop mates, without whom our grandchildren would have only one tale to remember. Jerry Forst was the prime motivator behind this book. He worked tirelessly to make contact with all the members and did all the arm-twisting to persuade them to contribute their experiences. His enthusiasm was overwhelming and contagious. His helpers, Derk Doornbos, Jack Snoeks and Ross Mortlock, did the best they could to help him as he strove to produce a book that demonstrates that the humanity of police officers is reflected in their fallibility as well as in the care they provide their communities.

—*C Troop*

NINE PRINCIPLES OF POLICING

IF THIS BOOK has a mission other than putting memories to paper, it would probably be an explanation of why we were the individuals we were. In doing so, we end up trying to explain our choice of being police officers rather than any other "trade." Instead of trying to enunciate the principles we chose to adopt into our lives, we share the following quote from an authority on the subject. Robert Peel (1788–1850) was the prime minister of the United Kingdom (1834–1835). He is credited with establishing the London Metropolitan Police Force and is known as the "Father of Modern Policing." His principles for policing follow:

1. The basic mission for which the police exist is to prevent crime and disorder.
2. The ability of the police to perform their duties is dependent upon public approval of police actions.
3. Police must secure the willing cooperation of the public in voluntary observance of the law to be able to secure and maintain the respect of the public.

4. The degree of cooperation of the public that can be secured diminishes proportionately to the necessity of the use of physical force.

5. Police seek and preserve public favour not by catering to the public opinion but by constantly demonstrating absolute impartial service to the law.

6. Police use physical force to the extent necessary to secure observance of the law or to restore order only when the exercise of persuasion, advice and warning is found to be insufficient.

7. Police, at all times, should maintain a relationship with the public that gives reality to the historic tradition that the police are the public and the public are the police; the police being only members of the public who are paid to give full-time attention to duties which are incumbent on every citizen in the interests of community welfare and existence.

8. Police should always direct their action strictly towards their functions and never appear to usurp the powers of the judiciary.

9. The test of police efficiency is the absence of crime and disorder, not the visible evidence of police action in dealing with it.*

It is our wish that our service be seen in this light. The exercise of humanity by police officers is often overlooked in the sensationalism of media interpretation of an event. The picture of an officer with gun in hand often finds more of an audience than an officer carrying a child to safety. Yet much of our work was protection rather than adversarial intervention. Hopefully, the lives depicted in the individual scenarios throughout this book help explain why we stand proudly after all these years.

—C Troop

* Ottawa Police Service. "Sir Robert Peel's Principles of Law Enforcement 1829." https://www.ottawapolice.ca/en/about-us/Peel-s-Principles-.aspx. Accessed August 6, 2020.

Introduction

ONE ROOKIE LITERALLY dodged a bullet that deflected at the last millisecond. It was his first week as a working RCMP constable. His training classmates didn't hear of his near death and his partner's severe injury until 30 years later, at their reunion in May 1996. The story startled the members of C Troop, as many had received no news of each other since graduation. Like many young adults, they had felt bulletproof. "I honestly do not recall ever thinking that I could die on the job," says Derk Doornbos. "I was simply enjoying observing the human condition."

Yet anything could have happened in 30 years, so there must have been some underlying sense of relief that none of their original troop had perished in the line of duty. After all, the reunion of C Troop, which first convened at RCMP Training Academy, "Depot" Division, in Regina on June 10, 1966, reintroduced members to people they cared about deeply, guys they had bonded with as very young men during more than five months of instruction. Together they had shared—and kept washed and waxed and shined—a 32-man dorm; shovelled manure from the stables at 6:00 a.m.; struggled into lace-up boots and breeches for twice-daily drill marches; exercised themselves into peak physical condition; obeyed profanity-infused orders from superiors; and struggled to stay awake during afternoon classes in report writing, first aid and the Criminal Code, among scores of other topics. "Long days and short sleeps took their toll, especially if the class was dull," says C Troop member Ross Mortlock. "Many times, a guy would fall asleep sitting up and, if caught, was sent to the corner to stand on his head for 10 minutes to get the blood moving again. It worked."

During their first reunion, they swapped stories about all of that, and of the police work they'd been dispersed to do since their graduation ceremony (Passout) in November 1966. Many of the tales reflected their own experiences. Others were completely surprising to them, especially if they'd worked only in one type of federal policing unit.

The array of possible locations the RCMP could have assigned them to across Canada included rural or northern detachments, and municipal policing units. Even in rural areas, there was astonishing variety, with some members working three- or four-man detachments with plenty of highway patrol work, while others might have found themselves at a two-man fly-in territorial post, enforcing the *Migratory Birds Convention Act* and registering births.

In the major cities, there was a similarly wide array of possible units, from the Drug Squad to Commercial Crime, Immigration to Intelligence. Some members had gone almost immediately into plainclothes duties and never worked in uniform again, while others were uniformed policemen their entire careers. Yet there was a common thread to the conversations. "We'd all made it through," says troop member Jerry Forst.

Unfortunately, two of their original group of 32 were gone by the first reunion in 1996. One died in a car accident and the other of cancer. But even those who had resigned from the Force long before retirement age, perhaps because of post-traumatic stress disorder (PTSD), had survived their RCMP experience.

They had top-tier coaching, but the timing of their service meant this group was fated to weather rapid and tumultuous change in the RCMP. Fifty-some years ago, a working RCMP officer's tools of the trade didn't include personal radios, computers or cell phones. DNA testing was decades in the future. Nor were members assured a partner in a patrol car. Working alone and without backup was often the norm in small rural detachments, and solo night patrols were also common in cities. Overtime was a foreign concept. You worked a minimum eight-hour day, often on a seven-day rotation, and if you were called back in for a demonstration, prison riot or murder, well, you went back in. If you were out of town, you left a number where you could be reached.

As well, there was very little time to get acclimatized to the job. Before heading to Regina for training, new recruits were already sworn-in police force members. After Passout, they were assigned to their first detachment as rookies for approximately six months, but they invariably encountered the difficult work of full-fledged members. For several, attending the scene of a mass murder or gathering up the body of a child at a motor vehicle accident was on-the-job learning that happened too soon.

As for love and marriage, well, that was literally a tale from a different century. The RCMP needed to staff police detachments in the far reaches of one of the world's geographically largest countries, and usually at short notice. "The easiest way was not to hire married men and to deny single members the right to marry for a period of three years after signing up," says Mortlock. "As a further restriction, a member had to request permission to marry, which also implied and ensured that he was financially stable, and his intended could pass a security screening as to her background."*

Meanwhile, if permission was granted and a young RCMP member married, his wife quite often became an unpaid extra member of the Force, answering phones at the very least, helping keep a small detachment running smoothly in many cases, and usually contributing daily as her husband's partner and as a visible role model in the community. Some members of the Force quit rather than have the progression of their personal lives dictated in these ways. Others saw their marriages crack and break from the strain of frequent, sudden moves to new homes. Remarkably, most of C Troop's members have had the same spouse for 50 years or more.

Updates to archaic policies are not the only changes that C Troop witnessed. In 1966, the RCMP was still very much a product of its history. It was formed in 1873 as the North-West Mounted Police, a quasi-military force of the federal government, established to keep peace in the wilds of the North-West Territories and modelled on the Royal Irish Constabulary. It became the Royal Northwest Mounted Police in 1904 and the Royal Canadian Mounted Police in 1920.

Despite the name changes, many aspects of national policing

---

*   Since its inception, RCMP regulations had stipulated that junior police officers were prohibited from marrying for their first five years of service, and after that, permission to marry required approval from a commanding officer, along with proof of a sufficient sum of money in a savings account to support a wife. Shortly after C Troop began serving, the waiting time was reduced to two years. Following the hiring of women in 1974, the RCMP abolished this policy and also allowed married men to join the police force.

had not altered much in the less than 100 years since the Force's inception. Yet hundreds, perhaps thousands, of working parts of the law enforcement profession were about to be overhauled or outright replaced during the decades when C Troop would serve—dramatically so. For starters, horsemanship was off the table. It had been a mandatory part of training when horses were a primary method of transportation, and even after vehicles were invented riding and grooming horses was considered a way to instil discipline in trainees. But in 1966, just a few weeks before C Troop was assembled, learning to ride a horse was deleted from the curriculum. The elimination of those classes meant that C Troop would no longer graduate in 1967, but rather in late 1966.

When C Troop arrived at "Depot" in 1966, there was little diversity among the ranks of the RCMP. The Force had only a handful of Indigenous members at the time, and no women. The RCMP's first female troop would not be formed until nearly a decade later. They graduated in March 1975. And it would take another 15 years, in response to a challenge from Sikh recruit Baltej Singh Dhillon, for the RCMP to allow observant Sikhs to wear beards and turbans.

For the members of C Troop, those were changes on their watch that took far too long. "We really needed women and people of all nationalities because how else can you police a multinational culture?" says Forst. "It really disadvantaged us to not have them."

The new trainees of C Troop ranged in age from 19 to 29. They hailed from all regions of Canada—from Vancouver, Toronto, and hamlets in Newfoundland and Nova Scotia, from Prairie farms, and the towns and suburbs of Quebec and Ontario. They were serious about launching careers and focused on a momentous task: they were going to uphold the laws of this country.

Some had institutional experience as teenage Army or Navy reservists, but their life experience was mostly limited. Few knew about domestic disputes, let alone the domestic violence incidents for which they would soon be the referees. As some discovered, and tragically far too early in their careers, dealing with horrific violence and its aftermath was also their difficult responsibility.

Preparation for the myriad tasks they would face was, to be charitable, a little primitive. To decide who knew how to swim adequately and who would need lessons, the young men were lined up on the side of the pool and ordered to simply "jump in," prodded by instructors' poles as they kept themselves from drowning. If you'd arrived at "Depot" with extra weight, you were assigned to the "Fat Boys Club." As Mortlock vividly recalls, they "had to do their routines—push-ups, running, chin-ups, running, weights, running, police holds, running, sit-ups, running, choke holds, running, squat thrusts, deep knee bends, and running—in green plastic garbage bags—until they reached the desired goal. C Troop adopted the timeless RCMP training slogan: 'There is the right way, the wrong way, and the RCMP way.' You can guess which prevailed!"

Firearms training was on six-chamber Smith and Wesson revolvers. Using a rifle or shotgun, which many full-fledged officers would soon encounter on the job, was somehow mastered later. C Troop members also say they were toughened up by being sent into confined areas with tear gas grenades tossed in after them. The first person to escape had to do push-ups.

However oddly, the RCMP training delivered some fundamental policing skills. It expertly served up two essential qualities that C Troop members would call upon throughout their careers: compassion and loyalty.

"That was the whole point of training, apart from providing skill enhancement," says Mortlock. "You would never let down a troop mate. You had his back under all circumstances. If he screwed up, you took the blame also, and the punishment as a troop was willingly accepted and you helped each other: no grudges, no hard feelings, because next time it might be you and he would be there for you."

Nor was it a stretch, at least at the outset, to transfer that compassion and loyalty for their troop mates to the public that they were about to serve, despite its challenging, often perplexing, and even infuriating character.

Possibly some of those qualities also took root while C Troop lived in a building that, at the time, was shared with the RCMP Police Museum. During their off hours, the young members could wander through the historical exhibits, absorbing information about the hardship and sacrifice that their predecessors had transcended while enforcing the law in a young country.

Certainly the rigours that awaited C Troop in the decades beyond 1966 produced some weariness and even cynicism. Not all its members continued policing throughout their working lives. But most hold such pride in, and respect for, the RCMP and what it represents that they decided to promote the RCMP's history by donating all proceeds from this book to the Mounted Police Heritage Centre that replaced the old museum.

To discover what caused that admiration in the individual members of C Troop, read on.

—*Helen Metella*

THE INSTRUCTORS

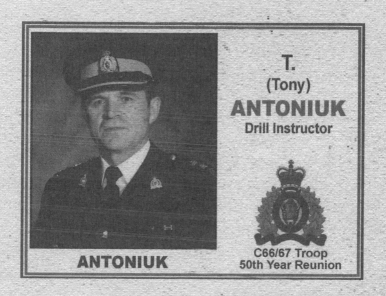

T.
(Tony)
ANTONIUK
Drill Instructor

C66/67 Troop
50th Year Reunion

ANTONIUK

IT WAS THE summer of 1966—the year the Beach Boys released their rock n' roll hit "Good Vibrations" and "mod" dress was in. Miniskirts were in vogue for women, while men sported low-slung, wide-belted, skinny, fitted pants, flashy printed ties on floral shirts—and long hair. In June of that year, 32 fresh-faced young men from across Canada travelled to "Depot" Division in Regina, where they would transition into adulthood and join the thousands who had gone before them in the RCMP and become Mounties. Some were eager to fulfil a lifelong dream of joining the RCMP, others were looking for a regular paycheque and a stable career. No matter their motivation, the 32 strangers bonded like brothers as they encouraged each other over almost six months of gruelling training that tested them physically and emotionally. To this day, C Troop credits Constable Tony Antoniuk for his part in developing them and the esprit de corps that exists among their members.

Ten years after joining the RCMP, Antoniuk was transferred to "Depot" as an instructor. At 31, he was just a few years older than the oldest members of C Troop. C Troop was Antoniuk's first group of recruits to instruct in drill and small arms—the use of revolvers and rifles. "I was responsible for them from Day One until the day they graduated," Antoniuk says.

During training, there were more than a few challenges. No matter how hard they tried, some recruits couldn't co-ordinate their arms and legs during the complexities of marching in drill. "The problem with some people, when they're trying to march, is they don't let their arms go," Antoniuk says. "If you relax, the arms will go up automatically. When you're tense, you have a tendency at times to move your right arm with your right leg. When you're marching, you're under pressure."

He was also under pressure. "How do you explain the intricacies of drill and firearms to two Quebec recruits who can't speak a word of English? I'm sure they had a difficult time, but they all succeeded," Antoniuk says. "This is where the troop helped them."

The purpose of drill was to teach the recruits to work as a cohesive unit. "We impressed upon the troop that they were only as good as the weakest link," Antoniuk says. "We expected them to work together and support each other. They had to be in a position where, at any time, they knew their fellow policemen were there to protect them and watch their backs."

The rigours of drill taught the recruits self-discipline, how to react to commands, and to think on their feet. "When you react to a given situation, you don't think of yourself," Antoniuk says. "You think, 'How can I help?'" Drill also instilled the importance of deportment—how trainees presented themselves, in and out of uniform. When recruits were out and about in Regina, they were expected to set an example by being neatly dressed at all times. "They were not permitted in those days to wear blue jeans," Antoniuk says. "They wore dress pants, and they were identified by their haircuts." No matter how long a recruit's hair was when he arrived at "Depot," it didn't take long before he shared the troop's cookie-cutter

C Troop in drill hall under the direction of Drill Instructor Constable Antoniuk, "Depot" Division, 1966.

haircut—shaved to the scalp. "Some of the barbers that we had would pride themselves on having a recruit in and out of the chair in two minutes," Antoniuk says, chuckling.

Training taught recruits to conform to strict standards of dress and behaviour, but also the importance of putting personal feelings aside in the face of tragedy. "They couldn't allow themselves to be overcome by emotion," Antoniuk says. "It's not that you're callous; you have feelings. But in a given situation, when there are people around and you show some emotion, you're not taking charge of the situation. The people around you expect that you, as a policeman, have been trained to know what to do and how to do it."

When Antoniuk took on training C Troop, he was sweating bullets to produce the best troop he could. "I knew that I was being assessed by the Training Officer and the Sergeant Major to ensure that my ability to act as a drill instructor was what was required." Antoniuk admits it was a heavy mantle, but says, "I was given a duty to perform and I was going to carry it out."

Many instructors yelled obscenities at recruits and shamed them. That wasn't Antoniuk's style. "Drill is self-discipline," he says. "We don't want to discipline the members. We want them to discipline themselves, and if they can do that, then there's no need for formal discipline."

To prepare the troop, Antoniuk went above and beyond the call of duty and he expected the same dedication from his men. Leading up to their graduation day, he asked the troop to "volunteer" for extra hours of practice—beyond the 80 periods of foot drill. "They volunteered, but they also knew that I expected them to come out," Antoniuk says. "Because it was my first troop, I went back to 'Depot' at night and I had the troop out doing drill—just to ensure that when graduation came they could be proud of their display. And they were." On graduation day, the 15-minute drill display was performed seamlessly in front of parents, the Commanding Officer and the Sergeant Major.

Members of C Troop looked up to Antoniuk as the epitome of a Mountie when they were in training. Their admiration for him continues to this day, which is why his story is an integral part of theirs.

Antoniuk was living in Bonneville, AB, when he was accepted into the Force. He joined the RCMP on May 29, 1956. Getting to "Depot" was a long journey. Born in Ukraine, Antoniuk was four years old when he, his three sisters, three brothers and parents travelled to Canada in 1939—about two weeks before the outbreak of World War II. "We were fortunate to be able to immigrate to Canada," Antoniuk says.

From the time he was 11, his heart's desire was to become a policeman. "There was an incident involving a family member and a police officer that happened in front of me, and I said to myself, 'I'm not going to let that happen to others—I won't do what he did.'" He had to wait a decade before he could fulfil his boyhood dream and join the Force. "I didn't have my citizen papers and I couldn't get them until I reached the age of 21," Antoniuk says. But finally, he was on his way.

Unlike C Troop, Antoniuk trained at "N" Division in Ottawa for nine months—the course was three months longer because it included equitation, which teaches horsemanship. Members of C troop were disappointed the riding program at "Depot" was discontinued just weeks before they started training. Although they didn't have the opportunity to ride, they still had to rise early every morning to perform the unenviable chores of shovelling out the stables and grooming the horses. Their stable duty ended on September 17, 1966, when 30 RCMP saddle horses, both trained and unbroken, were auctioned in Regina.

Antoniuk doesn't believe that discontinuing the riding program at "Depot" was a detriment to training. "Some people will say that dealing with the horses was good for the members who went through training because it taught them self-discipline, but we did that through drill," he says. "I don't think we lost anything."

After completing his training, Antoniuk was posted to Parliament Hill in Ottawa for three months before moving to a three-man detachment in Cornwall, ON. "While I was in Cornwall, the Commanding Officer, Ottawa Subdivision, arrived at the detachment and told me that I'd been selected for the Exhibition Ride, which was a jumping ride that we performed for one year only." Back to Ottawa he went, to be trained as part of the Exhibition jumping team. "We had 16 riders jumping in precision and, in a period of just over 10 minutes, we jumped 67 times," Antoniuk says. "You'd have to see it to really appreciate it." Over the year, the team toured nine cities—four in Canada and five in the United States.

When the ride was in Springfield, MA, Antoniuk was selected to have his picture taken for the local press. Dressed in Red Serge,

Constable Tony Antoniuk riding Knight, Springfield, Massachusetts.

he posed for numerous pictures— getting on the horse and sitting on it. "When I was on my horse, Knight, I pulled on the reins and squeezed my knees and reared my horse!" Antoniuk says. The next morning the dramatic photo of him on the rearing horse was featured in the local paper.

"I was performing stable duties when the officer in charge of the ride walked in," Antoniuk says. "He said to me, 'I see you were acting like Roy Rogers!' I said: 'Had I known they were go-ing to put that photo in the paper, I would have told them not to.' He said: 'You should have known better!' He turned and walked away, and I thought, 'I'm on my way home.'" But the chastened "Roy Rogers" went on to serve in many ways over many years.

Following the Exhibition Ride, Antoniuk had a series of rapid-fire postings to Saskatchewan: Nipawin, Hudson Bay, Colonsay, Lanigan and Val Marie. In those days, Mounties got precious little warning about new postings. They were expected to pick up and move at the pleasure of the RCMP. While Antoniuk was in Val Marie in 1965, the Commanding Officer of the Swift Current Subdivision called Antoniuk on a Friday and told him he'd been selected to go to "Depot" to take a three-month instructor course to determine if he could perform instructional duties at "Depot." "I said to him, 'But sir, I've already indicated I don't want to go to the training centre!' His reply was: 'You will report to "Depot" on Monday morning, no questions.' In those days, you went where you were told to go."

Antoniuk obeyed the order. But he was upset to leave his wife and three small children behind in Val Marie for three months while he and 11 other Mounties took the instructor course. "After eight weeks, we were told that we could go back to our detach-ments and await transfers," Antoniuk says. Of the 12 prospective candidates, 10 returned as instructors to commence a three-year posting at "Depot." "They were trying something different," Antoniuk explains. "They wanted to bring instructors from the field for a three-year period only and then transfer them out and have new instructors come in with field experience."

Hard work was peppered with humorous incidents, which often challenged Antoniuk not to crack a smile. One such in-cident occurred when Antoniuk was taking over another drill instructor's troop for a session. On parade square, Antoniuk gave the command: "To the front salute," and "they all saluted except for one," he recalls. "I approached him and said, 'Constable, why did you not salute?' And he said, 'Constable Antoniuk, I can't.' I said, 'What do you mean, you can't?' He said, 'I have a riding crop in my sleeve.'" Apparently, the recruit's regular instructor told him to bring a 20-inch riding crop to his next drill session and put it up his sleeve so he'd keep his arm straight. The red-faced recruit could not follow Antoniuk's order, much to his amusement. "I'm supposed to stand there and not even grin," Antoniuk says, laughing.

The light moment was a welcome reprieve from the heavy responsibility Antoniuk carried to perform well as an instructor. "If you don't play the part of an instructor, that's no place for you," Antoniuk says. For the first year and a half, he instructed drill and small arms at "Depot," and then moved on to teach in the academic section, which included the Criminal Code, all federal statutes and other related subjects. "It was all enjoyable," he says.

After instructing at "Depot," Antoniuk was sent to the Prince Albert Detachment. "I was there three months, and all of a sudden, a Telex came in that said I'd been selected to open a detachment in Creighton, SK, which is near Flin Flon, MB. This was on September 25, and the Telex read: 'Commence policing Oct. 1, no objections if you're there several days early.'" Antoniuk phoned his wife and asked if she was sitting down. "Her comment was, 'I know. I had a dream that before the boxes were unpacked, we'd be transferred.'" Following orders, Antoniuk and two single Constables opened the Creighton Detachment.

It was one of many times his family would be uprooted. Throughout his career, the Force transferred Antoniuk 16 times—eight transfers occurred within eight years. "Out of that, we spent three years in 'Depot,'" he says. "The shortest ones were the hardest, not so much on me, but my wife. We'd just get established and she'd start to make friends, and we were gone."

Early in his career, Antoniuk worked at three one-man detachments, which meant Nancy was his partner in crime. "The office was attached right to the house," he says. "One of the rooms that had been a bedroom at one time was made into an office. There was a police radio and a phone in there. They called the wives the Unpaid Second Man. Regardless of the time of night, if I was out and called on the radio, she'd try to answer it." Sometimes people would even come to the family's door.

The wives received no recognition until March 2013, when Commissioner Bob Paulson issued a certificate to be presented to all the wives who rendered assistance in those days. Signed by the Commissioner, the certificate reads: "In recognition of your steadfast and loyal support of the RCMP and its members."

In some instances, the family just got settled and within months Antoniuk would be transferred. He returned to "Depot" in 1987 as the Training Officer. The weighty position meant he was responsible for training programs and instructors. "I did notice that there were changes," he says. "Drill was still drill, but profanities were limited. Policies had changed and standards had increased. In the written exams, if I recall correctly, they had to have a minimum mark of 70 percent. If they didn't, they could be discharged or they could be back-trooped, which means being put back with another troop and repeating some of the subjects that they had trouble with." Unlike during his time at "Depot," trainees are no longer called recruits, but cadets. "Cadets are not members of the Force—they are there as students and they can be discharged at any time," Antoniuk says. "They don't become Constables until they graduate and are formally sworn into the Force."

All of Antoniuk's promotions were in the training field. He was in charge of training for Saskatchewan for about five years. During that time, he had a series of promotions: Sergeant, Staff Sergeant and Inspector. Upon being promoted to Inspector, he was transferred to Regina Subdivision as a Section Officer responsible for 10 detachments before he returned to Saskatchewan "F" Division headquarters, where he was the Planning Audit Officer for two years. In 1980, he was once again transferred to Ottawa. There, he was on the Commissioner's audit team for three years and, during that time, he travelled right across Canada auditing detachments.

In 1983, upon returning to Saskatchewan, he was posted to North Battleford as the Assistant Officer of the North Battleford Subdivision. "In 1984, we amalgamated the City of North Battleford, Town of Battleford, Rural Detachment, and Highway Patrol into one detachment, a total of 64 personnel," Antoniuk says. "I was transferred to the position of Detachment Commander for a period of three years and then I was selected to go to 'Depot' in 1987 as the Training Officer and remained in that position until retirement on May 29, 1991."

When he retired, Antoniuk had resided in Regina for a total of 16 years. He ended his career as a Superintendent and now lives on Vancouver Island. "I was fortunate to hold all of those different positions in the Force, and I hope that I left a mark." Antoniuk was devastated when Nancy died in 1998, but he was given a second chance at love and married his second wife, Nina, 13 years ago.

Much has evolved in training and the Force since Antoniuk was at "Depot," including mental health supports for members. "There are changes for the better," he says. "They have professionals who will provide them guidance and counselling. But years ago, you were told: 'Pull up your boot laces and carry on.' In those days, you were told that the work stays at the office. You didn't take it home. You weren't encouraged to discuss it with family. Looking at it now, there were probably times when a person should have discussed it with his family—told them how you felt."

Nevertheless, he was very pleased with the Force and the duties he performed throughout his career. "Regardless of the number of transfers, I felt that I contributed to the Force and the people that I dealt with," he says. "I feel like I set a good example. By the time I left 'Depot,' I really enjoyed the responsibility of both drill and the academic side, and I was very pleased that I was given that opportunity. I feel my 'Depot' experience, Division Training and my recent field experience helped me to qualify for the position of Training Officer, a position I never expected to achieve, but a position I really enjoyed."

Antoniuk is honoured that C Troop asked him to participate in their book. "I can assure them that it was my pleasure to have been their instructor, for they helped to mould my drill instructional duties," he says. "Once again, I would like to thank them for presenting me with a lovely clock upon completing their training. I wish them all good health and happiness during their retirement."

—*Pamela Cowan*

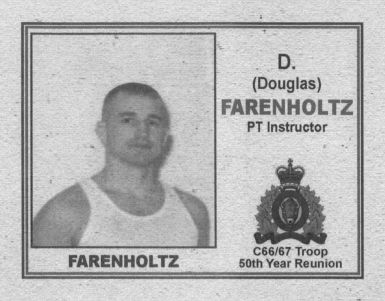

D.
(Douglas)
FARENHOLTZ
PT Instructor

C66/67 Troop
50th Year Reunion

FARENHOLTZ

To THE DISMAY of many in C Troop who had signed on to the Royal Canadian *Mounted* Police Force, when they arrived at RCMP Academy "Depot" Division in Regina in June 1966, horsemanship had just been eliminated from training. What a bummer. Yet all new members still had to muck out the stables and groom the horses until the animals were sold that September because, as their physical training and self-defence instructor Doug Farenholtz recalls, those skills were crucial in enhancing their psychological and physical fitness, discipline and confidence.

As well, "as a matter of course, the Staff Sergeant Major at each Division used the weekend stable duties as a 'disciplinary option' for recruits who had 'transgressed' the strict rules of the Training Academy," says Farenholtz. "Which obviously placed them on duty and limited their preferential use of free time."

Meanwhile, C Troop member Jerry Forst says, "Many of us recall some instructors using the fact we did not ride to push us more in other areas. Or maybe that was just me imagining

The PT staff, "Depot" Division, Regina, 1966. Left to right: Corporal Doug Farenholtz, M. Johnston, George Dury, Mike Prisk, Sergeant Bill Perry and Corporal George Duzak.

things." What Forst does remember with crystal clarity, is how vital Farenholtz's splendid training was when push literally came to shove as a working police officer. "I can tell you, I used the self-defence tips, and especially a modified Japanese stranglehold, many times. Being on Drug Squad, I kind of learned if you can't talk yourself out of a situation, you better end it quickly—something that came from training."

The skills Farenholtz imparted included self-defence based on situational encounters, arrest and control tactics, and basic martial arts. For Forst, training conducted by Farenholtz looms large in his memory of the "Depot" experience. "At the time we trained, PT (physical training) was 112 hours. We had weight training, police holds and self-defence. We learned the proper techniques on handcuffing, arm, wrist and choke holds, take-down moves, and how to take an object such as a gun from someone. One of the exercise programs had us carrying each other in our arms as we ran back and forth across the gym." PT also included running, weight training and flexibility exercises, says Farenholtz, with about a third of the hours dedicated to learning and practising self-defence from the different positions required in police work. These included when standing, when on the ground, when removing offenders from vehicles and when gaining control over a suspect while applying handcuffs from various positions. The carrying-a-person exercise actually had objectives that went beyond strictly physical fitness. "It was partly to instil discipline and confidence physically," says Farenholtz. "It was also to instil the mental commitment to assist and care for your fellow officers and the public in critical situations."

By training under Farenholtz, C Troop was learning from a multi-talented athlete and soon-to-be visionary athletic researcher who went on to help develop the physical abilities entrance standards that have been adopted by numerous law enforcement agencies across North America, as well as in many other countries. "C Troop were on the ground floor of subtle changes that would evolve over the next several years, as PT programs started to include timed activities such as circuit training and strength training using weights and isometrics to increase and improve muscular endurance," says Farenholtz.

Training programs were evolving from reliance on military-based activities to include more personalized applications, he says. These included progressive, measured physiologic-based aerobic fitness exercises, as well as the range-of-motion activities that supported the rigours of self-defence and are designed to encourage trained officers to adopt these activities into their lifestyles. "Running short intervals [anaerobic] and longer distances [aerobic] followed by some strength applications in controlled 'tussling' would eventually evolve to reflect and simulate the arrest and control of a suspect," says Farenholtz.

These exercises were the basis of the test standards that Farenholtz later developed. Before then, however, C Troop's vigorous training paid dividends. With team members Bob Swift, Carter MacDonald, John Seniuk, Ernie Stagg, Jack Snoeks and David LeBlanc, C Troop won "Depot" Division's athletic trophy and medals for the summer of 1966. That was a nifty feat, considering that several troops were participating in training programs at the same time as C Troop, and theirs wasn't the only one that Farenholtz was helping whip into shape.

Several C Troop members say that what they learned from Farenholtz may well have saved their lives and those of the people with whom they were interacting as working RCMP members. Forst still considers Farenholtz as his mentor, even though the latter was barely older than most of those he was training. Farenholtz had joined the RCMP in February 1961, at age 19.

C Troop's last PT class with Corporal Farenholtz, November 1966.

From "N" Training Division in Rockcliffe, ON, he graduated top of his troop, and won the light heavyweight class boxing tournament trophy while participating in a boxing tournament that involved the three or four troops then training there. After his graduation, he was assigned to be Troop Leader to guide the next troop sworn into "N" Division and assigned to the Physical Training staff.

Two months later, he launched his career in the field in the rural detachment of Olds, AB, then a town of 2,500 just north of Calgary that provided backup assistance to three smaller communities. There, in addition to fulfilling highway patrol duties, he developed rapport with his community's youth and families, as an assistant basketball coach and referee, and by helping start gymnastics and boxing clubs at Olds Agricultural College.

On at least two occasions, his Olds posting reinforced how essential peak physical fitness was for an RCMP member. On a summer day in 1962, while he and his Corporal were walking the beat in the downtown, the Royal Bank's alarm went off. "As neither of us was carrying our .38 revolvers, we first had to run back to the detachment to get our guns (which were locked in our desks) and then run back to the bank. So, essentially, we had to run around the block to get to the bank, whereas if we were carrying our guns, it would have been less than half a block. Fortunately, it was a false alarm. We did carry our guns during the night shift."

Later, while on a night patrol, he experienced his first gun-control incident while attending to a domestic conflict. He had quickly arrested the husband for assault and was walking him toward the police car. "As he seemed co-operative, I had not handcuffed him before leaving the house. This turned out to be a dangerous mistake, as once we got about halfway to the police car, he grabbed hold of the lanyard attached to my gun and yanked it out of the holster. I was able to grab my gun on the way by, and was able to gain control over it as he continued to wrestle with me for the gun. I threw and tripped him to the ground [but] the lanyard snapped, and my gun ended up several feet away on the lawn. I had to wrestle and applied an arm lock to ultimately gain control over him and put the handcuffs on him for his ride back to our cells. A lesson learned for sure." Not long after Farenholtz filed a report of the incident, the lanyard and the shoulder cross strap (neither of which served a useful purpose, he says) were removed from the uniformed patrol dress code, reducing the "handles" with which criminals could potentially gain control over RCMP officers.

Another of Farenholtz's athletic gifts was put into service next, when he was transferred to the RCMP Musical Ride for two years. The promotional event showcases equestrian skills of the Force in shows that are staged worldwide. For Farenholtz, it meant tours across Canada and the United States. Importantly, the posting also gave him the time to enrol in two university courses in preparation for studies toward a degree, and to continue his athletic training in judo, jujitsu and volleyball, among other sports.

After his stint with the Musical Ride, he returned to "N" Division as a PT instructor, training recruits in horsemanship, and then transferred to "Depot" in 1965 as a PT and self-defence instructor and Corporal. There he trained numerous troops, including C Troop, until 1968, when he entered the University of Saskatchewan to earn a degree in physical education. His studies were funded by the RCMP, contingent on Farenholtz completing the four-year program in three years, which he did.

While at university, he involved himself in the school's judo, jujitsu and wrestling programs, became an accredited wrestling official for the province, and was promoted to officiate over world-level wrestling championships. In 1979, as president of the Saskatchewan Wrestling Association, he chaired a special meeting of the Canadian Wrestling Association (hosted at "Depot" Division). At that meeting, the association voted on whether to take advantage of permission the Canadian government had given sports-aligned associations to allow their athletes to attend the 1980 Summer Olympics in Moscow, minus support from the

Constable Douglas Farenholtz riding Kayo, RCMP Musical Ride, Ottawa, 1964.

government, which had decided to boycott the Games. As association president and meeting chairman, Farenholtz cast the deciding vote to not allow the wrestlers to attend. "I felt comfortable making this decision in support of Canadian values and leadership," he says.

With this comprehensive background and experience in physical fitness, Farenholtz returned to "Depot" again as an instructor and began changing the Force's approach to fitness training, placing more emphasis on aerobic fitness, muscular strength and endurance, flexibility, co-ordination and balance. "I was able to influence a change in the focus of the recruit physical training programs, from the generally militaristic structure to one of maintaining a supportive lifestyle, and of physical fitness and self-defence and control tactics skills that met the requirements related to the duties of the RCMP," he says.

In 1974, Farenholtz went back to fieldwork. "I felt that I needed further field experience if I were to gain the general respect of my peers, and senior experienced officers, through reflective experiences that I had encountered in the real world of policing." Farenholtz asked to be deployed to a busy detachment, and Burnaby Detachment was the RCMP's largest at that time. "I felt that I would be able to get all the experience I wanted and needed when posted there." In Burnaby, he was the Corporal in Charge for two different zones before being promoted to Sergeant, supervising and co-ordinating all zones in co-operation with the Traffic, CIB (Criminal Investigation Branch), and General Duty sections.

During that time, he worked with several C Troop members, including Forst, Derk Doornbos and Colin Maudsley, and also completed the first study that analyzed first-responder calls to all zones, categorizing the locations and plenty of statistical data about the calls for assistance.

Farenholtz hoped that his conclusions could assist the administration in assigning capable officers to specific zones and ensure that training updates would enhance the level of policing in all calls for assistance. He was disappointed when, to his knowledge, there was no follow-up of that sort.

Still keenly interested in the fitness of RCMP members, during this posting Farenholtz also established and instructed a self-defence and control tactics program for members that included fitness and lifestyle discussions as well as martial arts instruction.

From Burnaby, Farenholtz was posted to Sechelt, BC, where he completed another crime analysis, this one prompted by the high comparative number of issues involving Indigenous people within the detachment area.

With several years of policing experience, along with increased levels of responsibility now under his belt, Farenholtz continued to be fascinated by physical fitness research. In 1979, he was transferred back to "Depot" Division as the Staff Sergeant in charge of the Physical Training Section. This gave him the opportunity to further his education and so he completed his Master of Science degree in Exercise Physiology. His graduate thesis, "A Comparative Analysis of the Effects of RCMP Physical Training on Male and Female Recruits" (1981), led to Farenholtz creating improvements within the approach and content of the RCMP's training programs.

This accomplishment, combined with a lifelong dedication to physical activity, prompted Farenholtz to adjust his career path. After 21 years of service, he retired from the RCMP to become the director of physical training programs at the Justice Institute of BC (JIBC), and was tasked with co-ordinating and instructing the physical fitness of police, sheriffs and corrections officers across the province. From that position, and with the assistance of E.C.

Rhodes, dean of the Kinesiology Department at the University of British Columbia, Farenholtz researched and developed the physical abilities entrance standards for the Corrections, Sheriffs and Police Departments in British Columbia. These are now known as COPAT (the Correctional Officer Physical Abilities Test), SOPAT (the Sheriff Officer Physical Abilities Test), and POPAT (the Police Officer Physical Abilities Test). Those standards, along with modifications, were later accepted by the RCMP as PARE (the Physical Ability Requirement Evaluation), by most other police forces throughout Canada (as POPAT), and in a number of US states and other countries, including Australia.

In 2014, Jeremy Lane, a former RCMP member who is currently a Sergeant with the Abbotsford Police Department, purchased Farenholtz's company, PTM Equipment Inc., and access to all of Farenholtz's research, along with his then-issued patents.

Farenholtz completed his last research project in 2016, at the age of 75, for the state of Arkansas, within a contract received by Lane. The physical abilities standard—which incorporated several of Farenholtz's patented products (including the Power Training Machine)—has been implemented by the Arkansas State Highway Patrol.

Among Farenholtz's copyrighted research is the task analysis in which he identified nine physical activities required by police officers in the pursuit of their duties: walking, carrying, jumping, pushing, lifting, climbing (stairs, hills), pulling, vaulting and running. Using that analysis, he designed and instructed the JIBC programs and created the POPAT and the foundation of the PARE tests, which develop both the mental and physical skills needed by law enforcement officers in carrying out all their duties, including protection of the public, and the arrest and control of people who confronted officers or resisted arrest.

To demonstrate the rational foundation of the need for entrance standardized tests of applicable physical abilities, Farenholtz also created the "Model of the Human Resource," which is copyrighted to both Farenholtz and Lane (LEPAT Inc.) It explains the accumulated level of knowledge and experience that must be psychologically controlled (the fight-or-flight response) during the transition between thought and taking the appropriate physical action while under duress.

Farenholtz based his research on observations and information he had collected from police officers he had trained, including the hundreds of recruits (among them, C Troop), and, additionally, on the behaviour of inmates serving their sentences in correctional centres located across Canada and in the state of Nevada. "Without the collective contributions of those I had trained and worked with—the combined experiences that they shared intentionally or otherwise (most often unknown to them)—I would not have been able to achieve the level of satisfaction that I experienced throughout my focused career," he says. "In that light, thank you to the members of C Troop for your past contributions."

—*Helen Metella*

C TROOP

Royal Canadian Mounted Police
C - 66 - 67 RCMP Troop
50th Year Reunion - 10th June 1966 - 10th June 2016
Regina, Saskatchewan

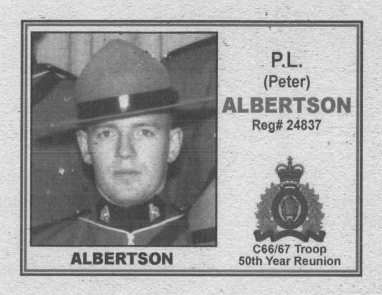

P.L.
(Peter)
ALBERTSON
Reg# 24837

ALBERTSON

C66/67 Troop
50th Year Reunion

PASSIONATE ABOUT PURSUING a policing career, Peter Albertson had just been accepted into the Vancouver City Police Service when he received word that he was among 32 men selected to form C Troop at "Depot" Division in Regina. Albertson had always believed serving in the RCMP would be "the ultimate career." The rigorous training would test his mettle, but could never fully prepare him for the highs and lows of policing.

The tide of emotions began after he drove onto the grounds of "Depot" and surveyed Saskatchewan's pancake-flat terrain. The seafaring young man felt a momentary wave of nostalgia for the West Coast. Before joining the RCMP, Albertson lived in Vancouver and served a three-year hitch with the Royal Canadian Navy, followed by a couple of years with the Canadian Navy Reserves.

After serving in the Navy, he was no stranger to regimentation and discipline, but even he was taken aback while touring "Depot" with other newcomers. "We were walking by this long building when horses came running out with recruit riders," he says. "One guy fell off in front of us, splitting his head open on the concrete curb, there was blood everywhere. Another guy came charging up on a horse, yelling, 'Who told you to dismount? Get back on that f--king horse!' Well!"

As classes got underway, Albertson discovered there was one major difference between military and RCMP training. "The military rebuilds you so you unquestioningly, and immediately, follow any order," Albertson says. "The RCMP tears you down to remake you into a person who knows how to think for himself, to make decisions and have the confidence to carry them out."

One of the older members to join C Troop, the 24-year-old was selected as the troop's right marker. Albertson was responsible for overseeing the troop, maintaining discipline and harmony within the ranks, and was the go-between for the troop and instructors.

From the beginning, he had a great deal of respect for Constable Tony Antoniuk, the troop's drill instructor. "I know the troop felt the same," Albertson says. "He knew his drill and knew how to teach, without profanity or put-down. We would have brief discussions on how the troop was progressing, and he was sincerely interested in our achieving the best possible results." In contrast to Antoniuk's even-handed approach, a lot of drill instructors were harsh and literally got in the faces of trainees, yelling profanities at them for the smallest of infractions.

On parade square, C Troop had its fair share of reprimands, but that was part of the training, Albertson says. "You've got to get used to that. If you can't take it, you're just not going to make it." While Antoniuk didn't verbally berate the troop, he wasn't an easy touch. "He wouldn't tolerate any fooling around," Albertson says. "You were there to learn. He came down on us a couple of times, but we worked hard to give him the responses he wanted."

The recruits also delighted in having fun at each other's

expense. Albertson was one of the instigators behind a prank that triggered more than a few chuckles during one inspection of the troop's uniforms and revolvers. Prior to being inspected, the troop had to ensure every article of their uniform was in pristine condition and their revolvers were polished to erase fingerprints before the guns were put in holsters. Bob Bossence wasn't in the dorm when three of his troop mates removed his gun from the holster, tied an unrolled condom around the tip of the barrel, then returned the revolver to its holster, condom first. With wide grins, the perpetrators marched off to the drill hall. "We were fully aware we could well be court-martialled or worse for this stunt," Albertson says, laughing.

The troop lined up and stood at attention with Albertson, as right marker, at the right front. On Antoniuk's command, the troop drew their revolvers and held them at 45 degrees in front of them. Within seconds of the guns being presented, a loud *fwap* was heard. "Bossence, at the rear corner of the troop, had attempted to yank the condom off, but it remained stuck on the gun sight at the tip of the barrel," Albertson says. Another *fwap* followed. Albertson, the first to be inspected, fought a losing battle to keep a straight face and he smiled as he heard Bossence's agitated efforts to get the condom off his gun. "A bewildered Constable Antoniuk asked me, 'Constable Albertson, what's up?' All I could answer was, 'I'm just so happy to be here, Constable!' He didn't pursue it and went on down the line," Albertson recalls.

Another *fwap* was heard. "Now, he's at Maudsley, a robust, reddish-haired Englishman, who was quaking with mirth at this time, complete with red glowing face. Constable Antoniuk said: 'You happy to be here too, Maudsley?' 'Oh yes, Constable!'"

The puzzled drill instructor moved down the line again. Stopping in front of Michel Laverdière, he got the same answer,

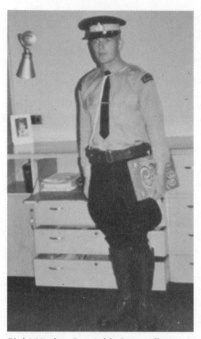

Right Marker Constable Peter Albertson standing in his pit, holding Troop marker board, 1966.

this time with a French accent, "Mon Dieu, Constable. H'am soo 'appee!" The only ones not smirking with each consecutive *fwap* were those unaware of the stunt and, of course, Bossence. To this day, Albertson doesn't know if Antoniuk saw the "protective shield" at the end of Bossence's gun. "Constable Antoniuk either didn't notice it or decided not to notice it," he says.

No one was exempt from being the butt of jokes, including Albertson. Throughout the day's activities, he carried a right marker board, which was a clipboard with two hinged wooden covers. The wood covers kept papers, such as the list of the troop's names, from flying around. One day in the drill hall, Albertson stepped forward and handed the book to Antoniuk so he could call the roll. Albertson rejoined the ranks, but was quickly summoned to the front after the Constable flipped up the cover of the book. "He showed me this *Playboy* pin-up, and I was as shocked as he was," Albertson says. "There was kind of a smile on his face, but he tried to hide it and he was OK. He knew by the look on my face that I did not know it was there. There were two or three people in the ranks who were grinning broadly, so there was no doubt who was responsible. It was a fun thing and he let it go. He was that kind of a guy."

Academic classes were fast-paced, with a lot of note-taking, but Albertson had a "secret weapon"—Barb, his future wife. He

Left to right: Bob Bossence, Jerry Forst, Peter and Barbara Albertson, Ernie Otway, Derk Doornbos and Colin Maudsley, all C Troop members at Peter Albertson's wedding, Vancouver, BC, July 13, 1968.

mailed his notes to Barb, an executive secretary. She used her skills to decode the scribbles, type the notes, format them and mail them back to Albertson. "Apparently, she would spread the notes out on the family living room floor, and her parents and older sister would help her decipher," Albertson says. "She was great. They'd follow along at home and know what we were doing, and I got top marks for my notes!"

Several days before Albertson's graduation Passout ceremony, Barb and his mother arrived in Regina. With time on her hands, Barb was exploring the grounds at "Depot" and entered the drill hall during a session. All eyes turned to see who had entered. "The drill instructor shouted, 'Don't look at her! Look at me! I'm more beautiful!' Barb was mortified and slunk out of the hall," Albertson recalls.

After six months of a hard grind, Albertson was ready to take on the world when he left "Depot." He was disappointed when he and Ross Mortlock were posted to the Edmonton Guardroom/ Detachment in Alberta. "It was boring," he laments. "There were no shootouts, no high-speed chases, and no rescuing fair maidens." The Guardroom held prisoners from outlying RCMP detachments who were brought to Edmonton for court, patients from a mental institution near Fort Saskatchewan, and individuals the RCMP transported to the city on warrants from the Edmonton City Police. "We'd pick them up by car or plane, hold them in cells, and disperse them accordingly," Albertson says. "We were almost like a clearing house."

Not only was the work a letdown, but some prisoners hadn't bathed or changed clothes for months so they "reeked to high heaven." Usually one unarmed Constable escorted the prisoners to compulsory showers, but two went if an individual was deemed dangerous. "Of course, you wouldn't wear your gun because if they jumped you, you may have a problem," Albertson says. The Mounties' fists were their only protection, but Albertson says there was never a problem while he was there. He recalls prisoners lathering up with a special kind of soap to kill lice. "You always felt like you had to detoxify when you finished a shift."

There were, however, some fond memories at the Edmonton Detachment, including one that occurred when Albertson returned as an escort on the prisoner bus. He was advised that the Edmonton Detachment wanted a member in Red Serge to talk to a group of young, blind children in the large "K" Division parking lot. Albertson, having just returned from attending the Edmonton Supreme Court in dress uniform, went to the parking lot. He was immediately surrounded by excited children ranging in age from 5 to 14 years. All were giddy about exploring every aspect of the marked police car.

"They'd listen to the siren and police radio and feel the dome light going around," Albertson says. "They wanted to touch everything—the communications equipment in the trunk, the traffic flares and emergency equipment." The children took turns putting on his Stetson and handcuffs, handcuffing their friends, and feeling the size, shape and texture of bullets. Under close supervision, they were allowed to touch Albertson's revolver. "It was a great feeling to see and hear these kids get so enthused about something they had only heard stories about in the past," Albertson says.

Members and civilian staff working in the offices above the parking lot looked out and saw the children jumping up and down in excitement. Later, many members told Albertson they would have given a lot to have traded places with him that day.

As a member of the Edmonton Detachment, Albertson took his turn observing autopsies for continuity of evidence in possible court proceedings. In his first year on the Force, he attended three autopsies—a duty he found extremely interesting. Before the first autopsy, he had wondered if he'd get queasy; he wasn't sure what to expect or how he would react. Instead, the scientific process fascinated him. "Everything came out and was examined, weighed, samples cut and catalogued," he says. "It was incredibly sterile, respectful, efficient, highly professional and very thorough. I was very moved by how complex the human body is." Staff encouraged his questions and took the time to fully explain what they were doing. "It was quite the experience!"

While working at a detachment between Edmonton and Jasper, Albertson was returning from Supreme Court (now the Court of Queen's Bench of Alberta) in Edmonton in a marked car on a summer day. As was the case when Mounties attended Supreme Court, he wore his Red Serge. Driving along Highway 16, a long line of tourist traffic moving towards Jasper suddenly halted. The car behind Albertson's cruiser couldn't stop fast enough. To avoid hitting the police car, the motorist drove off the shoulder, down the sloped bank, and the car rolled onto its roof. Albertson put on the cruiser's red dome light, drove to the shoulder and scrambled down the bank to assist. To his relief, he was able to get two uninjured adults and two children out of the wrecked car.

All traffic, including unimpeded traffic eastbound to Edmonton, stopped to gawk at the spectacle. People piled out of their vehicles and grabbed their cameras to take shots of a Canadian Mountie in Red Serge in action. Against the backdrop of the police car's flashing red light and a rolled-over car, babies and small children were thrust at Albertson with requests, "Here, hold this, I want to get a picture," or "Put your arm around my girlfriend." Traffic quickly became gridlocked. Albertson called for expedited backup. Officers in regular uniform arrived at the scene and were content to direct traffic, allowing Albertson to play reluctant "poster boy" for the Force.

One memorable call to the Sherwood Park Detachment came late one evening from a woman who was upset her dogs had become locked together in a variation of their mating ritual. "It was after hours so the vet's office was closed and she didn't know what to do or who to call," Albertson says. "I suggested dumping cold water on them. The phone was on speaker when she asked if I thought it would work. I gave the honest answer that 'It would work for me!' My partner, listening intently, almost choked on his coffee. She didn't phone back so the assumption was made that the case was closed."

Around 1:00 a.m. on another occasion, Albertson had just got out of a marked highway patrol car at a farmhouse near Sherwood Park when he heard two vehicles crash at the intersection of two highways less than a quarter of a mile away. "I turned to see a cloud of dust and headlights spinning in the air," he says. One vehicle had T-boned another. Albertson rushed to the crash and discovered a deceased woman on the ground and a man pinned under his vehicle by a hot exhaust pipe. Passing motorists stopped and offered assistance. Briefly, Albertson considered having them help lift the vehicle and pull the man out, but decided against it in case the vehicle dropped and crushed the man. Instead, he radioed an Edmonton tow truck driver he'd relied upon in the past. Albertson asked the driver to expedite the call and requested an escort for the tow truck from the Edmonton City Police. The tow truck driver arrived on the scene in record time. "He was fast and he was good," Albertson says. "He knew exactly what to do to get that car off the guy in a hurry."

Tow truck drivers are often forgotten heroes, he muses. "Not once have I heard recognition being given to tow truck drivers who so often are called to assist first responders in sometimes violent, tragic and traumatic situations," Albertson says. "There was no 'thank you,' no recognition, no commendation, no counselling. They just go home to their families, totally unsung heroes."

There were moments of pandemonium in the air and on the ground one day in the late 1960s when the RCMP in central Alberta was demonstrating how its aircraft patrol could nab speeders. An Edmonton media outlet had requested a photographer be allowed to fly in a separate plane to take action shots of the Force's new speed-detection system. In the "spotter" plane was a civilian pilot, accompanied by a spotter who was an RCMP member.

The spotter watches for obvious speeders and times them with a stop watch as they drive between two lines painted across the highway exactly a quarter of a mile apart. The speed is charted and, if necessary, the spotter radios to police vehicles further down the highway to intercept the speeding offender. The spotter plane circles and keeps the speeding vehicle in sight until it is pulled over. The system works well on the Prairies, where drivers can spot cruisers on the side of the road miles ahead and slow down to avoid a ticket.

RCMP aircraft monitoring speeds on an Alberta highway. It was a situation similar to this in which the RCMP plane was forced to crash land after being hit by the media aircraft's propeller.

On the day of the demonstration, Albertson was an interceptor in a marked police car, which was positioned as if a speeder had been stopped. In this case, the "speeder" was another member in an unmarked highway patrol car. The officers were instructed not to look skyward as the newspaper's photographer wanted to get a photo of the spotter plane and the ground vehicles in one shot.

"The two of us on the ground heard a loud *pop* and figured one of the planes had backfired," Albertson says. Then, over the radio they heard: *We're hit … We're going down.* "We looked up and saw one plane heading away in a slow curve. The other, the spotter plane with our member on board, was flying in a much tighter circle and losing altitude quickly. Both of us in the highway cars immediately sped off." Albertson turned off on one road, the other officer took another. "The other car radioed that he thought he was near them and told me to follow his road," Albertson says.

With the emergency lights and yelper siren activated, the first cruiser roared through an open gate and into a farmyard. Chickens went flying, dogs were barking, and the farmer, with his family, came running out of the house. "Two minutes later, [the officer] radioed he had found the aircraft just as I entered and passed the farmhouse with all emergency equipment on," Albertson says. "More flying chickens and barking dogs and a farm family looking very confused."

He followed flattened-grain tracks through the field to the plane. "We were very fortunate the civilian pilot turned out to be a senior pilot instructor trainer and was able to land safely," Albertson says. Meanwhile, officers at the Edmonton Subdivision could hear all hell breaking loose on the police radio and wanted updates.

. Apparently the plane commissioned by the newspaper had encountered turbulence and its propeller clipped the tail of the spotter plane. "We updated them immediately when the plane and occupants were safely found," Albertson says. "The other plane had landed safely in a nearby field. More damaged grain."

It was a spring day in central Alberta in the 1970s when Albertson responded to the most traumatic call of his career. He was just leaving his home at 7:30 a.m. to head to work at the Sherwood Park Detachment when Sergeant Ron Roth phoned Albertson and said there was "a situation" he needed help with and he'd pick him up in five minutes.

"There had been a light plane crash out of town. The exact location wasn't known, that's all we had," Albertson says. "We got near the area and got word a local farmer had phoned in a more precise location. We got as close as we could by car, then started hiking in." The officers located the plane's fuselage lying on the ground. The smell of aviation fuel was very strong, but there was no fire. "Other than the bent main frame, the roof and wall panels were virtually pancake flat, no bodies were apparent," Albertson says. "There was still no word on the number of occupants, if any, other than the pilot."

As the pair widened their search, they found a couple of bodies and, about 30 feet away, the plane's two wings, which had been sheared off. The officers got new information indicating more passengers were involved so they continued searching. "The remaining bodies were located, with the exception of the pilot," Albertson says. "All were whole, but indented 10 to 16 inches into the ground from the impact."

Recovery was a difficult, delicate task. While they were rechecking the cockpit area of the plane, looking for signs of the pilot, Roth admonished Albertson to be careful where he was standing. "I looked down and my shoe had uncovered a head I had been standing on! This was an investigation that left its mark."

At that time, the RCMP had nothing in place to help him or other officers deal with traumatic events. Albertson recalls re-hashing the unsettling details of the air crash with his wife many times. "Fifty years ago, we did not have the opportunity to debrief with anyone other than our wives or some members," Albertson says. "Just write a report, submit it and move on… It's much better now, but there's still a long ways to go."

While working in the Evansburg Detachment in Alberta, Albertson and other members from adjacent detachments around Edson were called to join in a manhunt for a murder suspect. A convoy of officers armed with rifles, revolvers and shotguns searched through thick, mountainous terrain, off the beaten path. Eventually officers found the suspect, who had killed himself with a shot to the head. After the initial investigation was completed, all of the team departed except for Albertson, the most junior member. He was tasked with waiting for officers from the Identification Section of the RCMP to arrive at the scene. Darkness had descended. With a rifle and revolver close at hand, Albertson strained his eyes watching for bears as he guarded the body of the deceased man. When the Identification team showed up, Albertson watched in fascination as they went about their work, taking pictures with the shutter open and painting the scene with a flashlight. He witnessed first-hand the scope of their job, which involved much more than taking fingerprints.

Another frightening incident occurred when Albertson was new to the Sherwood Park Highway Patrol and driving around to familiarize himself with the area. He'd been patrolling the highways and adjacent areas for a number of hours when he stopped around 2:00 a.m. at the Clover Bar gravel pit. "I drove the car along the top of a long gravel pile," he says. "It was getting quite foggy, and I decided to get out of the car and see where I could turn around to head back." His instinct to stop and check his surroundings was spot on. Huge excavators had eaten away the gravel just in front of his cruiser. "The base was about 200 feet straight down," Albertson says. "The front tires of the car had come to a stop about six feet from the edge of this drop."

While Albertson was working at Valleyview Detachment in northern Alberta, a local lad showed interest in joining the RCMP and asked if he could go on a ride-along. It was a blustery winter evening and the mercury had dropped to -30°C when Albertson and the young man began patrolling the area in a marked police car. All was quiet until a radio call came through indicating that a couple of "bad actors" in Edmonton had stolen their halfway house manager's car and were likely heading to their hometown, north of where Albertson and his sidekick were patrolling.

"We headed south on the highway from the town, then I

backed our car a short ways down a side road with lights off. We were hidden by a stand of trees," Albertson recalls. "We had the description and plate number of the 'borrowed' car, so we just waited." The second car that passed them appeared to fit the description of the suspect vehicle. "We waited a bit and then pulled onto the highway and gradually closed the gap so I wouldn't spook the driver," Albertson says. "Eventually we got close enough to confirm the plate number—our guys!"

From a glance at the suspect's car, Albertson knew it was faster than the police vehicle and guessed the driver would probably try to run. "I faded way back, and then floored it," he says. "I switched on the red dome light, the right flashing front fender light that read 'stop' and the yelper siren as I pulled alongside, encouraging him to drive off the highway into the snowbank." After the stolen vehicle disappeared into a white cloud, Albertson stopped and threw the cruiser in reverse so his high beams shone on the suspect's car. "His car was buried in snow, except for the two left side doors," Albertson says. "The two, in shock and blinded, were cuffed, searched and placed in the back of the police car, and it was game over!"

Perhaps unsurprisingly, a search of the trunk revealed rifles and ammunition. The pair was escorted to detachment cells in Valleyview. "The two of us called it a night and I took the ride-along home," Albertson says. "He picked up his RCMP application at our office the next morning."

One day, after driving into a farmer's yard to serve a subpoena, Albertson spotted a single turkey. By the time he got to the farmhouse door, four or five turkeys had gathered by the patrol car. When no one answered his knock, Albertson returned to his vehicle, where a dozen or more tom turkeys were jumping on the hood and trunk of the car and pecking at the windows. "Not wanting to disrupt the farmer's livelihood by damaging his birds, I turned on the siren to scare them away," he says. "They weren't intimidated in the least and all started closing in with menacing glares and beaks. Alfred Hitchcock's film *The Birds* came to mind." Surrounded by the frenetically flapping flock, Albertson started the motor and rocked the car back and forth a few times, and in the end, having dislodged the birds, triumphantly made his exit.

During the final stretch of his eight years with the RCMP, Albertson used his days off to assist his brother with his food business in Edmonton. The business was growing and Albertson's brother asked him to take it over. "I'd had my share of good, busy postings and knew that less desirable ones would probably be coming," Albertson says. "As well, my two children were nearing school age, and Barb and I wanted to take university courses that were only available in larger centres." His decision to leave the Force was reaffirmed when, on a visit to Edmonton, he came across an incredible opportunity to backpack for five months through New Zealand, Australia and Indonesia with his wife, two youngsters and sister-in-law. It was time to leave the RCMP.

"We had to sell our property at my last detachment and leave in very short order to take advantage," he says. "Everything came together very quickly." The last few days were rushed. "The second-last paper I had to sign at the office was for the return of my Red Serge," Albertson says. "I was sure there were options, but I had no time to argue or do research. I had to give up this uniform." In addition to the sadness he felt at traumatic scenes and during other aspects of police work, he recalls this as a low point in his career. However, in retrospect, "it was the only really low point," he says.

After leaving the Force, Albertson became president and managing director of Profit Pack Foods Ltd. in Edmonton from

1974 to 1978. The company prepared, packaged, and shipped food to most of the hotels and convenience stores throughout Alberta. It was a busy time. Between 1976 and 1977, Albertson attended Northern Alberta Institute of Technology in Edmonton as a full-time business administration student, and from 1974 to 1981 was president and managing director of World of Microwave Ovens Ltd. Based in Edmonton, the company had three retails outlets in Edmonton and one in Calgary.

As the 1970s wound up, Albertson entered the world of real estate and was a realtor in Sherwood Park for four years. More change was on the horizon. In 1983, the family moved to Vancouver, where Albertson was involved with security systems and electronic shoplifting prevention equipment until 1987, when he became director of sport development for the BC Ringette Association. During his tenure, the association's registration tripled in three years, and he established a Summer Ringette Camp and co-ordinated the implementation of a Player Development Instructors Clinic. Since 1989, he's been actively involved in the pet nutrition business through his distribution company.

After departing the RCMP, Albertson's business pursuits have been varied, but his training at "Depot" made an indelible mark. "'Depot' made me realize that I was capable of a lot more than I previously thought possible," he says. The training contributed to his organizational skills and self-discipline, and enhanced his self-confidence. "Field work after 'Depot' continued this process," Albertson says. "I'm sure these experiences contributed greatly to my life after the Force."

—*Pamela Cowan*

R.J.
(Robert)
ALLISON
Reg# 24845

C66/67 Troop
50th Year Reunion

ALLISON

WHEN BOB ALLISON was a child, his father was briefly a member of the Lethbridge Police Department, where he befriended a fellow officer whose wisdom Allison still quotes almost 70 years later. "He said, 'Just because you wear a uniform and have a gun, that doesn't make you any better than the person you're dealing with,'" says Allison. That perspective guided Allison through every incident he attended to while serving 33 years with the RCMP, predominantly in British Columbia's rural interior.

Those incidents ran the gamut of police work, from thefts, bar fights and murders, to domestic disputes, drug-smuggling, hostage-taking, a school bomb, customs violations, the expected ratio of car accidents, drownings and sudden deaths, and even a farm animal disposal.

In addition to remembering that he wasn't a privileged, god-like figure, Allison always kept another personal credo in mind. "I'm not a fighter," he says. "I think one-on-one communication, be it between fellow workers or the general public, is important.

Bob Allison spraying down his stable clothes and covering them in plastic before he puts them in his locker, July 1966.

In a domestic situation, say you're going to arrest a husband or wife, if you can spend an extra five or 10 minutes talking to the parties, and then walk out of the house without wrestling or forcibly removing them, everyone is better off. If you're notifying someone of a sudden death, take a few extra minutes not just doing your job but explaining things to them. Same if you're giving someone a speeding ticket. If time is available, by talking to people you can make the situation better."

Often the full impact that Allison had on people by taking the extra time to talk through a situation that required police intervention wasn't revealed to him for years. "In 100 Mile House, we had a fellow in a church threatening suicide," he said. "Everything turned out well, but four years later, I got a letter from his sister saying, 'I lost track of you and I want to say thank you.' She said the family recalled the incident each spring. The Force was experiencing criticism at the time and she felt the incident was handled professionally, with compassion and patience. The same compassion was then extended to the family and subject. I didn't think we did anything extra, but I think he had a rifle with him and we got him to put down the rifle."

During his first posting, covering general duties in the bustling Surrey, BC, detachment, Allison remembers covering many break-ins, as well as a job that's probably now considered a relic from a bygone era. During graveyard shifts he conducted property checks, which meant scanning for broken windows and shaking the doors of local businesses to see if they were unlocked. As a rookie, he was often startled by unexpected guard dogs left on the premises overnight. "Nowadays, I'm sure the members would say, 'You did *that*?!'"

When he moved to the Traffic section, Allison admits, "I wasn't what you'd call a dedicated traffic man. Some people deserve tickets, but we all make mistakes, so maybe I didn't write as many tickets as my supervisors wanted."

Raised in the small Alberta city of Lethbridge, Allison was not enamoured of the congested Lower Mainland, so he gamely accepted the transfer to Unit B Freeway Patrol because it was generally considered a springboard away from the district once those dues were paid.

For two and a half years, he worked eight-hour shifts on the roads from Langley to Vancouver's city limits and also the Upper Levels Highway (the local name for the Trans-Canada Highway as it traverses the Second Narrows Bridge into North Vancouver and flows to West Vancouver). The stint did pay off, in several ways. Allison met his future wife, Marilyn, while working in Surrey, and when his work on highway patrol was done, he indeed secured a transfer to a smaller detachment. It was in Grand Forks, BC, minutes from the US border in the logging and resort region of the West Kootenays. The posting marked the beginning of a career in which he served in several smaller towns, including 100 Mile House, Trail and Fruitvale, culminating in the bigger centre of Golden. "I liked the smaller detachments," says Allison. "There may not have been as many large, involved investigations, but you got your finger in a large variety."

In Grand Forks, that meant policing the rough-and-tumble behaviour of loggers, who played just as hard as they worked; ensuring that the recently calmed protests and roadblocks by the Sons of Freedom (a radical breakaway sect of the local

Bob and Marilyn Allison's wedding, April 12, 1969.

Doukhobor population) remained calm; and occasionally checking cars' contents for smuggled items, once travellers had cleared Customs at the border. "I remember we had one fellow at the border crossing at Cascade, he tried to smuggle some drugs, and he was in our cells for a month or so. This would never happen now, but he'd be outside washing the police cars with the guards sitting there watching him. At that time, I think the meals for the prisoners were being supplied by local hotels. They were famous for their borscht because the cooks were all of Russian descent. So, he wasn't suffering for it."

For a summer, Allison was also seconded to the popular holiday destination of nearby Christina Lake, where he was charged with "flying the colours" and making the RCMP's presence known, albeit with challenges. He recalls there being many traffic accidents within a short period of time, and lot of weekend parties to quell with modest resources. "We would do preventative boat patrols, but the boat was a wannabe boat that wasn't the fastest or the most modern. They also had an old houseboat there and had put a foundation under it. We lived there. The living room was the office and there was another cabin out back where the other member lived. My wife was the unpaid office assistant there. She did a lot. I think an Officer in Charge (OIC) in Nelson realized how much and thanked her, but that was the position. It was old school and a member's wife was expected to help."

In truth, Marilyn was often an unpaid member of the RCMP

in Grand Forks, too. When members were all out on the road, the detachment office's phone recording directed callers to the mobile phone in the patrol cars—which was fine if they were in their cars. When he knew he'd be away from the vehicle for an extended time, Allison occasionally directed the calls to his home, and then it was up to Marilyn to track him down.

The concerns of members' wives were often taken for granted in other ways, Allison says, recalling the story of a colleague in another small rural detachment. "His wife was a pharmacist, and when they transferred him, they didn't worry that there was no pharmacy in the town." Fortunately, the places Allison served always featured good schools where Marilyn was able to work, and provided a steady diet of unique learning experiences for him. "I remember one incident when a rancher's cows got on the highway and a few were injured and had to be put down. Of course [police-issue] .38 specials were not the most powerful. I had disposed of one cow when the farmer showed up. He was a dead shot with his .22 and *bang, bang, bang,* the rest were down. Then he gave me a rough time about my marksmanship."

Other incidents were more stomach-roiling. At 100 Mile House, some 200 kilometres northwest of Kamloops in central BC, Allison was called to accompany a coroner to investigate the sudden death of a person living in a cabin by a lake. "No one had checked in on him frequently and the person had been deceased for quite some time. I remember being in the cabin for a minute and then out of the cabin for fresh air and then back in, and out … the job had to be done and we did it."

In 100 Mile House, Allison discovered another truism about life in the RCMP at the time—transferring here and there throughout small-town Canada was subject to factors that even such a large organization couldn't control. While Allison was slated for a move to Prince Rupert that came with a promotion, the family had difficulty selling their house in the central BC town. Instead, he accepted a promotion to Corporal in the same detachment where he'd been a Constable, and learned the hard way that it's tricky becoming the supervisor of colleagues who were very recently your peers. "I didn't do a very good job during that transition," he says. "I overreacted at times. I should have been more laid back. I hope I improved upon that as time went on."

His superiors evidently felt he did, because when he was posted next to the city of Trail, Allison became the shift supervisor of a much larger policing area. Again, despite the rural environment, the files proved as challenging as any in a big city. One concerned a child who was being assaulted by her juvenile male babysitter. "We had very little support from the accused's family, but we did convict him," says Allison.

Next he became Detachment Commander in the quiet and much smaller Kootenay community of Fruitvale. It was a four-man detachment dealing with mostly routine general duties such as break-and-enters. That relative respite was followed by a long final assignment as Detachment Commander in the bigger centre of Golden. Many unique challenges awaited him there.

Known by winter visitors as spectacular snowmobiling and skiing country, Golden was also the perfect setting for growing "Kootenay Bud," due to the district's warm temperatures and the remoteness of many properties. That meant the RCMP dealt with both the primary and secondary crimes that revolved around marijuana production. "People would bypass the fuses on the electrical boxes and steal the hydro," Allison says. "They would rent houses and the whole house was turned into a grow-op."

Depending on the size of the operation, the RCMP would either chop down the plants immediately, or sit on the information and tease out the owners. Either way, the police still had to dispose of the product. "When I first went to Golden, we had a lot of grow-ops but we had to get permission to destroy the plants. There was a mill west of Golden in Donald that had this burner. I don't know how many plants we took out there to destroy, with all the employees saying 'what a waste.'"

Even then, Golden was a pit stop for the many motorists travelling the route between Calgary and Vancouver. That alone made it a busy place for policing. "I couldn't believe the number of people in Golden who didn't lock their houses," says Allison. "I'd say, 'Do you realize how many people go through here?' That amount of traffic included travelling criminals."

In fact, that subset of travellers brought to Golden one of the most memorable investigations Allison oversaw during his career. "This fellow from Calgary, his wife was having an affair. He killed [the other man] in Calgary and then drove out into the Fraser Canyon outside of Golden with his wife. He was going to commit suicide by driving over the barrier into the canyon. He had poured some gas in the car to set it on fire. But he didn't make it over the barrier. He survived, but his wife didn't."

Golden was also the site of an incident Allison cites as "one of the worst things in my career," which occurred less than a year after he arrived. In the summer of 1990, just east of Golden, a semi-trailer loaded with pipe failed to negotiate a sharp turn and lost its load. Pipes smashed into a bus headed from Calgary to Penticton, carrying a dance troupe of young girls. "Two were killed. I remember a doctor from Calgary had stopped and was helping, and the doctor said, 'I need help holding her.' I travelled in the ambulance with her, holding her down while the doctor attended to her. She reminded me so much of a girlfriend of my son's from Trail. I can't say for sure if she was one of the two who died. I will never forget her screaming. I attended numerous MVAS (motor vehicle accidents) throughout my career, but that one always surfaces."

For anyone, that portion of the experience would be more than enough trauma to process. For an RCMP member, there was more work to do. At the hospital, Allison was called on by one of the nurses who wanted a reporter thrown out of the hospital because he was trying to interview some of the injured girls. "So you're dealing with that," says Allison, who suddenly had to manage the media's comportment. Additionally, organizations such as dance schools didn't have communications at the ready the way they might today, when issuing updates on an unfolding event can be managed by cell phone calls. So, he and the chaperones from the bus became responsible for issuing public statements.

"Once that was finished, you had to make sure you did a complete investigation. Of course, we had an experienced traffic analysis person doing the work, but you had to make sure to get all the evidence you were going to need for court, and besides the court case there was a coroner's inquest on it, which was an entirely different thing." Tragic and shocking incidents have considerable ripple effects, too, says Allison. The town of Golden had just two full-time ambulance attendants; all the others were volunteers. "It affects not just the members at the scene; it affects the whole community."

There was a critical incident debriefing with a psychologist for RCMP members and the office staff following the accident. Allison is certain that talking about it helped, but he also knows that the comfort of intuitive silence also sustained him through many tough events as a law enforcement official. "You have to have a very understanding family. My wife reads me very well. There are times when I like to talk and times I don't like to talk."

Flexibility from families at other times was also crucial, as plenty of ordinary days were derailed by the demands of the job. One weekend trip to Calgary from Golden was abruptly cancelled when news of a Friday afternoon bomb blast at the local high school turned those plans to ash. The bombing had occurred in a boys' washroom and fortunately there were no injuries. However, insufficient evidence meant charges weren't laid. All that came of it was a disruption of the Allisons' downtime.

"Another time, I was having one of the best golf games of my life, and there was a hostage incident in Kimberley [a couple of hours south]. A bunch of us got called to that. I was the only one from Golden. It was accepted for a small town that if you were sitting at home doing something, the phone would ring. Or if you worked an afternoon shift to 3:00 a.m., quite often you'd be on call till 6:00 a.m." Since there were many occasions when "the bad guys would change plans in your private life," Allison almost doesn't find it ironic that he and Marilyn missed their 50-year troop reunion in May 2016, because they suffered serious injuries after their car was T-boned by a stolen vehicle in Kamloops a week before the gathering.

Having outside interests such as sports throughout his career was one beneficial way to survive the strains of the job, Allison says. He avidly joined baseball and hockey teams at most of his postings. He believes it not only countered the stress, but also provided him protection within the communities he served. "You meet people on a personal level and sit around afterward and have a beer and get to know them. Then, if there are places you go into where you're working by yourself, say you're called to a bar fight, the majority of the time there's someone else in that bar that I knew, if I got into difficulty, would step in and help me."

A high tolerance for hijinks also helped take the edge off many a tough week. "When I was at Golden Detachment, I went into my office one morning to find it completely rearranged. The large safe had been turned around, the desk was against the wall, and all the furniture—including fully loaded bookshelves—was stacked on the desk. A large sign was attached, stating, 'The FLQ [Front de libération du Québec] were here.' Needless to say, the only Quebec-born detachment member had left his calling card." The man was an amateur power lifter who was prone to pranks. "The type of guy, who, if you got back at him, you got double back," says Allison. "He accomplished this on his own and was not to be found when the furniture had to be put back in place."

Allison served in Golden for 10 years and lived there for another 10 post-retirement so Marilyn could continue to work at her job. They now live in Kamloops, enjoying close contact with their grandchildren.

Just as he never considered himself grander than any of the people he interacted with as a member of the RCMP, nor does he feel that police deserve the heavy burden of negative assessments so prevalent these days on social media. "Do police screw up sometimes? You bet. Everybody does. But people should also acknowledge that most of them are out there doing the best job they can." Throughout his career, Allison kept the goal of performing to the best of his ability at the top of his mind. It's the reason he thoroughly enjoyed what he characterizes as "not what you might call a glorified career, but one that was very satisfying to me."

Peter Albertson (left) and Bob Allison, (right) revisit their old pit during their 30-year reunion tour of "Depot," 1996.

—*Helen Metella*

R.H.
(Ronald)
BEAUCAIRE
Reg# 24832

C66/67 Troop
50th Year Reunion

BEAUCAIRE

RON BEAUCAIRE wasn't much of a swimmer when he arrived at "Depot" Division in Regina. "I learned to swim as a kid, but not that well. My father used to put a rope around me and let me jump off the end of the wharf," he says. However, by the end of his training, he met the Force's standards and had the skills to save a life. He'd do just that early in his policing career.

To his dismay, the 20-year-old was sent to the Force's "Fat Boys Club" to do mandatory exercises. As a youth, Beaucaire loved sports. He played lacrosse, hockey and football regularly, so he thought he was in good shape when he joined up. Not so, according to the RCMP. To meet the Force's stringent requirements, he had to take extra lessons in the pool, over and above the mandatory 60 periods of swimming. "In the pool, you almost froze to death because the water was so cold," Beaucaire recalls. Despite the discomfort, he went the distance and by the end of training he'd earned the Bronze Medallion. Little more than a year after

Ron Beaucaire was a non-swimmer when he arrived at "Depot." However, by the end of his training, he received his Bronze Medallion.

leaving "Depot," Beaucaire would put the lifesaving skills he'd learned into action.

Beaucaire grew up in an English-speaking home, but picked up French when he was playing with neighbourhood children in Ottawa. "I learned it on the streets, so it wasn't quite the same accent that everybody was speaking or wanted to hear," Beaucaire says. Being bilingual, he was destined to be sent to Quebec. His first posting was Montreal "C" Division. There he lived in barracks and, like any new member, learned the ropes. "I did security at the front desk and participated in inspections of some of the federal government buildings in Montreal and the surrounding area."

He gained more field experience in January when he was sent to General Investigation Services and did "a little bit of everything," including making arrests on outstanding warrants. In June he was transferred to the RCMP's Marine Division in the Port of Montreal and assigned to ensure safety on the water around Expo 67. He and an English-speaking member, Constable Hector Dawe, were assigned to the RCMP *Athabasca*, a 26-foot patrol boat. Together they patrolled the water and checked, among other things, the safety requirements on boats.

Beaucaire was at his new posting for just a few weeks when he had to dig deep to save a life. The call for help came late on

RCMP Marine Division boat the *Athabasca* was assigned to patrol the waterways around Expo 67 in Montreal. Constable Ron Beaucaire is on the front deck of the boat with Constable Hector Dawe operating the controls. The two constables were dispatched to rescue a young woman who had jumped into the water.

the evening of June 21, 1967, when Beaucaire and Dawe were notified of a suicide attempt by a young woman on the Montreal waterfront. The woman had jumped 30 feet from the pier into the fast and dangerous water of the St. Lawrence River.

Aboard the *Athabasca*, Beaucaire and Dawe rushed to the scene. When they arrived, the woman was on a boom, and darkness was nearly upon them. The officers had only the spotlight from the top of the pier to guide their rescue attempts. Despite the strong and treacherous current, Beaucaire jumped into the black water, fully dressed and with his runners on. He then hoisted the woman up so Dawe could pull her aboard.

The stressful night, however, was not over. The swift current made it difficult for his partner to manoeuvre the boat. Beaucaire was struck by the bow and forced under water. He was in the water for a considerable time before the patrol boat made it back

THE ONTARIO BRANCH
ON BEHALF OF

The Royal Life Saving Society Canada

PRESENTS

THE M. G. GRIFFITHS CERTIFICATE

TO

R.H. Beaucaire, R.C.M.P.

who by application of knowledge gained
through the programme of the Society

Saved the Life of a Fellow Man

CHAIRMAN — AWARD COMMITTEE   June 21, 1967.   PRESIDENT — ONTARIO BRANCH
DATE

"WHOMSOEVER YOU SEE IN DISTRESS RECOGNIZE IN HIM A FELLOW MAN"

M.G. Griffiths Certificate presented to Ron Beaucaire.

to him. "Thanks to his experience and seamanship, Hector pulled me aboard," Beaucaire says.

After the dramatic rescue, Beaucaire never found out if the woman survived the suicide attempt. "Our job was to pick her up and get her to the Port and the Port police looked after her," he says. Unbeknownst to Beaucaire, the Port authority contacted The Royal Life Saving Society Canada to provide details of the heroic rescue. It was a proud moment when the Royal Ontario Lifesaving Society honoured Beaucaire and Dawe for their personal bravery and presented each of them with an M.G. Griffiths Certificate.

Beaucaire's first and only encounter with death was when he went on a call to retrieve a body from the St. Lawrence River. Someone had spotted a floating dead body and advised the Port of Montreal. "They didn't have a boat at the time so they contacted us because they knew we were on the water with the boat," Beaucaire says.

As is often the case with emergency responders, Beaucaire was left in the dark about the elderly man's identity or the circumstances of his death. "With the way the currents on the St. Lawrence were, he could have come from anywhere," Beaucaire says. The image of the peaceful expression on the man's face remains etched in Beaucaire's memory. "He had a smile on his face as if at peace... It's a smile I will never forget!" Unlike what many police officers experience, it was his only encounter with death, and he considers himself very fortunate in that regard.

Beaucaire's duties were carried out on land when he was transferred to the Quebec City Detachment in 1968. For four years his work included serving income tax summons and warrants for the tax man. "We would go to court and present the documentation that we needed to have the individual fined," Beaucaire says. Usually people were wanted because they'd filed their income taxes late. Their fines varied depending on how delinquent they were in submitting their income tax. If they didn't pay, Revenue Canada would issue a warrant for their arrest and forward it to Beaucaire to execute. "Further, my duties entailed attending court in Quebec City and in La Malbaie, 90 miles north of Quebec City, to present documents for income tax purposes. I also carried out investigations on a nearby First Nations reserve, assisted with the Drug Squad, and enforced the *Migratory Bird Act* on the St. Lawrence around Quebec City."

Beaucaire met his future wife, Candy, at a beach party in Ottawa, and the couple kept in touch while he was in training. Candy attended Beaucaire's graduation at "Depot" on November 16, 1966. "We were married on June 8, 1968," Beaucaire says. "It just happened to be two years to the day that I joined the RCMP."

Ron and Candy Beaucaire's wedding in Ottawa, on June 8, 1968. Left to right: George Piccott, Carter MacDonald, Candy and Ron Beaucaire, and Michel Laverdière.

Over time, their family grew and Candy stayed at home to care for their two sons and daughter. Unlike the wives whose husbands worked in detachments, Candy didn't take calls and messages from the public. But she nevertheless had her hands full. "It was fun, especially when Ron started shift work," Candy says, laughing. "That was another story. He was trying to sleep through the day and there were two active little boys running around. When our daughter was born, that was the first week he started working nights. That was tough!"

Looking back at Beaucaire's career, Candy says she rarely worried about him coming home safely, except when he was posted in Quebec City and he went out with the Drug Squad as a backup. "Then at 3:00 in the morning, I'd be wondering, 'Where is he?' But aside from that, I never experienced any scary moments. We were fortunate."

Beaucaire served a stint at "A" Division in Ottawa from 1972 to 1985. That's how he came to be in the thick of a riot on June 3, 1976, when more than 5,000 angry Quebec farmers clashed with RCMP on Parliament Hill. The demonstration started peacefully enough at 1:30 p.m., but quickly escalated. The mob was met by a small squad of RCMP behind barricades. According to news reports of the day, by 4:00 p.m. the crowd broke through a line of Mounties guarding the steps to the House of Commons.

About 70 members of the riot squad rushed in to assist the regular force, preventing demonstrators from entering the Parliament Buildings. The huge police presence on Parliament Hill included RCMP officers from the "A" Division office and Headquarters. "The riot squad was directed by Headquarters," Beaucaire says. "There were at least a few hundred members on Parliament Hill itself, and there was also the Ottawa Police Department looking after the streets in front and around Parliament Hill." It was a frightening experience; the situation was volatile. "You didn't know what to expect," Beaucaire says. "Everybody got excited and started to push." Under a barrage of liquid milk, powdered milk, bottles, sticks and cans, officers managed to push the crowd back from the steps of the House of Commons.

Meanwhile, Agriculture Minister Eugene Whelan was meeting inside with a delegation from the Union des producteurs agricoles. The demonstrators kept chanting and calling for Prime Minister Pierre Trudeau and Whelan to come out and talk to them. Trudeau wasn't at the meeting, but Whelan, who had gone to bat for dairy producers, stepped outside.

He faced an angry mob. The dairy farmers were enraged because the federal government had rejected Whelan's proposal for a dairy subsidy to compensate for low prices. Whelan barely had time to say "I'm your Minister of Agriculture" before protesting

Iconic award-winning photo of Eugene Whelan, Minister of Agriculture, being doused with sour milk on Parliament Hill, Ottawa, June 3, 1976. Constable Ron Beaucaire deflects the milk jug from directly hitting Minister Whelan. *Photo courtesy CP Press. Used with permission.*

producers pitched a jug of milk at him. Whelan was hit on the forehead and doused with milk despite the best efforts of Beaucaire, who was standing next to him and put out his arm to shield him from the milk bath. A Canadian Press photo of Whelan wiping milk from his face with Beaucaire by his side was featured in papers across the country.

After the four-hour protest ended, it took a while for Beaucaire's adrenalin rush to subside, and the incident left him sour. "We had to throw away our riot helmets because they smelled like sour milk," Beaucaire says. "We washed them and our clothes, but the smell just wouldn't go away so we had to throw everything away." Reflecting on the incident, Beaucaire says today's Mounties have more defined roles on Parliament Hill. "They're all in dedicated areas," he says. "In our day, it was more fly-by-the-seat-of-your-pants and hope for the best."

In his stint at "A" Division, Beaucaire worked in various areas, including Organized Crime, Customs and the Mint. He also provided security for the grounds of Government House and the Prime Minister's residence. Typically he wore plain clothes when he was on duty at Government House. But on one unforgettable night, the bodyguard of Governor General Jules Léger was dressed to kill—so to speak. "We went out to the National Arts Centre to see a ballet, so I wore a tuxedo," Beaucaire says, laughing. "My only regret is that I don't have a picture of me in my tuxedo."

While on security detail at Government House, Beaucaire recalls Margaret Trudeau and her children coming out to greet the King and Queen of Jordan. "Justin took off his boots and had two different socks on," Beaucaire says. "He started a trend, which is still popular with kids today. I think the King and Queen were amused."

Following his time at Government House, he was assigned to the Traffic Division, patrolling National Capital Commission property in the Ottawa and Gatineau area. Beaucaire then worked at Security System Headquarters from 1985 to 1987 before moving on to the Security Evaluation Inspection Team headquarters in Ottawa, where he remained until 1999.

The team of Mounties and civilians inspected federal computer sites all over Canada. "The civilians checked the hardware and software because government departments were only allowed to use certain types," Beaucaire says. The RCMP was in charge of administrative work and ensuring the computer rooms were secure. "We checked all personnel who had access to the computer room to make sure they had all of the proper clearances and required access to the computer room, and we made recommendations on how to strengthen security."

While serving his country, Beaucaire travelled across the nation. "It was wonderful because I visited all the provinces in Canada," he says. "I was happy." After spending 30 years in the Force, Beaucaire was proud to receive his long-service medal in Ottawa. He served three more years with the RCMP, but had hoped his career would be longer. "I got a letter saying they no longer required my service after 33 years," he says sadly.

Beaucaire retired from the Force as a Sergeant. "The only regret I have is the way I was let go," he says. "I'm sure at Headquarters they could have found me a position so that I could have gotten my 35 years. But I did have some good jobs and the members I worked with were always good to me, and I tried to be good to them."

—*Pamela Cowan*

C.L.
(Carmen)
BROWN
Reg# 24831

C66/67 Troop
50th Year Reunion

BROWN

"A GOOD PORTION of police work is common sense," says Carmen Brown, who trusted his practical judgment plenty during 38 years with the RCMP, and certainly while deciding which direction his working life should take in the first place.

Brown grew up in Springhill, NS, a town forever known to most Canadians for two reasons: it's the hometown of singer Anne Murray, and was the site of the Springhill mining disaster of 1958, the most devastating underground earthquake in North American mining history. The event that killed 75 miners occurred just two years after a similar explosion in one of the town's other coal mines had killed 39. Those two terrible tragedies took place when Brown was 10 and 12 years old, respectively, and surely helped solidify his desire to get into the larger world as soon as possible.

"Being a town boy, mining was a way of life," says Brown, who spent a summer picking the coal that spilled from overloaded trucks, making $50 per 50-pound bag. "I knew that was not for me early in my teen years."

As the fifth son in a family of nine boys, with a father who ran a neighbourhood grocery store from the front of the family home and also drove a soft drink delivery truck to support his family, Brown also knew his prospects in Springhill were limited and mostly unpalatable. While his two years of training as a student reservist had turned his thoughts to some sort of policing, the local police force did not tempt him to stay in the Cumberland County town.

"It was too small, too much local politics. I wanted to get out," he says. As well, "the RCMP seemed more professional, more up-front." That assessment was no doubt reinforced after another dreadful dose of reality hit when Brown was about 15. Helping his father make soft drink deliveries, he was in the truck going down a rural road when a young boy with some mental incapacity broke away from his older sister as they were standing at the edge of the pavement. He abruptly ran in front of Brown's father's truck and was killed instantly. Brown doesn't recall much of the incident besides a terrible sorrow for everyone involved, but he does remember being a witness at the inquest. While the experience wasn't the sole reason he was interested in policing, "It was a factor, obviously."

Brown applied to both the Armed Forces and the RCMP. The RCMP replied first, so Brown was on his way to Regina a few weeks after his twentieth birthday. On the train, he befriended fellow C Troop recruits Carter MacDonald, Dave LeBlanc and Joe Dennis, who had all boarded in Cape Breton. At "Depot," one of his strongest friendships was with pit partner (roommate) René Charbonneau, a future Deputy Commissioner of the RCMP, who credits Brown for helping him enormously by allowing him to practise his limited English through patient conversations.

"It's like anything else, in sports or whatever, you meet somebody and you either like or dislike him," says Brown. "I liked René. He was up front. He wouldn't be boasting about anything. He had common sense, good clear thinking. He was somewhat like me—serious, he kept to himself, and he knew what he wanted, what he was there for."

Carmen Brown, "Depot" Division, Regina, July 1966.

While Brown was too focused on his training to experience many humorous moments at "Depot," at least one portion of the training that bordered on a prank is seared into his memory. "When you were on night patrol, you basically covered the whole training area. Part of training was to teach you to be responsible; you had to sign in the books, and one stop where you had to sign in was the morgue. That really turned me off, but I guess because as police you're in the morgues all the time, you have to learn how to react. On patrol, it all comes down to your nerves and shaking it off. In the morgue, there was always an instructor who would be checking the night patrols. They would hide in that damn morgue and scare the living crap out of you, by walking up behind you to test your nerves." Luckily, for all the players in these eerie vignettes, "It was in the early part of training and we never carried guns," says Brown.

Brown's preference for common sense behaviour prevailed once he was assigned to his first detachment in Newcastle, NB,

Carmen Brown, "Depot" Division, Regina, November 1966.

and true to his philosophy, it produced a far more satisfying result than would have been likely with scare tactics. Assigned to general duties and highway patrol, he stopped a young woman named Anne Marie McCarthy for speeding. Enjoying his interaction with the talkative and attractive local, he wrote up a ticket but in the space reserved for "registered owner of the car," he wrote "Daddy" and then tore his copy of the ticket out of his book so that it never showed up on a court docket. When he met Anne Marie a few weeks later at a social event, he presented her with the ticket. That application of goodwill led to their courtship, marriage and three children together.

Anne Marie never objected to the several transfers away from New Brunswick that the RCMP required of their family, says Brown, although she had good reason to be irate at one aspect of the job. "I found it funny, but Anne Marie didn't," says Brown. "When our son was born, I was the only one covering the shift. I took Anne Marie to the hospital, the Hotel Dieu in Chatham, bid her good luck and farewell. I didn't feel good about that at all, but I also knew I had to go out and work. I lived with that one for a long time."

Brown spent six years in New Brunswick's Miramichi region, working Richibucto as well as Newcastle and Chatham, investigating the usual assortment of small-town complaints: property damage, sudden death, motor vehicle accidents, alcohol abuse and arson, while also guarding prisoners, and providing other security and court-related matters. "One of the big things you learned was how to deal with people in a respectful manner even though they want to rip your head off for giving them a ticket and making them go to court."

In fact, when Brown arrived for his first posting and stayed overnight in Moncton before driving to Newcastle, the Superintendent in charge of the Subdivision made a point of asking, "Can you fight?" "He said that where he was sending me was a very rough area," Brown recalls. "I told him I grew up in a large family of boys." Knowing how to wrestle didn't come in that handy during one baffling incident early in the Newcastle posting, however. Brown had arrested a drunk driver whose English was scant, save for some choice locker-room slang. It was 1967 and the breathalyser was a relatively new device. When Brown asked the man to "blow into the tube," the fellow jumped up, apparently mistaking Brown's demand for a crude phrase that described an act of a sexual nature. Hollering that he was not doing that, the man barricaded himself inside a closet. "It took a while to get him out of the closet. I had to get another member who was more experienced to help, and he just started laughing."

But true to the Superintendent's warning, Brown did experience some nasty physical incidents in the Miramichi. One was a fight in a small restaurant in Chatham. Two youths were involved in the altercation, but as soon as the police arrived they "became the best of friends," says Brown. And then they turned on him. "I lost a shirt; it was ripped right off my back. That was my first encounter with Allan Legere. He was just a young kid," he says, referring to the notorious rapist, arsonist and serial killer who in the late 1980s became known as the Monster of Miramichi, and who is still imprisoned for his violent crime spree.

During Brown's close encounter with another well-known tough guy, he leaned heavily on his common sense. Yvon Durelle was an internationally famous champion boxer from Baie

Sainte-Anne, a fishing town on Miramichi Bay. He retired in 1965, and by the late 1970s was on trial for shooting and killing a man who attacked him in the bar Durelle's family owned. He was famously acquitted of that on the grounds of self-defense by lawyer Frank McKenna, a future premier of New Brunswick. Brown's encounter with Durelle was several years before that, during a highway check he conducted as a one-man patrol unit.

"He had this rifle lying across his back seat, and I asked him what he was doing. He said he was working for lands and forests, for the purpose of paying his taxes—which he never paid. When I took the rifle out of the car and was standing in the ditch, the damn thing went off. It had a feather trigger, it was loaded, and he was driving around with it. I emptied the gun and gave him a warning."

Having grown up around guns, Brown wasn't in any danger handling that one. Yet what made a 21-year-old rookie RCMP officer decide to take the high road with the careless gun owner? "No specific reason other than that you're in a neighbourhood where the relationships between the police and fishermen are not good because basically we were either taking their licences away or putting them in jail. I was trying to make a better relationship."

Sometimes, the relationships just weren't there to cultivate and common sense had to kick in full force. "I remember one night I was at the Big Cove Reserve [now the Elsipogtog First Nation, on the Richibucto River] and there was a good friend who was working at the detachment. The two of us ended up going to a dance hall on the reserve, but when we got to where the problem was supposed to be in the dance hall, they shut the door and shut the lights off. It didn't take us long to get out that door!"

Not every call featured antagonistic citizens, but many of the calls to reserves were unnerving and demoralizing, says Brown.

For one thing, the poverty was gut-wrenching. "I felt sorry for the people themselves because they were not being treated well," he says. "But when you go into a so-called new house and find the walls have been half torn down and the 2×4s being used in a fireplace, it's shocking."

For calls like that, Brown did the most sensible thing he knew, using techniques to defuse and not escalate a situation. "I'm not known as a talker, but in those situations you talk a lot. You also do a lot of listening and look for faces you can recall, because a lot of times you're dealing with the same type of people or even the same person. You remember their face, their attitude. It helps that you're on guard right away. Or, do you know their friend or parent? I've stopped people for speeding who I should have given a ticket to, but as opposed to that, I'd say, 'I know your father. He and I are going to have a talk about this.'"

Coupling sound judgment with a stern tone also allowed Brown to prevent a few stories from becoming far worse for the people he caught red-handed behaving stupidly. In Richibucto, during a "saturated patrol," in which three patrol cars descend on a small detachment and do a blitz of road checks and traffic stops, Brown stopped an American vehicle that "was literally flying low. When I asked for his driver's licence and registration, he gives it to me, and underneath was a $20 bill. That ticked me off, so I gave him back the money and said, 'This appears to have been stuck to the back of your licence.' In another incident, there was an ex-police officer I stopped for speeding who wouldn't roll down the window. I didn't speak French and he was a francophone. Finally, I told him if he didn't produce his driver's licence through the window, I would have his vehicle towed with him still in it. He kind of changed his attitude, rolled down the window and spoke English."

While Brown let those people know precisely how thin the ice they were skating upon was, he was happy to help those who seemed less entitled. Near Rogersville one day, he stopped a young male driver who appeared unnecessarily nervous. When Brown asked to inspect the car's trunk, he found several brand-new power tools. A few more strategic questions and the young man admitted that he worked for a hardware store in Moncton and had stolen the tools with hope of selling them. Impressed by the youth's quick confession, Brown seized the tools, told him to keep quiet and that he'd be in touch. Then he phoned a co-worker in his detachment and asked him to call the hardware store and pose the question: If the tools were returned, would that be the end of it? It was. "I was young once too," says Brown. "It was just his reaction that made me help him. 'I did something wrong here and it was my fault.' I never had a problem with him again. It kept him out of court, kept his record clean, and the tools went back to the owners. What was to be gained by sending him to court?"

In 1972, Brown transferred away from general duties, to Divisional Headquarters in Fredericton for off-road administration, staffing and personnel duties, overseeing applications of those who wanted to join the RCMP. "It was fun. You were making decisions about whether people should be going into this career or not. You'd ask them general questions, give them the opportunity to talk it out, and if they couldn't talk it out or if there wasn't some indication of them making a decision or having a reason for the decision, then police work was not for them. The surprising thing was, every once in a while you'd get a candidate who was gung-ho and after the interview was done, I'd say, 'I cannot recommend you, for these reasons,' and I can't tell you how many of them thanked me. It was like I was taking the pressure off." Brown did similar work when transferred to Ottawa, doing performance and promotion evaluations while working on national staffing for Security and Intelligence employees involved in crime scene investigations.

Keen to move back to New Brunswick, Brown was refused because he wasn't bilingual. Instead, he took a post based in Halifax, which required him to be on the road each week conducting personnel interviews full-time. With his long experience in staffing issues, he was the obvious choice when a troubled detachment in Tantallon, west of Halifax, needed a firm-handed Supervisor as its Non-Commissioned Officer. The Staff Sergeant who had been in charge there had taken sick leave, distressed because a member of his unit had been caught stealing drug exhibits from the locker and selling them—a crime that drew federal prison time. Brown was brought in to restore order and equilibrium.

"That was difficult. People, maybe not intentionally, resented the implication that they were party to what had happened, that they were not clean, that somebody had to be brought in. They resented that." Nor did it help that a local publication wrote an article heralding his appointment entitled, "There's a new sheriff in town." Once again, Brown turned to the trustiest tool in his kit—good old-fashioned common sense. "You give them space, you let them do their normal thing, and if there's something not within policy, you let them know."

The posting, which lengthened from a couple of months to more than a year, also helped stabilize Brown's life, which was turned upside down when Anne Marie died in 2001. "It got me through a very bad period. It gave me a purpose, something to do."

Brown retired from the Force in 2004, as a Staff Sergeant, but continued to do personnel interviews on a contract basis for another two years. Since then, he's been happily fulfilling the duties of doting grandfather to four grandchildren, and living in Lower Sackville, NS.

In addition to the RCMP providing him a satisfying career in which he was personally rewarded by being able to help others, the nearly four decades of policing refined valuable qualities that complemented the lessons in level-headedness he learned from his father and brothers, says Brown. "You learn to listen. There's always some truth in everything somebody says. It's just that some people are skilled at twisting the truth."

—Helen Metella

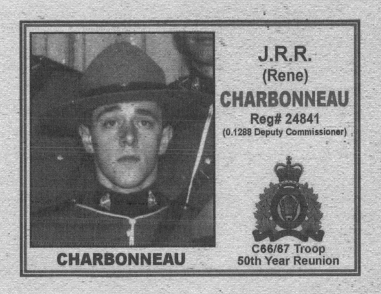

WITH HIS NAME on many a mobster's hit list, René Charbonneau made a habit of looking over his shoulder and watching his surroundings. Moving up the ranks from Constable to Assistant Commissioner, he was a target for the thugs he brought to justice. And there were many throughout his storied, 37-year career in the RCMP.

Charbonneau was the "money man" in high-stakes undercover drug stings. He busted clandestine drug labs, tracked down counterfeiters, and skillfully gained the confidence of informants who held top positions in the Hells Angels and other biker gangs. "I was handling informants—that's the worst of the worst, you know. Yet I felt comfortable doing that. Some people can't do it because they're too nervous. But staying in the office was worse for me than spending time at the street level."

For Charbonneau, undercover work was like flipping a switch, transforming him into a different person. "When you're on, you play a role when you're working undercover. But it's important when you get out and go back to the office that you turn the lights out. There is nothing better for me than when I'm finished to go out and look at the sky, look at the sun, look at the beautiful mountains—I enjoy that."

Charbonneau's hard work was recognized with regular promotions that culminated in him reaching the second-highest position in the RCMP. He credits his professional success to teamwork, which began at "Depot" Division in Regina.

At "Depot," Charbonneau and 31 strangers from diverse backgrounds and different parts of Canada lived together as C Troop for six months. "At the end of training, we were one," Charbonneau says. "That's something the Force has that not many organizations have."

But it took time and incredible effort. Charbonneau's sole language was French and he knew all of the training was in English. He got his first taste of what lay ahead when he got on a train in Montreal and met recruits heading from the Maritimes to "Depot." "When we had breakfast, whatever they ordered, I said, 'The same.' That's all I could say." Until they reached Regina, the menu choices of his new troop mates were his. Likewise, at "Depot," Charbonneau played "follow the leader" in classes, particularly in drill when he couldn't understand the English commands. During the first couple of months in Regina, when Charbonneau wasn't in class, he was in the barracks studying and learning the language.

Passing the time while confined to barracks, September 1966. Left to right: René Charbonneau, Derk Doornbos and Carter MacDonald.

When he went into training, he had three strikes against him: he couldn't speak English, couldn't swim and had little experience driving because his family couldn't afford a vehicle. Gradually, Charbonneau learned English and his driving skills improved, but his crowning achievement was at the pool: "I went to the swimming pool every evening and I worked very hard to get my Bronze Medallion in swimming."

While learning English, Charbonneau credits Carmen Brown, his pit partner in the 32-bed dorm, for his "incredible" support and patience. "In the evening, we'd talk and I'd have a hard time to talk to him and answer him. He often had to repeat what he said, but I learned to know the guy and we talked about personal things—our families. That's something that I'll always remember."

After graduating from "Depot," Charbonneau returned to Quebec. Posted to Montreal, he worked in uniform at the Expo 67 site or at the airport when VIPs arrived for the World's Fair. Following Expo, he went to work in the Montreal Drug Section. That six-year posting was the beginning of what became his life's calling.

The hours were long, with many shifts exceeding 12 hours at a time when there was no overtime pay. Despite this, these were heady times for the young Constable. Charbonneau was deeply involved in the so-called "French Connection," a scheme by which heroin was smuggled from Turkey to France and then to the United States via Canada. It proved to be a major operation, with one seizure totalling 3,400 pounds of hashish. As the main investigator, Charbonneau spent five weeks in court beside the crown prosecutor. But before any major trial began, there were many loose ends to tie up. "We had to re-investigate things. We had to be more precise on certain evidence, and that was quite an experience," Charbonneau says. "I was able to bring a witness

[who] was supposed to be charged, and flip him to be our witness." However, throughout the trial, he had to provide around-the-clock protection for the man, his wife and daughter because, "If we didn't have him, we had nothing."

The tension rose as they built their case, with Charbonneau receiving numerous threats from the mafia. "I travelled to the courthouse on the subway and I was constantly looking around and watching my back. Lots of times, I wonder how I did it."

The nerve-racking trial ended with a successful conviction, but it came at a tremendous cost to the witness and his family, who went into the witness protection program and received new identities—one of the first relocation cases for the Force. "My superiors approved it, and he was out of the city and out of the province forever. His wife had a hair salon and she had to sell it and they had to sell their place. They lost a lot!"

While working in the Drug Section, Charbonneau upgraded his education. "Going to university opens your mind," he says. "It's not about the degree, but to open your mind. I've always been curious, but the best thing about the job was the human relationships." Charbonneau enjoyed his job and university classes, but the load was heavy. He felt a sense of relief when a colleague suggested he apply for a recruiting job, which entailed preparing files on candidates accepted into the Force. "I had pressure to stay in the drug unit, but I'd had enough. I'd really had enough and I needed a change."

With the move to recruiting, Charbonneau was promoted to Corporal. He kept regular hours while he did security checks on the backgrounds of RCMP applicants. His days were busy because at that time the Force was hiring a lot of men. As Charbonneau sorted through the applications, he was particularly interested in determining if the candidates could work with others. "Teamwork is so important. That was a special skill that you needed because, just like a troop, you will depend on others and others will depend on you. It's just like a family."

Although he found the work interesting, after 18 months Charbonneau missed the action on the street and he asked to be transferred to a two-man border detachment at Rock Island, along the Canada-US border. His request was granted and soon he was caught up in a fast-paced job that involved immigration, customs and the border patrol.

While at Rock Island, Charbonneau launched a massive drug investigation in collaboration with the Drug Section in Montreal. The mission was to keep close tabs on a Rock Island resident who was collaborating with Montreal drug dealers. The RCMP sent six men to assist him, but the undercover cops couldn't work out of the detachment because they'd be easily identified in the small village.

To get the inside track on the drug deals, Charbonneau got approval for wiretaps—the first time the surveillance tool was used outside of Montreal. "I had to go to Montreal every two months to get approval from a judge. They had party lines, so that was a complication." His team kept the Rock Island suspect under surveillance as he frequently drove back and forth to Montreal, but the unmarked police cars along the drug dealer's route had a hard time keeping pace. "He was going 100 miles per hour and with our stupid police cars we had a hard time to stay close to him," Charbonneau says. "We lost him many, many times." Despite the challenges, he and his men made numerous busts for possession of hashish.

After two years in Rock Island, Charbonneau moved to a larger detachment in Joliette, a city about 50 kilometres northeast of Montreal. Promoted to Sergeant, he covered many miles in the large rural area doing drug and counterfeit investigations, discovering clandestine meth labs and tangling with the Hells Angels.

In 1979, Charbonneau was transferred back to familiar territory—the Drug Section in Montreal. He wasn't enthusiastic about returning to a posting where he'd already spent six years, but he followed orders. "I was in charge of the clandestine labs that were mainly run by the Hells Angels making speed and all kinds of other dirty drugs," Charbonneau says. "That's tough work, very tough work. You've got to be very, very patient."

Prior to the seizures, the RCMP worked hand-in-hand with chemists from Health Canada. During covert night operations, the cops tailed the bikers to their drug stash in the countryside and snatched samples of the drugs, which they passed on to Health Canada for testing. "You have to know when the stuff is ready before you bust because if it's not at the right level, then you have nothing. We did make quite a few seizures. It was special work."

René Charbonneau, drug undercover photo.

In light of his successful work on clandestine labs, Charbonneau was put in charge of the undercover team in "C" Division (the Montreal Drug Section) where, as he says, "We worked mainly with the bikers. We were making all kinds of purchases and we had a lot of fun." The undercover cops would buy LSD, PCP, cocaine and heroin. The buys started off small with purchases of 125 pills. Eventually the size of the purchases would begin to increase. "We'd say, 'Can you get us 900?' and the guy would say, 'You have to go to someone else.'" Ultimately the aim was to identify and get close to the main players of the drug supply chain.

As the buys increased, Charbonneau and his team eventually bought kilos of cocaine at a time. "Once, I ended up in Quebec City and I had $200,000 in my suitcase. I was older so I was the money man. I went to the room and I opened the suitcase and there was $200,000, and I said, 'If you're ready, I'm ready. You go back to your men and bring the stuff.'" The responsibility for so much cash weighed heavily on Charbonneau. Had the money been stolen, he would have lost his job.

Just like during his training days back in Regina, Charbonneau always developed a sense of camaraderie with his co-workers. However, this could sometimes end in heartache. For example, he was devastated when two of his mentors, a Senior Constable and Staff Sergeant, "went bad and ended up in jail. There are times in your life when you are vulnerable, and I believe that is what happened because these two guys were not bad people." In the case of the Constable, he took heroin from the evidence locker and sold it. "When you're working undercover and handling informants, you're playing with dynamite," Charbonneau says. "But you don't have a choice, so we have to have the right people and you have to have the right managers also to say, 'No, we don't do that. Stop the operation.'"

When he wasn't making drug buys, Charbonneau taught undercover courses to provincial police and instructed RCMP members at the division level on the handling of informants. "I did have quite a few informants during my years—very, very high-level people who were at the top of Hells Angels and other bikers. I had expertise. I had made many mistakes in my younger years so I now knew what I was talking about. This is why they wanted me to give these courses."

The Force recognized Charbonneau's remarkable work ethic and as time went on, promotions followed. In 1983, he successfully passed the exams to become a commissioned officer and went on to the next step—a formal interview. Waiting outside the interview room, Charbonneau didn't look the part of a senior officer: he was dressed in a shirt and tie but, in keeping with his undercover work, his hair hung to his shoulders. In the end, the length of his hair didn't impede his progress and he was promoted to Inspector.

He landed in charge of security at the Montreal International Airport (Mirabel) but after about 18 months he was called back to Montreal's Drug Section. "I was Detective Inspector and, a few months later, Officer in Charge. I didn't want to go back there. I'd spent too much time in the Drug Section, but there were problems," and his expertise was required. The backlog of challenges included the arrest of a Staff Sergeant who had helped an informant move several kilos of hashish. The unit's morale hit rock bottom.

Gradually, Charbonneau turned the situation around by bringing in officers who worked well as a team. "To me, that was the most important—the rest will follow. We had some very good operations, we had fun. No [officers] got arrested and no bad things happened while I was there, and that's the most important thing for me."

However, there were also drawbacks. After working long and hard to get convictions, the frustration of Charbonneau and his fellow officers grew when drug dealers were acquitted on technicalities. "I often thought, 'What am I doing?' They've got all of the money and they're laughing at us.' We got no support from the government—that's how we felt at times. But then, you go back to work."

From Montreal's Drug Section, he became the Officer in Charge of personnel for "C" Division, which covered the entire province of Quebec. Recruiting was a welcome change from the difficulties of the Drug Section, and the new posting ran from 1989 to 1992. From his Montreal office, he enjoyed speaking with each candidate before he or she left for "Depot" in Regina. "I was in charge of recruiting, but also all of the transfers in the whole Division," Charbonneau says. "I really liked the job, and that is something that I like about the Force. You can go from Personnel to Training—there are all kinds of jobs."

It wasn't long before Charbonneau's superiors wanted him to move to Ottawa. He didn't want to go and started thinking about leaving the Force. He changed his mind when a headhunter for a major bank offered him a job heading their security operations. Instead, however, he accepted a transfer to Quebec City in 1992 and took over as the Commanding Officer of the Quebec Subdivision. "I had three beautiful years in Quebec City. That was a promotion to Superintendent."

The idyllic posting was marred when he received the tragic news that a partner he'd worked with earlier in his career had taken his own life. "I spent days and nights thinking about what the hell happened—why? [But] the Drug Section is a very demanding position. These jobs are high intensity and sometimes you become vulnerable. That's the only explanation I have. Sometimes you work so much that you don't take time to look at the sun or the flowers."

While in Quebec City, he wrote an exam to become Chief Superintendent and was transferred to Ottawa's Drug Enforcement Branch. "That's the heavy stuff. That's the approvals for the major operations across Canada, so I travelled the country and also outside Canada."

In 1995, he was promoted to Assistant Commissioner in Charge of enforcing federal laws, including drugs, money laundering, customs and immigration. At the time, the RCMP worked with 10 other countries on drug investigations. In November 1996, Charbonneau was sent to Cuba to share his expertise in drug enforcement. Over the course of his three days there, Charbonneau developed a good relationship with his Cuban counterparts that helped down the road. "We transferred some equipment to analyze drugs, we brought them to Montreal, to Ottawa and to Regina, and we brought them to special meetings. This is about being Canadian. We're open and everywhere I went, we were told, 'We want training from Canada, from the RCMP.' That made me proud."

Charbonneau was pleased when the liaison officer in Lima invited him to Peru. "Meeting heads of criminal operations in other countries is crucial to the success of our operations," he says. In Lima, Charbonneau flew in an army plane to the jungle where commandos were trained to detect mobile labs. In these labs the process of making cocaine from coca leaves began. "They take the leaves and with chemicals they make a pasta—a powder—out of it. The pasta is then packaged in big, multi-kilo bundles and moved to a certain place in the jungle, and an airplane lands on a very small strip to pick them up." From there, the pasta was taken to Columbia to make the final product, cocaine. As Charbonneau noted, "The fact that they brought me to their secret base in the jungle was a gesture of appreciation for our Force."

The criminals constantly moved the labs in order to avoid arrest by the army. Once, during a briefing on the work of the commandos, Charbonneau was told they had taken down a Colombia airplane that was picking up the pasta being made in the labs. At the end of the meeting, Charbonneau gave the leader of

Assistant Commissioner René Charbonneau, second from the left, in the jungle training centre in Peru, where Peruvian police train to arrest cocaine producers.

the commandos a gift from the Force. "He looks at me and says, 'I have nothing to give you,' and he took off his jungle hat and he gave it to me. And I still have it. It was sweat-stained, the hat of a working man, and it was one of the most beautiful gifts I've ever had. I remember the man. He had to leave his family and work in the jungle because it was a secret place, well guarded."

From the jungle, Charbonneau went back to Lima where he had an appointment with General Vidal, who was in charge of Peru's security. He laughs when he recalls the crazy trip to see the General. "I've never seen anything like it!" He was in a Suburban with a motorcycle escort, and as the entourage made its way through Lima's heavy traffic, police officers on motorcycles kicked any vehicles in their way.

The meeting with the General went well and ended with Charbonneau promising the RCMP's assistance in the fight against drugs. "I said, 'Whatever we can do to help, we have to work together to help each other.'"

Following the trip to Peru, Charbonneau went to Bogota, Colombia, to give a workshop on money laundering. When he arrived, he spent the morning with General Rosso José Serrano, who was in charge of the Colombian National Police from 1994 to 2000. Serrano was one of the masterminds behind the dismantling of the Cali and Medellin cartels. In the afternoon, Charbonneau was heading back to the Academy in Bogota where he was to officially open the workshop. General Serrano was also heading to the Academy, so he offered Charbonneau a lift in his military helicopter. "It was equipped with machine guns," Charbonneau says. "The cartels wanted the general's head so he was under full protection. When I got on the helicopter with him, there were all kinds of soldiers around us with strings of munitions across their chest… It was surreal."

Investigators from 10 countries in South and Central America attended the money-laundering workshop. In his address, Charbonneau emphasized that "everything the RCMP did in Colombia was done with respect for their country. That was applauded, let me tell you," he says. "We respected them and that is the Canadian way… I worked with Interpol and I was asked by many countries for training from the RCMP. They said, 'We want you to give the courses.' We gave the courses, but always with respect."

Once a year, Charbonneau attended senior management meetings in Regina. A course in 1999 coincided with a wave of Chinese people immigrating to British Columbia. "Immigration Canada wanted to go to Peking to meet the Chinese officials and they wanted the RCMP to be along with them." RCMP Commissioner Phil Murray put Charbonneau in charge of leading the Force's delegation to China.

Charbonneau and a colleague in charge of Intelligence stopped in Bangkok, Thailand, on their way to China. There, he met with a general to discuss co-training, then went on to Hong Kong for a quick meeting before going to Beijing.

In strategic areas around the world, the RCMP have liaison

Assistant Commissioner René Charbonneau (far right) at the opening of money-laundering workshop, Bogota, Colombia. Third from the left is General Rosso José Serrano, who is featured in the Netflix series *Narcos*.

officers who act as the link between law enforcement agencies in Canada and their host country. At the time of Charbonneau's trip, there were RCMP liaison officers in many major centres around the world, including London, Paris, Amsterdam, Bogota, Hong Kong and Lima, but none in China. "I think only the Australians had a liaison officer in China, but we wanted to have our own people there. They were opening the economy a lot and they needed help with credit card fraud. I offered our co-operation but I said it would be much easier if we had our own liaison officers here."

Charbonneau met with the Canadian ambassador and the Chinese Minister of Security, and during the short meeting he earned the Minister's trust. "I gave the Chinese Minister of Security an RCMP tie with the rider and the Maple Leaf, and he was so happy, he thanked me three or four times. I said: 'Sir, we would have liked to have a liaison officer here in Beijing with you,' and he said: 'What? Don't we have one already?'" As quick as that, a deal was struck. "The ambassador was very pleased and

I think within four to six months afterwards we took our liaison officer from Hong Kong and moved him to Beijing. That made me proud."

In 2001, Charbonneau was promoted to Deputy Commissioner of the RCMP—one step below the position of Commissioner. Despite his rank, he never lost sight of the work being done on the street. "The higher you go, you must always stay focused on the fact that your position exists because of the people that are doing the work—especially the Constables," Charbonneau says. "This is something that people who want to rise in the ranks sometimes forget—that the important people are the ones doing the job at the street level."

Charbonneau talked the talk and walked the walk. After a meeting in Vancouver, he changed into civilian clothes and walked around the city's Downtown East Side—an area known for junkies, poverty, crime, mental illness, the sex trade and homelessness. Earlier in his career, he'd been to the Downtown East Side many times. He wanted to see what had changed, so he talked to frontline officers and people on the street. After completing his survey, he gave his assessment to the Force's brass and advised strongly that they prioritize spending on human resources. "Don't put all of the money into computers and equipment for the big people in Ottawa," he told them. "Keep some budget and think about the job at the street level."

Charbonneau retired in 2003, and he and his wife, Johanne, moved closer to his hometown and bought a house in a Quebec ski area. Family time is precious to Charbonneau. It was something he had very little of when he was serving his country. That's changed with retirement, and he spends a lot of time with his wife, three children and six grandchildren—"a gift that life gives you," he says.

In 2001, 25 years after receiving his own badge, Deputy Commissioner René Charbonneau (seated) returned to "Depot" Division to present badges to graduating RCMP cadets.

On the job, Charbonneau immersed himself completely in catching criminals, but during his downtime he took solace in the beauty of nature and life's simple pleasures—the sound of children laughing in the playground, birds singing in the trees and the brilliance of bright blue skies. It was a fine balancing act. Now that he no longer has to transform himself to fit into the underworld, he can fully enjoy each day's moments of innocence. "When I listen to children playing, it makes me smile. It makes my day."

When asked what he learned most from his years in the Force, Charbonneau says that he feels privileged to have worked within Canada and outside its borders. "I met people who worked very hard. If we just respected people, we'd have a better life. Human relationships are important."

—Pamela Cowan

J.J.B.
(Joseph)
DENNIS
Reg# 24824

C66/67 Troop
50th Year Reunion

DENNIS

Introduction *by Jerry Forst*

As one of the C Troop members behind this book, I think it is important to explain how Joe Dennis's story came to be part of it:

> While reaching out to troop members to attend our thirtieth and fiftieth reunions, in 1996 and 2016, and later to solicit their participation in this book, I emailed and spoke with Joe Dennis several times. But before these contacts, I was not aware that Joe had left the Force at his five-year anniversary. Nor was I aware, other than through news stories at the time they occurred, of the details of two tragic murders that I would later learn about from Joe. During the late 1960s and 1970s, there was no real way of contacting other troop mates unless you phoned or wrote them, or kept track of their transfers on RCMP

dispatches. Thus, there was no communication between me and Joe until our 30-year reunion.

As newly sworn-in members of the RCMP, Joe Dennis, Carter MacDonald, David LeBlanc and Carmen Brown met for the first time when they travelled by train together from Cape Breton and Halifax to Regina, to start their training at "Depot" Division as members of C Troop. In Montreal, they were joined by René Charbonneau and Michel Laverdière.

During training I spent a lot of time teaching Joe Dennis how to drive; Derk Doornbos and I were duty drivers who helped new drivers in our off time. One time, when we were a senior troop, Doornbos and Dennis got into a wager over who was tougher—a Maritimer or a Prairie boy. To settle it, they slept in a spare two-man room one weekend with no bedding and with the windows wide open. I remember snow on the floor and the wind howling, but neither Derk nor Joe would give in and leave the room until Sunday night when they had to rejoin the troop.

Joe was a very dedicated troop member who was very well-liked and spent a lot of time in barracks. One of the funniest stories I remember about training involved Joe. One day, when we were close to being the senior troop, we were scheduled for foot drill on the parade square with our instructor, Constable Tony Antoniuk, after the noon parade. The troop was dressed in boots and breeks, wearing our brown serge with our Sam Brown hats, and we had our white RCMP lanyards attached to our .38 revolvers. However, Joe Dennis was missing a vital part of his equipment—his revolver. While changing at noon, Joe had misplaced the key for his revolver cabinet.

I was one of the few who knew this—Joe had told me as I hurried to join the troop outside. Moments later, Joe came running out to join the troop and it appeared he had found his key as he had his lanyard in place hanging from his holster.

After the noon parade, we stayed on the parade square and Antoniuk put us through our drills. One of the drills we were practising for our Passout was a revolver drill, where we would present our revolvers on command, then re-holster them. This drill was not always part of our session, but it was that day. Antoniuk had us lined up in two rows of 16 members each and he gave the order to present arms. I was in the front row with Joe.

Antoniuk had us remove our revolvers so we were holding them in our hands, when out of the corner of my eye I saw him walking down the front row toward me. At the same moment, out of the corner of my other eye I saw Joe with his right hand extended, the white lanyard attached to his index finger, and I quickly realized he had *not* found his key and trouble was headed his way.

Seeing Joe, I wanted to laugh but I didn't, and somehow neither did anyone else. Antoniuk walked past Joe without seeing that he did not have a revolver in his hand. When we were ordered to re-holster our revolvers, I began to giggle as did several other of our troop mates who knew what had just happened—a close call.

When I reached out to Joe about the troop reunions, we had a number of amazing conversations. I shared my story of leaving the Force after 12 years and he told me his. I knew that Joe had not wanted to leave the Force any more than I had, but I also knew that Joe, like Bob Dolhy, John Turnell, me and a few others in our troop, suffered from PTSD. The difference was that I had sought treatment.

After my discussions with Joe about this book, I received an email from him that had attached to it the story you are about to read. Joe said he wanted to support the troop by telling his story. He knew he had not covered his whole story, but he was willing to share some of it for his troop mates.

I read what he'd written and, just as I had done in my discussions with other members, I told him that he might not want to share it because it could reopen up the wounds, anxiety and other feelings that the tragic events of which he was a part had scarred him with. That is exactly what happened to Joe and others, including me, in the storytelling for this book.

During the writing process, our writer and I asked additional questions of Joe to clarify the facts of his story, and carefully assessed the dangers of doing so. When Joe got the questions from the writer, he made a decision not to expand on his story because he began reliving the tragedies all over again.

I thought it appropriate to address this before you read Joe's story so that, first of all, other RCMP members know that they are not alone, and secondly, that, personally and collectively, our troop mates hope that those who need to do so will seek help for their PTSD.

Now, a few words about the content of Joe's story: these terrible events occurred soon after Joe's time at "Depot." He had only been out of training since the end of November 1966 and he worked on one mass murder less than a year later—in August 1967—and another in January 1969.

Like Dolhy and the others, Joe had no assistance program from which to seek help; the Force had not yet recognized that such a program was needed. Fortunately, PTSD has now been recognized as an issue, though getting members to seek help remains a problem.

In an email in mid-March 2020, Joe told me that on March 3, 2020, while listening to a radio story about the 1969 axe murders at Buffalo Narrows, a case on which he had worked, he learned that two children of the family (who had been at their grandmother's for the night and who, therefore, had not been slain) had not been provided with help to deal with this tragedy. Nor had their brother, Donny, the sole survivor of that event.

It is very apparent in talking to Joe, and to other troop mates, that all of them are more worried and concerned for those they perceive as victims in a murder, traffic accident, shooting or rape than they are about themselves.

I think it is important for the reader to know that during the writing process I sent out a request for stories from all our troop mates. Three members who served with Joe Dennis spoke about the hurt they felt when he left the Force. All spoke about how dedicated and mature Joe was in dealing with these tragedies.

Joe Dennis is a hero, as are the other members who suffer from PTSD, and their wives. Joe credits his wife Darlene's love, strength and support for pulling him from the pit and guiding them to where they are today. He sees her as his rock and his hero.

Here is his story.

NOT ALL OF the members of C Troop enjoyed long and satisfying careers with the RCMP after graduating as exultant Junior Constables in November 1966. While all entered their careers excited and energetic, and most were deployed to introductory assignments that suited their backgrounds, abilities and proficiency in one or both of Canada's official languages, all were still destined first for front-line police work.

And police work can be brutal.

The lucky ones didn't discover the worst of it until they had a few years of routine experience to create a balanced basis for comparison. Others, such as Joe Dennis, had the bad luck to slam head-first into a horror-filled incident before they had put in a full year on the Force.

Dennis's initial duties in the case, which included attending the crime scene, were dreadful enough to be life-changing. But these were followed by several common terrors that shake police officers' lives and are seldom visible to the public. One was Dennis's "close call from a mass murderer." Another was the almost unfathomable coincidence that he would attend another horrible and nearly identical crime that occurred, mercilessly, very soon after the first.

On August 15, 1967, just nine months after leaving "Depot" and in just his second posting, Dennis was called in to give direct support to the North Battleford Subdivision (Saskatchewan), which was adjacent to the Blaine Lake Detachment where he was posted.

Nine members of a farm family in the tiny rural community of Shell Lake had been massacred in what was considered Canada's worst-ever random attack. A father, mother and seven siblings were shot to death by a stranger while most of them were still sleeping; a four-year-old daughter somehow survived.

As Dennis explains what happened next, it's impossible not to compare the scene of danger and poor preparation that he stumbled into to the ambush and murder of four Mounties in Mayerthorpe, Alberta, in March 2005. Both incidents concerned a mentally unstable man who had frightened his rural community for years without recourse, and young RCMP officers, including several rookies, who were unaware of the magnitude of threat he posed.

As Dennis recalls, "Blaine Lake was a two-member detachment with a Corporal in Charge, located on the border of Prince Albert Subdivision and the neighbouring subdivisions of North Battleford and Saskatoon. At that time the Corporal in Charge was on vacation and had been temporally replaced with a senior Constable (Constable Ken Bullock). Neither of us was very familiar with the detachment area or its residents. Shell Lake fell within the jurisdiction of the North Battleford Subdivision. However, it was located adjacent to the Blaine Lake Detachment area and we were assigned to give direct support in response to the tragedy at Shell Lake (as were pretty well all forces in the area and throughout the province). The following days and nights were filled with road blocks and vehicle checks, following up on leads

96

from the public, and so on. Our lack of local knowledge placed Constable Bullock and me at somewhat of a disadvantage.

"On the afternoon of August 18, a request for assistance was received from the Sergeant of our neighbouring Detachment at Shellbrook. He had received information from the public that Victor Hoffman, a young resident of the Leask area, had recently been released from the North Battleford mental facility, and that he had a history of violence towards animals that should be looked into. Leask was in the Blaine Lake Detachment area; however, we were not familiar with him or the location of his residence. The [local who had provided police with the lead] was contacted. He knew where the Hoffman farm was and would guide us to the location.

"Constable Bullock, our guide, and I met with the Shellbrook Sergeant and his Senior Constable. We proceeded in two vehicles to the Hoffman farm, a short distance from Leask. The farm was separated from the gravel roadway by a heavy growth of trees. It was a typical small farm with a barn, several sheds and the house somewhat separated from the other building by a grove of trees and bushes.

"As our vehicle pulled into the farmyard, a young man and an older man [Victor Hoffman and his father] were working on a farm vehicle a distance of approximately 25 feet from where we parked our vehicle facing them. The Shellbrook vehicle entered the yard a short period of time behind us and parked to our rear. A large barn was located approximately 50 feet to our left, and there were several smaller sheds just beyond where the Hoffmans were working.

"There was an older model vehicle [which proved to be Victor Hoffman's] also parked to our left, sort of between us and the barn, and approximately 75 feet from where the Hoffmans were working. We stopped more or less between their work site and this vehicle.

"We were in the lead vehicle and as we stopped, naturally the Hoffman men, who were working under the hood of the vehicle, looked up from their work. The older man appeared normal, a curious look but nothing out of the ordinary. However, Victor Hoffman's reaction, though only momentary, was very different. I thought it curious at the time but just summed it up to surprise on his part. However, later it would speak volumes. He had what I now would describe as fight-or-flight body language and a shocked facial expression. Several times, in rapid succession, he looked at us and then at his vehicle. These reactions lasted only a second or two. As the Shellbrook vehicle entered the yard, Victor appeared to become calm and went back working on the vehicle. Later, I discovered that none of the others in our party had observed what I had.

"Our guide from Leask remained in our vehicle. As the members from Shellbrook Detachment investigated, Constable Bullock and I exited our vehicle but remained in the background, standing by if required. The Sergeant and his Constable approached the Hoffmans and commenced a discussion with them, mainly with the father. After a relatively short period, the members and the father walked to the farmhouse [approximately 100 feet beyond the car], which was partially screened by a grove of bushes and trees. Victor Hoffman continued working on the vehicle. We remained near our vehicle, casually observing Hoffman, and engaged in general conversation with our guide.

"After approximately 15 minutes, we walked over to Victor's vehicle and observed two firearms on the rear seat. Upon inspection, they proved to be an Enfield .303 and a Browning pump action .22, and both rifles were loaded. Constable Bullock removed a fully loaded 10-round magazine from the .303; I removed 12 .22 long-rifle rounds [12 rounds of .22 calibre] from the tubular magazine of the .22. Bullock put the magazine in his pocket, and I placed the loose rounds in mine, together with a partial box of .22 rounds, which were also on the seat. We returned the firearms to the seat of the vehicle.

"While we were examining the vehicle, Victor had stopped work and had entered a small shed a few feet from the work site. We thought he was obtaining supplies or tools from the shed to continue the job.

"We commenced walking towards the farmhouse to inform the Sergeant of our discovery. We met the other members as they were returning to the farmyard. The Sergeant was carrying a pair of rubber boots belonging to Victor. [At the scene of the murders, the killer had left a boot print in Mr. Peterson's blood on both sides of his body as he stepped over it to exit the house. The prints had a distinctive pattern, and the Sergeant felt the tread on Victor's boots might match that pattern.]

"As we all approached our vehicles, Victor was observed entering the barn from the direction of his vehicle. I retrieved the .303, opened the breach, and handed it to the others. I then picked up the .22, and as I always do when I handle a firearm, worked the action. To my amazement, I ejected four .22 calibre long-rifle rounds from the firearm. I was certain I had fully emptied the firearm previously and confirmed this with Bullock. We were to learn later where these rounds had come from, and the close call we all had just experienced.

"With the discovery of the boots and a potential murder weapon, Victor Hoffman graduated from being a person of interest to a suspect in the mass murder. However, the Sergeant did not wish to have any further contact with him at that time. Bullock and I were instructed to take up a position on the road where we could observe the only access/egress to the farm and to intercept Victor if he attempted to exit the farm. The Sergeant and Constable from Shellbrook Detachment returned our guide to Leask, then continued on to Shell Lake to have the boots and .22 firearm examined by the crime lab, which had been set up at the temporary police headquarters. They then returned to join us in watching the farm.

"In the predawn hours of August 19, we received confirmation that the boots' tread matched the bloody boot prints, and the firing pin on the .22 matched the indentation on four expended shells retrieved from the murder scene. We were instructed to continue on watch, and that a General Investigation Section (GIS) team was en route from North Battleford to the Hoffman farm to effect Victor's arrest. We remained on station until the GIS arrived, and Victor Hoffman was arrested without further incident. He provided them with an extremely detailed confession, admitting he had committed the murders.

"In time, Victor Hoffman was tried for the Shell Lake murders and found not guilty on the grounds of insanity [paranoid schizophrenia]. He was incarcerated in a home for the criminally insane in Ontario, where he died of cancer in 2004.

"The following are interesting details of the horrible event:

- Victor was released from the North Battleford mental hospital on medication a short period before he committed the murders. At his trial, a representative for the institution admitted that an unmedicated Victor might have been capable of the act for which he was charged; however, his unsupervised medication treatments corrected that possibility. The problem was that Victor stopped taking the medication because it was making him sick, and he started seeing the devil, who kept tempting him to do a terrible act. At night, he would drive the rural areas while the tempting continued. He was able to resist until the early morning hours of August 15 when he came upon the Petersons' farm, which stood out on a hillside, whereupon the tempting overcame him and nine people he did not even know died.

- His initial plan was to shoot all his victims in the head, cut off the heads, and dispose of them so ballistics could not be obtained from the bullets. However, Mr. Peterson lunged at him and he had to shoot him numerous times in the body before he collapsed in the doorway, thereby ruining this plan to cover his tracks. He shot Mrs. Peterson as she tried to escape the house through a kitchen window carrying her one-year-old child. He then went around to the four bedrooms, shooting six of the Peterson children. He left one four-year-old girl alive. As he left the house, he shot the one-year-old, who was crying by the mother he thought was dead [published reports say she later died in hospital]. He said he thought the child would starve.

- As a follow-up, Victor repeatedly poured grinding compound down the barrel of the .22 firearm he had used and fired hundreds of rounds in order to alter the gun's rifling and thereby the ballistics of any bullets. It worked, because the lab advised they could not get a match on the recovered projectiles from the victims. However, the firearm, which he had apparently stolen from a house party he had attended several years previously, left a very unique imprint on cartridges, as the original firing pin had been replaced with a homemade one by the rightful owner. Victor had attempted to pick up all the spent casings at the scene but he missed four that bore the imprint of the homemade firing pin.

- During his questioning Victor Hoffman provided answers to several of the queries I had:

Q. What was the meaning of his immediate actions, which I felt I had observed, upon seeing us entering the farmyard, the momentary panic and fear, the rapid back-and-forth looking from us to his vehicle?

A. Our Blaine Lake vehicle entered the farmyard several seconds ahead of the one from the Shellbrook Detachment. Upon seeing us, he immediately realized why we were there, and his first reaction was to get to the loaded firearms in his vehicle and initiate a firefight. That course of action was foiled upon the entry of the Shellbrook members into the yard. He then decided to wait and see how things developed.

Q. Where did the four rounds that were in the .22 rifle when we took possession of it, come from?—a firearm I was certain I had completely unloaded a very brief period before.

A. I'm afraid our complacency and failure [for whatever reason] to restrict Hoffman's movements or keep him under closer or direct observation afforded him the freedom of movement that could have cost us dearly. He advised that as we were checking out his vehicle, he stopped work, entered a tool shed, left by another door and made his way to the barn without being observed. Then, when we left the area of his and the police vehicles to inform the Shellbrook members of the discovery of the firearms, he got to the off-side of his vehicle, again without being seen. By means of the driver's side rear door he got to the firearms. He had reactivated his plan to "shoot it out," which he almost abandoned again upon discovering that the magazine for the .303 had been removed. However, as he had the .22 calibre ammunition with him, he decided to continue with only that firearm. He was in the process of loading the .22 when all four of us started to come back to the vehicles. He only had time to load four rounds, which was not enough to carry out his plan. Replacing the rifle on the seat, he walked back to the barn."

As harrowing as the Shell Lake massacre and its aftermath were for Dennis, his trial by fire in the RCMP was far from over. Just 17 months later, in early 1969, he was temporarily transferred to the Buffalo Narrows RCMP Detachment in northern Saskatchewan. He was there to take over detachment duties so that the regular detachment member could focus on a mass murder that had occurred on January 30.

A schizophrenic young man who lived in the tiny village murdered seven people—a mother, father, two of their daughters, two of their sons and a family friend—with an axe, also while this family was sleeping.

The parallels to the first mass murder are jaw-dropping, and included the fact that the second family's name was Pederson (the first was Peterson). Dennis described the murder scene as "a slaughterhouse." It is difficult to conceive how he carried on policing, especially when, not long after, he lost two RCMP colleagues with whom he'd served—a Sergeant and a Senior Constable who were killed while responding to a domestic dispute. Then, life dealt him yet another cruel blow when his long-time girlfriend broke off their engagement and returned home to Nova Scotia.

Unbelievably, viewed through the lens of everything that has been discovered about PTSD and policing since the 1960s, Dennis did not receive counselling.

"I never thought about burnout," says Dennis. "I guess I had the naïve belief that my superiors would not burden me with more than could be managed. That belief was replaced by a sense of betrayal and abandonment ... but that is history and I really don't wish to dwell on it."

—Joe Dennis and
Helen Metella

R.J.
(Robert)
DOLHY
Reg# 24847

C66/67 Troop
50th Year Reunion

DOLHY

RCMP MEMBERS LEAVE the Force for their own reasons, in their own time, but few in C Troop had as dramatic a reason or came to that decision in as short a time as Bob Dolhy. Dolhy quit the Force in October 1967, less than a year after graduation from "Depot." Yet his brief stint in policing, which involved a close-range gun ambush in which he was unarmed, a startling and horrifying on-duty event a few days earlier, and subsequently undiagnosed PTSD, represents a major turning point in his life.

Dolhy grew up in Larder Lake, ON, then a small mining and forestry municipality, 200 kilometres north of North Bay and just a few kilometres west of the Quebec border in northeastern Ontario. "There wasn't much opportunity," says Dolhy, whose father worked in the nearby gold mine. "I really didn't have any prospects—I was maybe looking at the forestry industry. At 16, I got a summer job for the Ministry of Natural Resources, in fire protection." After Grade 11, Dolhy quit school to work in the mines too, but returned to school about a year later when his father died. While finishing his Grade 12, he spotted an ad in the paper for RCMP recruits. He applied, was interviewed in Kirkland Lake, and "managed to pass the tests," all in a short time.

"Before I knew it, I was on the train to Regina," says Dolhy. "It was the first time I'd been anywhere and it was quite a large city compared to where I'd come from. I knew no one, and it was my first time on my own. I was 20."

Two incidents that occurred on the same day, during a break from RCMP training, foreshadowed how suddenly and unequivocally a person's life could change. One summer weekend, Dolhy and several other C Troop members, including Carter MacDonald, John Turnell, Dave LeBlanc and Peter Albertson, were enjoying their day off at Regina Beach, "looking at all the girls—we were of that age."

Dolhy had already begun chatting up a young woman named Janice to whom he'd been briefly introduced a few days earlier by his troop mate Jerry Forst. He had offered to buy her a soda when a commotion stirred up among the beach patrons. People began yelling that a young man was missing and feared drowned. "We all ran into the water and held hands to form a line to cover a large area in quick time, and started walking, trying to find him," says Dolhy. "We soon found him, pulled him onto the beach, and someone began CPR immediately until the paramedics arrived." Despite everyone's best efforts, the young man did not make it. "It was a sad and emotional day," says Dolhy, "but a significant one."

He did buy Janice that soda, they continued to talk and "I did manage to meet her again." A few dates later and they were officially a couple, well in advance of Dolhy's graduation from "Depot." They married in 1968.

Between graduation and marriage, however, Dolhy took up his first assignment for the RCMP. It was in Minnedosa, MB, a rural farming community half-way between Brandon, MB, and Riding Mountain National Park. Dolhy was not impressed with where his first job in his new career had installed him. "I did not want to be posted to a small town." While Minnedosa was small, its RCMP detachment was responsible for patrolling a nearby First Nation reserve near Neepawa, and a national park, as well as several busy highways that intersected. That meant the

Bob Dolhy (right) and Mike Hampel (left) at C Troop Passout, November 1966.

RCMP's contingent was relatively big, certainly too large for all the Force members to be accommodated in the quarters available at the station, which was situated above the town's post office. "They had no place for me to stay, so I had to get a billet in somebody's house, just a room and a bathroom, in the north end of town. I didn't have anybody to talk to, or my own phone, but if there was a call from work, I had to go all the way back to the station, which was six or seven blocks away, because when we finished a shift we had to lock our revolver in the desk drawer. I had to go back to the station, get to the desk, get the gun and then go to the call."

While the inconvenient rules around gun storage sound like a plot point from a slapstick Keystone Cops silent film, Dolhy had been on the job for less than a week when he learned just how serious things could get in this small town—and how quickly. "One of my first days, I was riding with a fellow officer. He was showing me a little bit of the town. Somebody reported black smoke south of town, on a sand road off Highway 10. We found a car fully engulfed in flames, just off the side of the sand road. As we rode by, a person's arm was sticking out of the window and it fell off … it just fell off onto the road. The owner of the pool hall had gone bankrupt and he had burned himself in the car. That stuck around in my mind for a few days, I had to find my way around that."

If only that had been the most difficult scene to remove from his mind's eye.

"A few days later, I was working the day shift, still learning the lay of the town because I also had duties in the office. I finished my shift and locked my gun in the drawer, and I was going to head home. But I really didn't want to go back to my room and just sit there. I wanted someone to show me around, so I asked an officer who was going on night shift if he could let me ride along, to show me where places were. His name was Ken Bullock."

Constable Bullock had shown Dolhy several places around town before the two spotted that the red light atop the station's post office location was lit. "That's how we knew someone had called in," says Dolhy, explaining that there was no one besides Bullock on duty that night to take phone calls, so the light was their alert.

"We answered the call and it was coming from The 4 and 10 Restaurant. Someone had entered the property at a high rate of speed, hit the gas pumps and they blew up. The driver had left the scene, but the owner of The 4 and 10 recognized the car and passed the information on to us, including where the driver lived. It was actually near my billet. We drove to that location. It was dark, it was night, and the house was also totally dark. We parked our car across the street, about 30 or 40 feet from the house. We got out, Ken on the side toward the house and I got out on the other side, and we started toward the house. Halfway across the street, a shot rang out, and Ken dropped to the ground in front of me. It was totally dark, and I couldn't see anything. I ran behind the car for cover and heard another shot. I dove back inside the car. I had no gun—it was locked up in the office—and as I looked around the car for some kind of weapon, all I could think was, 'Oh my God, this guy is going to come and get me.'"

Dolhy didn't know it then, but that second shot he'd heard as he rounded back toward the passenger's side of the car had hit the red dome light on the roof of the patrol car. "Apparently my head was behind the dome because I felt the spray of glass, I felt the heat. It was that close."

Back inside the car, he heard the driver's side door rattle. "I thought it was the shooter coming for me. But it was Ken. Ken got inside the car to drive because he had the keys. He looked at me and opened his mouth and blood sprayed out, all over me and all over the side of the windshield. He got the keys in the ignition and was able to drive, but he didn't say anything because every time he did blood came out. I remember reaching over and trying to turn the windshield wipers on, but of course that didn't help—the blood was on the inside. He rolled his side window down and was able to see the road. Good thing he could drive because I didn't know where the hospital was. Nobody had showed me yet. I called Brandon on the car radio, but there was no answer. It was too far. I later found out they got the distress call, but I did not get their reply."

The hospital was on the south side of town, about half a mile away, and by the time they arrived, Bullock was woozy from loss of blood. "We entered at the Emergency entrance at the back and it was under construction," Dolhy says. "I remember they had a plywood ramp for wheelchairs that went about 30 or 40 feet and inside the hospital. I got Ken out of the car, supporting him on my shoulder. But his legs were getting weak, he was getting heavy and no one was around. I got him into the hospital and finally found an empty room, got him on a bed. He was bleeding from his mouth, and his neck was bulging at one side. His tie was choking him. I cut his tie and then ran up the hallway, yelling for help, and finally somebody heard me."

While part one of the nightmare was over, another stretch of agony, one with several chapters and which has lasted right up to the present day, was about to begin.

The hospital staff shooed Dolhy outside the room where he was left standing alone. He called his Sergeant, who drove over to pick him up, and then took him to the station to retrieve his gun. Then they both returned to the scene of the crime: the gunman's house.

"We surrounded the house with whoever [from the RCMP] was available. It was still totally dark and there were no more shots. After maybe 20 to 30 minutes, one of the officers said the shooter was down. He was lying on the porch, still breathing. I know, because I stepped over him. He had shot himself in the head. Ken had been shot in the face, in the cheekbone. The bullet glanced down into his mouth, shattering a tooth, and down into his neck, causing a lot of trauma there and in his throat. The doctors were able to operate on him that night. He ended up OK. The shooter died on his way to the hospital, as they were taking him to Winnipeg."

Since Dolhy was immediately tasked with writing up the entire incident as best he could, there was no opportunity for him to make a private call from the station's phone to his family or to his girlfriend, to let them know what had happened and that he was unharmed. Unfortunately, Janice heard the news the way the rest of Canada did.

"It was a Saturday morning and I was working at Simpsons-Sears [in Regina]," says Janice. "I got up and was getting ready for work and it came over the radio that there'd been a shooting in Minnedosa and an officer had been shot. I knew that's where Bob was. I tried calling and nobody answered the phone. I tried calling all day, but I had to go to work. I was worried all day. I got home from work and still hadn't heard anything. Bob called me the next day. They'd had him doing paperwork and he wasn't able to call his family."

Bob Dolhy, who graduated on November 16, 1966, was instrumental in saving the life of his partner, Ken Bullock, who was shot on November 25, 1966. Photo taken in Minnedosa, Manitoba, December 1966.

That was certainly not the only glaring gap in the RCMP's post-shooting practices of the day. Dolhy doesn't remember any kind of debrief happening nor any conversations, either formal or informal, with colleagues that might have helped him cope. Living at the billet, he was physically removed from the rest of the members, so had very little communication with any of them. Especially in the succeeding nights, "when I didn't sleep for many of them," he was left to deal with the aftermath alone.

In retrospect, that seems especially cruel, since nothing in the "Depot" Training program prepared any of the new members for the kind of dreadful experience that police officers are likely to encounter at some point in their careers—a gun fight and a close call.

"I kind of just thought, you're just out of training, you're supposed to be brave, this is your job," says Dolhy. "Training was

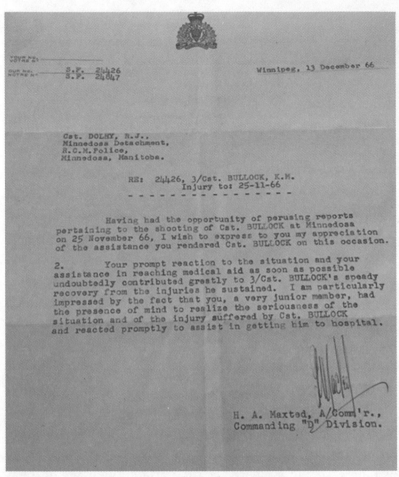

Letter of appreciation sent to Bob Dolhy after the shooting.

more regimented than anything. There was the schooling, like criminal law, and the swimming and marching, but not a lot of contact with people."

Just how close he had been to losing his own life became even clearer to the rookie policeman a week later. "I was asked to pick up the patrol car. It had been cleaned and repaired and there was a box next to the car, full of parts. And there was the red dome light, in pieces. I realized the bullet had ricocheted off the dome."

Compounding his distress was the fact that Dolhy was still on duty patrolling the town, which often required him to drive past the site of the terrible incident. "I could have used support. Maybe it would have helped me. At the time, I was just surviving with the job I had and doing what I was taught to do. I didn't get much sleep. I was always tired and went through this scene in my head a million times."

By the sixth or seventh month, Dolhy was "beginning not to like the job very much. I thought about it a lot at night—what am I doing here?" Yet, like every other new member, Dolhy faced a huge practical obstacle. At the time, the RCMP signed its new members to five-year contracts (which included their training time), and if members wanted to break that contract, they had to purchase their way out of the remaining months. "You had to have enough money to get out, and I barely had enough money to eat," says Dolhy. Nonetheless, he saved the money and made the decision to leave, not even hashing it over with Janice first. "He made the decision on his own and said he was going back home," she says. "We were already engaged then. I didn't want him to go. I didn't know what was going to happen with our relationship."

Back in Larder Lake, jobs with a future were still scarce, so Dolhy became a fire control officer, travelling around Ontario for the Ministry of Natural Resources, fighting fires. That winter, he went back to the mines, and the next summer he returned to firefighting, becoming a fire crew leader. "I really enjoyed it, but I was never home and we had married in 1968."

On the suggestion of a friend, he began working as an apprentice machinist, working on diamond drill bits and other mining equipment. Qualifying for machinist's papers took 16,000 hours, which Dolhy earned over eight years working in Kirkland Lake, North Bay and Regina.

Then some friends who had moved from Regina to southern California invited the Dolhys to spend Christmas with them in El Monte, east of Los Angeles. Enamoured of the climate, Dolhy discovered that there were plenty of machinist jobs available in the area, which was a bustling hub for manufacturing in the oil drilling and aerospace industries. With his professional machinist certification, Dolhy landed a job easily and the family moved in the spring of 1982.

When that company pulled up stakes, Dolhy found work with a subcontractor for NASA, just as new computerized machines were being installed to work on rocket engine parts. "I got in at the right time," he says. "I watched them build them and learned how to program these machines."

Employed first as a machinist and eventually as a plant supervisor, Dolhy collected scores of priceless experiences: he worked on elements of the Space Shuttle, the landing platform for the Mars Rover, and on the gears that turned the solar panels on the International Space Station. He attended test firings in the desert, seminars and static launches, and met numerous astronauts, including John Glenn, the first American to orbit the Earth, and Jim Lovell, one of the first three human beings to orbit the moon.

Although Dolhy returned to Larder Lake each summer, none of his friends from his early life in the RCMP knew what had become of him. Then, in 1996, Jerry Forst began planning a 30-year reunion and tracked Dolhy down. Dolhy attended the first reunion with delight, and was instrumental in advocating for the fiftieth anniversary gathering. Since re-establishing contact with his colleagues in policing, he has stayed close to them. Many have visited him in California, and he has made annual trips to spend time with several of his pals in Canada. "Living together so tightly for six months, the first time away from home for many of us, we got pretty close because all we had was each other," says Dolhy. "They were like family. The connection was always there. We just needed to spark it and the reunions did that."

Like family would, his RCMP colleagues also understand—without speaking of

Bob and Janice Dolhy at C Troop's 50-year reunion, 2016.

it at length—that Dolhy certainly suffered post-traumatic stress, something that he acknowledges has never completely gone away. "While I was working with this job [in aerospace], that was really demanding, I wasn't thinking about it," he says. "Just lately, because I was thinking about this interview, it's been manifesting and getting worse. I wake up at night and I'll be awake a couple of hours through the night, going through it. Hopefully, it will go away again soon. We've just purchased a home in Palm Springs, so a new chapter in life begins again."

—*Helen Metella*

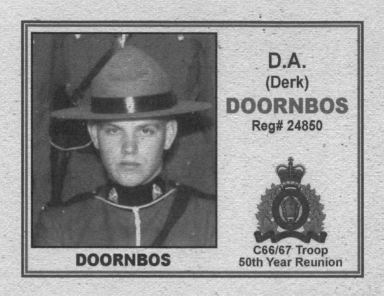

DOORNBOS

D.A.
(Derk)
DOORNBOS
Reg# 24850

C66/67 Troop
50th Year Reunion

MOST PEOPLE WHO hear about Derk Doornbos's life in law enforcement invariably respond, "I didn't know the RCMP did that!"

During a 35-year career, almost half of his service was abroad, representing the RCMP in Hong Kong, New Delhi, The Hague and Vienna, toiling at tasks as varied as security interviews in the refugee camps that housed Vietnamese "boat people," and conducting drug-trafficking investigations throughout the Indian subcontinent.

Despite the exotic locales, the work could be far from glamorous. One of his regular duties on the drug-trafficking file in India was to stay in contact with the police in Nepal, one of whom was an airport inspector at Kathmandu Airport. "I said, 'If you become aware of Canadians and you don't like the look of any of them—think hashish or drugs—I'd be very happy to have that information,'" says Doornbos. "So, he'd send me information sometimes, and then he'd forget, and so every few months I'd go to Kathmandu, and we would talk and then have tea and cake in the airport cafeteria. After I'd met him several times, this one occasion he said, 'No, let me buy *you* a cup of tea.' He summons a young lad, in Nepalese, and pretty soon two cups of tea arrive, and we talk. About half an hour later, as I'm leaving the airport, I see this tea lad. He's across the road, washing the darn glasses in a ditch! After the first few months, I never travelled anywhere in the subcontinent during my New Delhi posting without Imodium and Gravol," says Doornbos. "I was diagnosed with amoebic dysentery four times while there and on return to Canada had to see the tropical diseases people at the DND hospital."

Yet as a young RCMP Constable who had grown up in Calgary (where his Dutch parents had settled their young family), he began his career where every new graduate did, handling general duties in a Canadian detachment. Doornbos's first posting was in the Vancouver suburb of Burnaby, at the time the largest detachment in British Columbia's Lower Mainland. In General Duties and in the General Investigation Section, and later in the National Criminal Intelligence Section at RCMP Vancouver Subdivision headquarters, he learned the nitty-gritty of policing in the heart of a city—shadowing robbers and drug dealers, servicing (primitive) wiretaps and cultivating sources. He quickly fell in love with a job where he found that there was something to wonder at daily. "The dumbass things people do still amaze," he says. "You had to see the humour in things—albeit it is often quite sad."

Sometimes even he and his colleagues could be included in the first half of that statement. There was the Senior Constable, for instance, to whom Doornbos was assigned a few days into his first posting. While the rookie drove their patrol car on the midnight shift through torrential West Coast rain, with only a tenuous idea of which direction in Burnaby he was driving, the Senior Constable shed his jacket and hat and climbed into the backseat for a nap, telling Doornbos to "Call me if something comes up on the radio."

Then there was what Doornbos calls, in retrospect, "one of the dopiest and scariest things I took part in" while seconded from Burnaby General Investigation Section to a Joint Forces Operation in Vancouver. Assigned to a building overlooking Woodward's department store on Vancouver's busy Hastings Street, he had his RCMP-issue .308 rifle, sans scope, trained on the entrance. A group of thieves, who had been identified as a Montreal-based gang, had been holding up armoured car cash deliveries in the Lower Mainland. The RCMP and Vancouver City Police had learned that their next target was the Woodward's on Hastings.

The thieves' well-known modus operandi was to hotwire vehicles that regularly sat in a parkade near the site of their next job to use in their getaway. When one of the cars they'd planned on using at the Woodward's job wasn't there, the robbery was aborted. That was lucky all around, says Doornbos. "I was pretty good with a rifle because I'd had a .22 at age 14 for shooting gophers out on the prairie. But I had no sniper training. It was 10:00 a.m. on [consumer-busy] Hastings Street. I thought it was fine at the time, but it was a bit of a hare-brained approach."

Doornbos's training and equipment were a bit scant on other fronts, too. The late 1960s and early 1970s saw several protest demonstrations outside prisons in the Burnaby area. One was at the (Oakalla) Lower Mainland Regional Correctional Centre, which a Burnaby mayor who was employed as a guard there in the 1970s later called "probably the easiest prison to escape from in all of North America." Doornbos was part of the detachment's riot troop of 32 sent to help quell matters during one demonstration. "We're marching up Oakalla Hill, and there were a large number of people demonstrating outside the gate and in front of the property, but also people along the side of the road, clapping and cheering for us as we came along," says Doornbos. "We've got helmets and long hickory sticks to confront the demonstrators. That's it. On regular patrol, our duty belts in those days consisted of a .38 revolver, six extra rounds bouncing around in a too-large pouch [no speed loader] and a set of handcuffs. Have a look at any policeman's duty belt nowadays." (They are generally loaded with a firearm, several magazines of ammunition, two sets of handcuffs, pepper spray, baton, cell phone, taser and often a body cam. That equipment can now weigh up to 35 pounds.)

Constable Derk Doornbos in 1970, flying above the 401 Freeway, Burnaby, BC, in the first helicopter being tested in Canada for use in police work at the Burnaby Detachment.

Doornbos also twice ended up at the notorious and overcrowded BC Pen as part of a riot troop deployed due to a prison riot. "I remember one time, just outside the perimeter fence, some of our guys were shooting tear gas projectiles into the yard where [the prisoners] had taken weight sets apart and they had these big metal bars. We did not have any tear gas masks. I thought, if those guys in the yard make it through the single fence, if they make a concerted effort, our guys will have to start taking action and might be called on to start shooting."

Doornbos came away from those calls none the worse for wear, but was present at an early close call, which occurred during his stint with the General Investigation Section while he was with his fellow troop mate, Jerry Forst, as his partner. "We were the Youth Squad, clearing a lot of break-and-enters but also a lot of drug busts, to the extent that we became the de facto Drug Squad, as there wasn't one in Burnaby. Jerry and I were on to a group of people originally from Saskatchewan who were trafficking in amphetamines. We were following them into Vancouver one evening, and stopped their vehicle. Jerry was on the passenger side, me on the driver's side. Jerry yelled something about a gun, and it turned out that the female had a sawed-off .410 shotgun in her hand. Later investigation found that the shell in the gun had been struck with the firing pin and so it misfired. Jerry was one lucky guy." The event had other elements to recommend it, too. The amphetamines they recovered formed the largest seizure of the substance made to that point in the Vancouver area.

Derk Doornbos and Jerry Forst, C Troop members, worked as partners on the Burnaby Detachment Drug Squad. This is the .410 sawed-off shotgun that was pulled on them and misfired. Firearms tests showed the gun misfired every nine times.

In 1975, Doornbos moved to the RCMP National Criminal Intelligence Section in Vancouver and became responsible for the Asian Crime Unit. One of its tasks was to identify a number of retired and corrupt Hong Kong police officers who had accumulated millions of dollars in bribes during their careers. Those retirees then bought residential and commercial properties around the world, and a great deal of it in Vancouver, where many installed their families and concubines in upscale neighbourhoods such as Oakridge and Shaughnessy. The most notorious of these were known as the Five Dragons, and one of those was Hon Sum.

"We had heard rumours in the community that they were sneaking back into Canada, sometimes by land, via Seattle," said Doornbos. "We had a regular surveillance routine, and one morning my partner Gary Spence came back to the office and said he thought he'd seen Hon Sum walking near his home in Little Mountain Park. We were able to confirm this the next day, and then we contacted the ICAC [the Independent Commission against Corruption] in Hong Kong. Hon was arrested on a provisional warrant. After the initial hearing he was released on bail ... and fled. But the matter went to the Federal Court of Appeal for a favourable ruling that effectively kept the Dragons out of Canada."

The crux of those kinds of victories was simply fundamental detective work, says Doornbos. Translation: lots and lots of time spent pounding the pavement on surveillance and looking for leads. "Intelligence is all about gathering little tidbits and you build it up," he says.

To find those tidbits, Doornbos and Vancouver City Police Detective Bill Scotland "wandered around Chinatown trying to develop sources. It wasn't easy. But you check with the jails, see if somebody is being released, and you talk to him, get some tidbits. They won't tell you exactly what is happening, but they might say, 'This is the guy you should be looking at.' And you carry on from there."

If his experiences in the 1970s weren't carried out at exactly the same pace as TV cop shows of the era, Doornbos's police work nonetheless existed in the same ethos. While seconded to the Joint Forces Organization, which was a mix of Vancouver city police and RCMP units, he and others often worked collecting evidence from wiretaps (mostly not divulged, as those were the days before Part VI of the Canadian Criminal Code, which now requires judicial authorization).

The unit used to hang the wire from poles or switch boxes needed for the taps, he says. "A team would canvass for what were deemed to be upstanding citizens and a wire would be run down to a garage or somewhere where we could securely hide a voice-activated tape recorder. We would run a trap line, picking up tapes on various cases several times a day. At the office, we had old Uher reel-to-reel tape recorders on which we would manually slow the tapes to such an extent that we could count the dial back to determine what numbers the crooks were calling—all done digitally and remotely, and with a warrant nowadays."

With his solid foundation in all manner of big-city investigative techniques, in 1979 Doornbos was transferred to the RCMP's Hong Kong Liaison Office, the largest of its offices abroad at the time. "I came home on the Friday of the Labour Day weekend and told my wife, 'We are transferred to Hong Kong. We have to be there the first week in October.' My wife started packing up the house mostly by herself, with the help of our two boys, six and seven years old" because Doornbos had to go to Ottawa for briefings.

It would not be the last time that his wife had to undertake most of this on her own, as "something urgent in the way of work always seemed to come along," says Doornbos. Later in his career, while the family was packing up in Ottawa to go to The Hague, a Nova Scotia coastal town woke up to an inordinate number of Sikhs wandering around. "A human smuggling boat had offloaded, and it was determined that the vessel may have come via Antwerp, Belgium," says Doornbos, so he was dispatched ahead of schedule to The Hague and on to Belgium. Again, that left his wife to look after a household with some goods going to The Hague and some into storage, all while organizing a boarding school for the boys.

"My wife never flinched at the foreign postings; she always took all the myriad cultural adaptations in stride and was active at every post," says Doornbos. These included "extra courses in Hong Kong, working at the International School library, and as a stage manager for the community theatre in New Delhi, as president of the Canadian Women's Club in The Hague, and the community co-ordinator at the embassy in Vienna."

For 15 months while posted to Hong Kong, Doornbos and an RCMP partner accompanied Canada Immigration into the refugee camps of Mong Kok (now a congested commercial district of Hong Kong) and Macau. Outside Quonset huts, they vetted, through interpreters, people who had escaped on rickety boats when South Vietnam fell. Many had been in the camps as long as two years, and all desperately wanted to immigrate to Canada.

The screening was rudimentary. "My partner Don Kilpatrick and I asked questions, using some basic interview techniques," says Doornbos. "We had some sources developed in camp, and the interpreters would keep their ear to the ground if they heard any rumours, but we had to be careful of that. Somebody could inform on a family of six, so maybe his family of seven got ahead in line. Most of these people were just trying to get away from very bad situations," he says, reflecting that history will never record how many people attempted the journey through the South China Sea and did not make it. "I don't recall too often that we said no. But I'm sure we probably let in some people we shouldn't have. As a humanitarian, I knew we had to take these families, but we really didn't know who these folks were."

During his last year in Hong Kong, Doornbos was involved in drug and customs fraud investigations. "Hong Kong was always a source of heroin. But we also had customs cases, often with phony declarations and evaluations of shipments. We had to find the original business documents and compare them to the customs forms. These were mostly clothing and toy manufacturing businesses, and if you can send out four shipments a month and save a thousand dollars in customs duties on each one, that adds up."

Derk Doornbos with secretaries Indirani Gopal and Angela Wong, High Commission Grounds, New Delhi, 1985–86.

Both work and life became more interesting at his next posting in New Delhi, which Doornbos remembers as a marvellous kaleidoscope that engaged all the senses. He was eventually promoted to Staff Sergeant. His wife and two young sons had access to the Canadian High Commission's nearby pool and tennis court, and they enjoyed comfortable housing with a servant and many driving excursions throughout northern India, travelling as far as Islamabad, Pakistan. Doornbos recalls that these excursions bothered the High Commissioner, who was concerned for their safety. "There was virtually no ambulatory service in the rural areas, and severe accidents on Indian roads were frequent." But the family fell in with experienced and intrepid Canadian Foreign Service personnel who had been to similar countries.

Doornbos's area of responsibility covered India, Nepal, Sri Lanka, Bangladesh and the Maldives, and his duties mostly concerned the drug trade and immigration fraud. Unfortunately, Sikh terrorism was also rampant. In June 1985, a bomb aboard Air India Flight 182, flying from Toronto to Delhi, exploded off the coast of Ireland, killing 329 people in the largest mass killing in Canadian history. A connected explosion at the New Tokyo International Airport (now called Narita International) killed two baggage handlers and wounded four others.

Both crimes were perpetrated by Sikh militants from the Vancouver area, who checked unaccompanied suitcases onto Canadian aircraft that connected with the Air India flights. During the ensuing investigations in Canada and India, Doornbos was the conduit between the Ottawa Justice Department prosecutor, the then-National Transportation Safety Board investigation and the Indian Commission of Inquiry authority. "I was basically just the go-between," he says. "I do remember one assistant commissioner in the Indian Central Bureau of Investigation taking a chastising tone with me about Canada having allowed the likes of [ringleaders Talwinder Singh] Parmar and [Inderjit Singh] Reyat into Canada. I had to forcefully remind him that part of our then-function with the RCMP had been to submit the names of Indian males between the ages of 18 and 65 applying to immigrate to Canada to Indian authorities to check for criminal and or security records. But the Indians had poor central records. Even state and local records were sadly lacking. When Parmar emigrated, had they informed us he was wanted for murder, he would never have got to Canada."

Sikh terrorism had become so fierce that India's central government suspended the Punjab state government. Travel to the state was restricted, but Doornbos had been asked by Canada

Immigration to look into a particularly glaring case of misrepresentation of family members wanting to emigrate. The Canadians suspected there were children being claimed that were, in fact, not really part of the same family. "If you could get these children into Canada [collecting a fee from the real family], then later, when they were regularized, they could claim not to have been aware of the goings on, then sponsor their own parents and other siblings," says Doornbos.

He received the requisite documents to travel, and with a High Commission driver (who doubled as an interpreter) went to a town called Hoshiarpur on the National Highway in Punjab. It was raining and everything appeared dismal and muddy. Housing had been arranged in a government guest house where the only other occupant was a colonel commanding the regional military. He was escorted by his pickets, who loudly brought themselves and their automatic weapons to attention every time the colonel came and went. Not keen about staying there, as he was a potential target, Doornbos went to examine the decades-old musty tomes in the town police station that recorded all births and deaths, and on which the issuing of state documents was based.

"The erasures, fill-ins and write-overs were so obvious as to be laughable," says Doornbos. "Little coming out of that register could be trusted. The legitimate documents themselves issued by the state often appeared to have been put together very haphazardly. But the appearance of the town where that family was likely eking out a living, you could see that the family would resort to fraud to get themselves out of there."

After a two-year posting to RCMP HQ Ottawa as the Administrative Non-Commissioned Officer (NCO) in the Foreign Service component, and French-language training, Doornbos was sent to Europe—first to The Hague, where he worked mainly on drug and money-laundering operations. He was also a liaison to a special war crimes prosecutor in Amsterdam in the case of Jacob Luitjens, a University of British Columbia professor who was a Nazi collaborator known as the "Terror of Roden." Luitjens had lied on his immigration application and was eventually deported to Holland, the first Canadian ever to have his citizenship revoked for war crimes.

Although the prosecutors did successfully prove their case, as witnesses were being called, Doornbos encountered another one of those baffling human behaviours that has amazed him throughout his policing career. A Holocaust survivor with first-hand knowledge of Luitjens's deeds agreed to testify in Vancouver, but only if Canadian prosecutors also paid the extra travel expenses for him and his wife to go to California to visit their son. "I know I can't imagine what people suffered during the Holocaust years, but I thought to myself, 'You've got to be kidding. You're really serious about this, but you're suggesting you won't go unless we pay for you to go on vacation?' This disappointed me."

The things people overlook in their own self-interest emerged under quite different circumstances during Doornbos's subsequent posting to Vienna. While on a regular liaison visit to Sofia, Bulgaria, he was waiting on the steps of the Sheraton Hotel for his Bulgarian police contact to pick him up when he spotted a red Dodge Durango suv roll into the far end of the parking lot. A thuggish sort in a black leather jacket exited and left. A North American vehicle like that is a rarity, says Doornbos. He took a closer look at the truck. "It had Ontario plates on it. I grabbed the vin and then got on my cell phone to our hq. The plate was stolen, as was the Durango. I asked my police contact to make a detour from our scheduled appointments and we stopped off at the Organized Crime unit first. We had reported stolen cars to them before, but nothing much got done."

This time, "the foreign police officer had seen it himself," so the police apparently quickly tracked and arrested the Durango's driver, and he immediately told them where other cars were stored. "Several hours later, I was loaded into an old Lada police car with a barely working light and siren, and we drove madly, ending up at a lot where a total of 13 vehicles were parked, all late models, all stolen in Ontario," says Doornbos. "Stolen cars were a big deal there. There were people who had immigrated to Canada who had worked for the Bulgarian intelligence service, guys who knew how to produce documents and could be very convincing. They would lease a car in Canada with false ID, stick two to a container at a dry land port, and ship them to the port of Varna on the Black Sea. We had reports of a Customs man in Varna driving a new Jeep Cherokee. Would some patrol officer not have tried to check or ask about a bright red Dodge Durango, 'Where the hell did one of those come from?' Wouldn't some police at a traffic stop ask? Corruption was very much alive in Bulgaria. I don't know where those 13 cars were headed but I guess the Customs guy in Varna got his up front."

As for the 13 stolen vehicles that Doornbos's observation unearthed? "There were roadblocks and changing rules, and requirements for translation to Cyrillic thrown up at every turn. By the time I left the Vienna post, we had not been able to recover a single vehicle."

There are other career memories that stick in his mind, says Doornbos: "Bodies found in awful circumstances, many drug searches and kick-ins, being cover man on six- and nine-month undercover operations [cover men form teams of three to five other police members who are always surreptitiously nearby,

backing up and protecting an undercover officer in the field],
RCMP drug and money-laundering teams coming to the foreign
posts. But I long ago destroyed my notebooks and have forgotten
much."

After two and a half years in the RCMP's Drug Enforcement
Branch in Ottawa, Doornbos retired in 2001. Yet almost immediately, he went back to law enforcement, working as a sheriff in the
Court Services Division of the Alberta Ministry of Justice, now
the Alberta Ministry of Justice and Solicitor General, at the Calgary Court Centre. He worked full-time for several years and still
does, part-time, because "I really like the people I work with, and
I am still amazed and often amused at the things people get up to."

In his spare time, among other things, Doornbos volunteers
with the RCMP Veterans' Association at Fort Calgary and was on
the board of the Fort Calgary Preservation Society for four years.

Doornbos was just seven years old when he and his family
came to Canada from Holland and settled in Calgary. He recalls
being impressed by the Mounties he saw on the highways and in
the nearby Banff townsite during the early 1960s; he knew early
on that he was going to be either a conservation officer or an
RCMP member. The RCMP won out and he's never regretted the
choice.

"I have been very fortunate," he says. "An immigrant kid who
got to wear the coveted red jacket."

—*Helen Metella*

J.A.
(Jerry)
FORST
Reg# 24851

C66/67 Troop
50th Year Reunion

FORST

As SEVERAL OF his former colleagues in the RCMP say, with the utmost affection, Jerry Forst is not easy to dissuade once he has an objective in mind. That trait not only propelled Forst into and through an action-packed career with the RCMP, it ensured he won counselling assistance and compensation for the PTSD that ended his police work there after 12 years.

"I was one of the first members who put a [PTSD] claim into Veterans' Affairs," says Forst, who was just 31 when he left the Force, but 46 before he decided he deserved help with the psychological scars he was carrying. Although PTSD wasn't properly identified and acknowledged for another 10 years, Forst's focus on his objective prevailed. "I went to see a psychiatrist, at the request of my doctor and Veterans' Affairs, and I took a binder with me with all the stories that led to this," says Forst. "I said, 'Because I'm a policeman, I'm bringing proof to you.'"

Among the many stories was one about relocating his family to another city, almost overnight, because he was being stalked by mentally unstable criminals who threatened to kidnap his children. Another heart-stopping incident involved his narrow escape when a drug dealer's wife pulled the trigger on a sawed-off shotgun aimed at Forst, during a traffic stop in which his partner, Derk Doornbos, had found drugs on her husband. Forst was spared only because the weapon misfired.

As he did for the psychiatrist, meticulously assembling information, confronting counter-arguments head on, and filling any gaps with still more information is how Forst approached his entire RCMP career, including preparing to join in the first place.

Before his early death in a plane crash, Forst's biological father, Jim Mulcahy, and his father's brother, Jerry, were both members of the Edmonton Police Department. His mother, Winnifred, later became an Edmonton police matron. Yet Forst considered other careers dedicated to helping people, including being a minister or a mortician, before becoming a civilian cadet with Edmonton's police right out of high school, at age 18. He worked there a year, in the Identification Section, fingerprinting vagrants, prostitutes and other prisoners. Insatiably curious, Forst used the opportunity to educate himself about policing and also about human nature.

A young Jerry and his uncle, George Williams, who was a member of the RCMP stationed in BC. Years later, Jerry got to work with George when he was posted to the Lower Mainland. Jerry's father, James Mulcahy, died in a plane crash when Jerry was only three years old. James and his brother, Jerry Mulcahy, were both Edmonton Police officers.

"I just saw them as people, not as criminals," he says. "If they'd done something I'd never heard of, I'd ask, 'What's safe-blowing? What's nitroglycerin?' I remember this one prostitute, she was really mad. She'd been arrested for Vag. C [prostitution] and she started talking to me, saying, 'This is not prostitution! I was having sex with my dentist. I needed a bridge; he needed some help!'"

Rounding out this self-directed education in policing, Forst took advantage of a special duty request to work as a department store detective for Eaton's. There he was trained by two savvy female in-store detectives on how to spot shoplifters. "You would watch for people who wouldn't be looking at their items," he says. "They'd be holding them and looking out for clerks. If they were stealing suits, they had topcoats with pockets sewn in the side of them. They could roll suits into those pockets and could take two suits at a time. Women wore belts with a hook on them inside their pleated skirts, and they could take four pairs of pants at a time. One woman was a kleptomaniac, and we didn't stop her. We'd write down what she stole, and her husband would come in later and pay for it."

As illuminating as all this was, Forst realized that if he joined the Edmonton Police, he wouldn't be allowed to walk a beat until he was 21 years old. He was also keen to make it on his own merit without any help from police officers who had known his father. So, he applied to the RCMP, following in the footsteps of his mother's brother, George Williams, a Staff Sergeant Major Forst idolized.

When he graduated from the RCMP Academy "Depot" Division, Forst was still just 19 years old with a baby face that betrayed his youth. He soon turned that into an asset, though, during a plainclothes posting with Burnaby, BC's, General Investigation Section youth detail (which later morphed into the Drug Squad).

ALL CORRESPONDENCE TO
BE ADDRESSED:
THE COMMISSIONER
ROYAL CANADIAN MOUNTED POLICE
OTTAWA 7, CANADA

TOUTE CORRESPONDANCE DOIT
ÊTRE ADRESSÉE COMME SUIT:
LE COMMISSAIRE
GENDARMERIE ROYALE DU CANADA
OTTAWA 7, CANADA

HEADQUARTERS — DIRECTION GÉNÉRALE

YOUR NO.
VOTRE N° K.425A-36-66

OUR NO.
NOTRE N° G.425A-149-66

OTTAWA 7, CANADA

April 22, 1966

Mr. Jerry Arthur Mulcahy,
6207 - 90th Avenue,
Edmonton, Alberta.

Dear Sir,

Further to your application for this Force, a new troop will commence training approximately June 11th, 1966. Should one of the men intended for this troop be disqualified, you will be selected as his replacement. If no replacement is required, you will be engaged to commence training with the next troop to be formed, providing you are medically fit.

Arrangements are being made for your medical examination and you will be advised separately as to where and when you should report for that purpose. Your particular attention is drawn to the fact that all dental repairs must be completed at your own expense prior to your medical examination.

For your information, the first period of engagement is for 5 years. Initial engagement will be as a Third Class Constable with a salary of $ 4,309.00 per annum, paid semi-monthly. Your salary is subject to deductions for Income Tax, Pension 6%, room and board at the rate of 40¢ per meal and 50¢ per day for lodging whilst in training, and thereafter, when such are provided. When attested you will be posted to either "N" Division at Ottawa, Ontario or "Depot" Division at Regina, Saskatchewan for recruit training.

If you are in doubt on any matter connected with engagement, please do not hesitate to request information when you report for your medical examination.

Yours truly,

Insp. for
(D.W. Horn), Supt.,
Senior Personnel Officer

Engagement letter for Jerry (Mulcahy) Forst.

He and his partner, John Grady, easily struck up conversations with young people hanging around pool halls, which allowed them to put together leads on car thefts and other crimes. "John was athletic and coached rugby; I coached hockey," says Forst. "We were young, we listened, we never tried to condemn. One youth would tell you about another youth, and we'd go to work."

Corporal Les Holmes was Burnaby Division's NCO in charge of the Burglary Squad at the time. "I had to personally deliver the break-and-enter stats to the Officer in Charge (OIC), Jack Gibbon," said Holmes. "He insisted that the Burnaby solved rate be higher than the regional average every month, without fail. I recall that the solve rate was 16 or 17 percent. Many months, thanks mainly to Jerry Forst and John Grady, we far exceeded the average. Sometimes I would be getting a bit antsy towards the end of the month, but somehow we always came through."

Youth detail success soon found Forst seconded to the Drug Section in Vancouver for a few weeks, learning about heroin smuggling and trafficking, and the organized crime syndicates beginning to infiltrate the city. Back in Burnaby, he received rigorous training from Staff Sergeant Bruce Northrop, who later became a Superintendent, and from his boss in Burglary Squad, Corporal Les Holmes, who later became an Assistant Commissioner. "They had a method. You'd attack a crime with a whole bunch of people and constantly refocus," says Forst. "I never assumed that anything anyone ever told me was the truth, never came up with a theory first. We learned to look at the facts and then if someone tells you something, to see if you can prove or disprove it. You look at the whole picture, so nobody can fool you. You keep going over stuff and checking and rechecking. That's how I learned to investigate."

That method proved itself sound when Forst was assigned to rake the lawn of the victim's home on a 1970 homicide case. His diligence uncovered particles of a very specific model of headlight. The tiny fragments were tied to a vehicle used by the prime suspect in the murder of nightclub dancer Jackie Lampen, who had been killed in front of her six-year-old daughter in an organized crime hit.

The investigative technique also gave Forst faith in the system when he took a 23-year-old Indigenous mother to the hospital after she was raped and severely beaten just weeks after having had a Caesarean section. Forst obtained her statement and sat with her during the trial. Seeing her aggressively cross-examined by the defence and hearing racist remarks from court attendees that "Aboriginal women could not be raped," Forst was relieved when the detailed police work of his similarly trained colleagues in the Burnaby Detachment helped convict a serial rapist. Forst believed that an investigator's role was to present the evidence he had gathered and let the courts make the final decision on guilt or innocence. However, he worried that the decision might be affected because the young woman was Indigenous, and told his wife, Ruth, that if that were the case, he would quit police work. Fortunately, justice prevailed.

Between those early triumphs and the circumstances that eventually convinced him to leave the RCMP, Forst experienced the entire gamut of what police work in Vancouver entailed during a formative period of its growth from sleepy coastal city to major international port. Walking the beat, he quickly learned how to improvise and hold his own with biker gang members who were stealing motorcycles, altering their serial numbers and then registering the new numbers.

After spotting an obviously stolen bike and having it towed away, the next night Forst was checking doors behind a closed mall when he was confronted by a massively built and livid biker, backed up by half a dozen others. As the biker dismounted his bike, Forst drew his gun and told him to halt or he'd shoot. The biker scoffed, saying, "You can't get us all." Forst replied, "No, but I'll shoot you dead. Now get the hell out of here before you end up dead and the rest of you end up in jail." Common sense kicked in and the bikers fled. Forst took deep breaths and thanked his maker.

While that moment went well, many others, when the work was ostensibly more routine, produced trauma that can and still does mess with Forst emotionally. At the milder end of that scale, on Christmas Eve 1975, he responded to a car accident on a freeway and found that an impaired driver of a glass-company truck had struck the car of a 70-year-old female motorist. Her injuries seemed minor, but while being loaded into an ambulance she asked Forst to ensure that the small Pomeranian and the Christmas presents in her car were delivered to her son. Forst agreed and began transferring the presents to his trunk. Alas, the Burnaby firefighters who had finished sweeping the road of broken glass decided to help him and opened the car's door before Forst could yell "No!"

Six firefighters chased the tiny escapee dog down the roadway to the 401 Freeway while Forst followed in his lights-a-blazing police car. When he caught up, it was too late. "They handed me what appeared to be a frozen flat rug. The dog had been run over." It was left to Forst, a lifelong dog lover, to meet the woman's son at the hospital, explain what had happened and pass over the evidence. Apologizing profusely, Forst asked if there was anything he could do. "No, Corporal, I think you have done enough," said the son. It was one of Forst's saddest Christmas Eves, and its memory can still cast a pall on the season.

Even rougher realities of police work were established earlier than that, however. Seven months into his career, while walking the beat in South Burnaby, Forst was introduced to a young Constable just two weeks out of training. Terry Tomfohr was 19, and eager to chat with someone his own age and of similar experience. "When we sat down for coffee in the lobby of the

Astor Hotel, I could sense the excitement and eagerness he had for the job," says Forst. Forst assured him of how good his training partner was, they chatted about the RCMP's hockey team, and about the life insurance the newcomer had bought that night before coming to work. Then Tomfohr and his trainer departed to investigate a complaint about youths throwing rocks at houses.

"About half an hour later, I was walking the beat when one of the members stopped by to tell me I was needed to help search for Constable Tomfohr," says Forst. The newbie had split

Constable Terry Tomfohr, 19 years old and a new recruit two weeks out of training, shared a coffee with C Troop member Jerry Forst on June 3, 1967. Half an hour later, Constable Tomfohr died when he fell off a cliff on Burnaby Mountain. At the time no memorial was held, and detachment members were expected to carry on with their duties as usual.

off from his partner when he heard noises coming from a bush area. "I had worked the area before, and knew the dangers of the deep cliff drop-offs the bush area covered up," says Forst. Indeed, in the darkness and on unfamiliar terrain, the young Constable had unknowingly run off the edge of a cliff, dropping 30 or more metres. He died of his injuries. For each of the members working that evening, it was the first time they'd lost a policing colleague. For Forst and his colleagues, it was when they first lost their belief in the invincibility of being a Mountie.

"I am sure this was an accident; however, I know that this experience started a change in me," he says. "I knew the youths he was chasing, and I arrested one of them several times after this

The memorial to Constable Tommy Tomfohr, shown above, was erected at the Burnaby Detachment on June 2, 2002, 35 years after his death.

incident. Although I believe I was open-minded throughout my career, and tried to treat every investigation or encounter with an individual as a new one, my mind changed a little bit to where I started to think it was us good guys against them, the bad guys."

The RCMP had no protocols then to deal with the death of a member on duty, so Forst and his colleagues were not debriefed. No local service was held because Tomfohr's body was transported home to Alberta for burial. Not until 2002 did the Burnaby Detachment commemorate Constable Tomfohr on-site with a memorial. Whenever he is in Regina, Forst visits the RCMP cenotaph at "Depot" Division, where Tomfohr is honoured. "It brings back a flood of memories, which I describe as 'innocence lost,' thinking of how tragically this young member died in the line of duty."

There was more innocence to be lost, of course. Forst was called to investigate more than one suicide at the notoriously overcrowded Oakalla Prison Farm in Burnaby. One aching memory involves an inmate in the next cell over who explained to Forst that he did not call for help because he believed the man who had hung himself had lost hope and "was in a better place." In another still-haunting incident, a heroin dealer was shot in the head 14 times, not long after Forst convinced him to provide information about the organized crime syndicate that supplied him. "The reality of drug trafficking and addiction is heartache," says Forst. "I felt sorry for him and his family; however, I also thought about the many people hooked on drugs who were slowly having their lives sucked out of them, and their families, as the drug dealers profited from their misery."

Despite the grittiness of his work, pitting his smarts against smug and devious crooks was a culmination of everything Forst felt he was destined to do since he was a teenager. During the 1970s, for instance, while training a new female officer, he relayed to her something he'd realized while creating fingerprint files in Edmonton: "Although prisoners might change their names, use aliases or different birthdates, one thing they normally did not change was the answer to where they were born," he says. That trick of the trade soon helped the policewoman and another RCMP member identify and charge suspects responsible for four bank robberies.

Occasionally, however, Forst's shrewd policing instincts made investigations uncomfortable for him. Incredible as it now seems, Forst says that during the 1970s, criminals shipped their weapons, masks and other robbery-related gear by airplane and by bus inside wooden cases that purported to be filled with work tools. So, in a joint RCMP/Vancouver Police operation, Forst and an attractive policewoman were assigned to pose as recently arrived passengers and watch the baggage claim area of the Vancouver Airport for two trunks being shipped from Montreal. When the suspects claimed one trunk but kept waiting for the other, the policewoman realized the suspects were viewing remaining passengers with suspicion. She slipped her arm around Forst's waist with a smile and, playing along, he ducked his head toward her, causing his nose to dip into her hair. Raising his eyes to maintain his surveillance, Forst spotted his father-in-law looking directly at him from the waiting area beyond the baggage claim. But the suspects' trunk had arrived, so Forst and his undercover partner grabbed their dummy bags and marched past his father-in-law, in pursuit. "I wanted to call my father-in-law and explain, but with no cell phones and a night of surveillance, that wasn't going to happen," says Forst. "It was three days before I could talk to him." It was considerably longer—many decades later, in fact—before he found the incident amusing enough to share with his wife, Ruth, even though she was remarkably unflappable about every aspect of his police work.

Much of what feels funny in retrospect was problematic when Forst lived through it, however. While he was Corporal in Charge of the Crime Prevention Unit, a young Constable named Dave worked with him. Constable Dave, who had just returned to uniform, came to see Forst early one Sunday and asked for guidance because he'd briefly had his patrol car "stolen." While stuck in a muddy trail during a park patrol, he'd accepted a passing senior citizen's offer to give the police car a push. At the last moment, Dave had worried that the older gent might suffer a heart attack, so he put him behind the wheel and pushed the car himself. They got the car moving and into a wide clearing when suddenly the red lights and siren went on, and the senior gunned the gas and took off, doing a few donuts on the park grass. When Dave eventually regained control, the senior was exultant: "I've always wanted to drive a police car like that!"

Dave drove the unrepentant man home but was unsure how, or if, he should report it. "I asked him if anyone else knew," says Forst. Luckily, no one did. So, Forst paid the senior a follow-up visit. After confirming the facts, he asked, "Are you planning to tell anyone about this?" The man grinned, "I'd like to tell somebody." Forst's response was immediate and grave, "If you do, I'll have to charge you." So, the man promised he wouldn't tell anyone. "I went back to the station and said to Dave, 'Don't ever tell anyone else!'"

Despite such lighthearted memories, and considering that his RCMP career lasted just over a dozen years, Forst was involved in a high proportion of complicated, headline-grabbing, adrenalin-pumping operations. Several illustrate how dramatically Canadian society was changing and the pressures this exerted on its police. One of those was the infamous riot outside a 1972 Rolling Stones concert.

In 1970s' Vancouver, multiple flashpoints were sparking. American draft dodgers and hippies from across the United States and Canada had drifted west where, in summer at least, it was warm enough to sleep outdoors. Drugs and free love were in abundance. Meanwhile, a group of teenagers from low-income families on Vancouver's East Side, known as the Clark Park Gang, became the roughest of the city's "park gangs." While they'd started as layabouts and young offenders, sleeping, drinking and doing drugs in the park, some had become violent thugs, friendly with Satan's Angels (later to become Hells Angels). Others were being approached by shady, politically subversive groups who, it was believed, encouraged them to stir up trouble at events.

Indeed, the Clark Parkers were blamed for having roles in several previous riots, including one in Gastown and another at a November 1971 concert featuring Chuck Berry at the Pacific Coliseum. When an undercover operation in which Forst participated discovered that a potential problem was about to erupt at the Stones' June concert at the same venue, the Vancouver Police Department put a few patrols out front, as well as officers in another building on the nearby Pacific National Exhibition

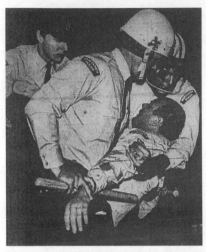

The 1972 Rolling Stones riot in Vancouver.

(PNE) grounds. RCMP plainclothes members (including Forst) were stationed outside throughout the day, to mingle with the crowd, gather intelligence and monitor the situation. If things started to heat up, the inside officers were to deploy, in uniform, undercover and on horseback, as a show of force. However, because of criticisms that they'd been too aggressive in previous altercations, they planned to react with caution.

Forst saw Clark Parkers mixed in with ticket-scalpers and concert-goers, and then watched the mood darken as it became obvious many of the latter held counterfeit tickets. "At 9:00 p.m., Stevie Wonder opens [the show] and there are 2,000 concert-goers outside the Coliseum, trying to crash the doors," he says. "Someone threw a smoke bomb, and rocks broke the glass doors leading into the Coliseum." Rocks were also thrown at police who had exited the PNE building. Wine bottles were stuffed, lit on fire and hurled. A bomb landed under a Burnaby RCMP vehicle that had inadvertently turned onto the street where the rioters were. Rioters tore wooden slats from house fences to use as clubs.

"It was very scary, personally," says Forst. "I, like the other plainclothes officers, didn't know where to go to be safe as the rocks, bottles, smoke bombs and Molotov cocktails were flying everywhere. The [uniformed] officers were not a trained riot squad; they were street officers. They had no riot equipment other than helmets. I remember thinking the police officers and the officers on horseback were sitting ducks."

It took 15 minutes before police received the command to rush the rioters and start making arrests. Peace was restored just as the concert let out, although some 50 police officers were injured. "It was like a movie and suddenly it was over," says Forst. "I could not understand and still do not understand why the order wasn't given sooner."

Two other high-profile events in which Forst and other Burnaby GIS section (plainclothes officers) played a role, underscore the fact that serious crime was escalating in the Vancouver area. The first was the robbery of the Dairyland Credit Union in Burnaby on May 8, 1970, by two heavily armed men.

The suspects had been followed by the GIS to the credit union, where Forst and the other officers saw the robbers pull on masks and rob it. A chase ensued. The robbers lost control of the stolen car they were driving and fled into a bush area. When police confronted the robbers there, the thieves refused to surrender their weapons and instead pointed them at police. Forst's partner, Don Brown, shot one of the robbers, apparently ending the group's criminal plans.

Except it didn't quite end there. In 1973, when those robbers were in jail, it was determined by members of the Co-ordinated Law Enforcement Unit (CLEU), which united members from the RCMP and several Lower Mainland municipal forces to combat criminal activity, that a second robbery was being planned by associates of the first group. CLEU, to which Forst was seconded, conducted a lengthy surveillance of two robbery suspects, and determined they were targeting the Canadian Imperial Bank of Commerce in Burnaby's Lougheed Mall.

Still, Forst and his CLEU colleagues were mystified when, on

On May 8, 1970, a robbery suspect was shot by Burnaby RCMP after two heavily armed masked men robbed the Dairyland Credit Union. Left to right: Corporal Don Brown, suspect, Constable Jerry Forst, Staff Sergeant Paul Starek.

Sunday, December 16, the suspects' vehicle disappeared into the underground garage of an apartment building behind the mall. Unbeknownst to police, the suspects stole a vehicle from the garage and drove it to the home of the bank's manager, forcing their way in. Five children and an adult in the manager's home were bound, gagged and left in the home while the robbers took the manager and his wife to the rear of the mall where two maintenance workers were taken hostage. All were moved through a back door of the bank and held hostage in its coffee area.

Not knowing where the suspects were, the CLEU surveillance team, guided by their leader Tom Charlton, entered the mall at 5:15 a.m. to surveil the bank. Charlton and Forst gained access to the Hudson's Bay store, which was located beside the bank in the mall. From the wall cavity where the glass mall doors were stored during opening hours, voices could be heard in the bank. Police now knew where the robbers were and had to ensure the safety of the hostages. Meanwhile, a bank employee assigned to check and open the bank that morning entered the bank, and was quickly compelled to bring the other staff in when the robbers told her they had the bank manager's children as hostages. The other staff members entered the bank as directed, while the CLEU officers secretly kept watch.

The police did not reveal their presence; the heavily armed nature of the credit union robbery led Forst and his colleagues to expect the same calibre of resistance. Only now there were many hostages. Instead, they let the suspects leave the bank with the holdup proceeds and the manager's wife as a hostage. Police posing as shoppers then confronted the robbers and rescued the hostages without firing a shot. During the ensuing struggle, however, two RCMP officers—Jim Bell and Brian Leicht—and the bank manager's wife were wounded by a shotgun blast from the suspect's gun.

Solving violent crimes like the one pictured here is an everyday part of the work of RCMP officers across Canada.

Ruth and Jerry Forst were married on June 24, 1969, in New Westminster, BC.
Left to right: Ruth's sisters Linda and Donna, Jerry's sister Judy, Ruth's best friend
Ruth Muir, Ruth and Jerry, Derk Doornbos, John Rowland, Frank Richter and Bill
Glover, a member of Edmonton Police Service and Jerry's best friend, along with a
mini Mountie, were part of their wedding party. Jerry says the wedding was
the second best day of his life; the first was the day he met Ruth.

As nerve-racking as each of these front-line situations was,
only when combined with shadowy dangers that threatened his
own family did the high stress begin that would eventually cause
Forst to leave the RCMP.

On December 21, 1974, while Forst, his pregnant wife and
young son were living on a Langley acreage not far from four
other homes inhabited by RCMP members, he was awakened at
2:30 a.m. by the doorbell being rung repeatedly. A drunken man
and his girlfriend were demanding entry. After Forst refused,
the two ran toward the home of another RCMP officer across the
street, and Forst noticed the man pull a rifle from behind a tree.
Ruth Forst called the other member's home, warning him not to
open the door, while Forst shone a flashlight on the couple, who

were now on the member's doorstep. The young man ran back toward the Forst residence, and shots were fired over the home. Forst and the other RCMP member neighbours—Andy Lucko, Ed Gallagher and Al Chaytor—chased the two suspects into a wooded area. With the help of the Langley Detachment, the perpetrator was arrested and eventually sentenced. Afterwards, says Forst, "I saw a change in my wife. She became more protective, although at no time did she ever say anything about the incident, even though I asked her if she was worried."

Ruth's calm nature was constant and reliable, even when, a couple of years later and in another home, the family began receiving credible threats about two arsonists Forst was investigating. When the RCMP received information that the criminals were intent on kidnapping the Forst children, the police installed an alarm with wire that surrounded their house. "That didn't work very well because there were raccoons in the neighbourhood [that triggered the alarm]," says Ruth. "During that time, I remember Jerry sleeping with his service revolver under the pillow." Forst responded to one false alarm at his home, as did several other members of the detachment. He recalls being

Threats against the Forst children played a large role in Jerry Forst's decision to leave the RCMP. The children are now adults—one a police officer and one a pilot—but Forst still has concerns about their safety and well-being.

distressed knowing that he went to work carrying a gun but was leaving his wife and two young children alone.

When Forst told his Sergeant about his stress and asked for a transfer, he received a startling reply, one reflective of the expectations made of police officers during that era—to never show vulnerability because it could affect their career progress. "He said, 'I think your wife is stressed. I'll put in a memo that says your wife is stressed,'" says Forst. "I thought it over, but I knew I had to get the hell out of there. I signed that, but I still feel bad about it. It wasn't my wife who was stressed."

In December 1977, the family was quietly transferred 1,200 kilometres north, to Fort St. John, BC. While they liked the smaller centre, within a year Forst decided to resign altogether. He was carrying a sense of betrayal and abandonment, he says, because in his view the Force didn't realize how serious the threat to his family had been, and the potential it had to dangerously change his outlook. "When you've been in a shootout, you get used to it and roll with it, but when it gets personal, it's possible you won't do what you know is right."

Forst developed several absorbing careers after leaving the RCMP in 1978. First, he joined the coroner's office in New Westminster, BC, for three years, and on the side ran a pub in Chilliwack with a retired RCMP Inspector. Next he became a Labatt's salesman in BC, and then one of its managers in New Brunswick for 12 years. Returning to Edmonton, he managed investigations for the Alberta Securities Commission for 13 years, and provided local and international investigations services for PricewaterhouseCoopers for another nine. He wound up his career as the assistant general manager of investigations for ATB Financial.

Despite all his professional successes, Forst had mood swings brought on by memories of his RCMP experiences, a state of mind he calls "walking a black dog."

He started aggressively defending people "and it got me into trouble." While playing recreational hockey, he was suspended for two games after taking such umbrage over another player's hit of one of his teammates that he knocked the player out cold. He found himself unable to watch violent movies or television shows. Of all things, he hurled a profanity at a traffic cop issuing him a ticket. During early attempts at group therapy, Forst remembers having irrational outbursts. Family gatherings that became too noisy made him irritable and unable to concentrate. But three years of group therapy, coupled with his successful campaign to be compensated for his PTSD, and subsequently becoming a Christian in 2002, have helped him curb his anger issues. "I think I am still dragging them around," he says. "I think I've become overprotective, and sometimes overbearing. Every so often that black dog comes up. It's hard to know what sets it off. I do know that my wife has been my rock, and that her faith and prayers, and my own faith, are what helped me the most in dealing with PTSD." It also helped when he continued to extend to people the empathy that prompted him to choose police work.

Both avid motorcyclists, Forst and Ruth bought their own Harleys and joined the Christian Motorcyclists Association of Canada (CMA), where he served for 15 years as the Canadian prison co-ordinator, speaking at prisons and churches across Canada. Forst's connection to young people continued as he, Ruth, and other CMA members volunteered weekly at the Edmonton Young Offenders' Centre for 15 years. Through the CMA, he met a former inmate and outlaw biker for whom he and Ruth provided a place to live in their home for six months. That unlikely friendship resulted in the man, who became a preacher,

Jerry and Ruth Forst are members of the Christian Motorcyclists Association of Canada. The Forsts serve as Canadian Prison Ministry coordinators. Both have led prison ministry outreaches—along with other CMA members who minister in young offender centres, jails and homeless shelters—for the past 17 years or so. Jerry credits their faith and PTSD counselling, along with support from his peers in the RCMP, in helping him with his ongoing battle with PTSD.

officiating at the funeral of Forst's mother and at the interment of Ruth's parents. After Forst suffered a heart attack in November 2019, the man immediately travelled from central Alberta to be at the hospital to pray for and comfort Forst.

Forst's policing instincts are still intact—he can recognize with a glance that the teenager at the next table in a coffee shop is a struggling meth addict—and so, too, is his legacy. His daughter, Tanya, who he presented with her badge when she completed training, is now a veteran member of the Edmonton Police Service, and his son, Robert, is an airline captain.

Forst realizes that the RCMP, like other police forces, didn't understand and wasn't prepared for the effects of PTSD on its members. He credits the strong esprit de corps of RCMP members, and his friendship with RCMP and City Police members with whom he worked—in particular Don Brown, Jim Simpson, John Grady, Bill Glover, Mike Hampel, Ernie Otway, Ross Mortlock, Bob Dolhy, Joe Dennis, Bob Swift, Wayne Schauer, Scott and Sue Coomer, Richard Wenham, Ken Doern, Frank Richter, Les Holmes, Jack Ewert, Mel Rioux, Jim Bell, Glen Delwisch, Eric Stenberg, Chris Windover (née Mackie), Howie Larke, Derk Doornbos (and their respective spouses), along with Eric Spink, Dr. David Wong (psychiatrist, C Troop) and the RCMP Veterans' Association for helping in his recovery.

"Whether members serve one day or a whole career, it is extremely important for the members and their families' mental and physical health that they be recognized by the Force, its Veterans, by serving members and the public, so that the members know that their service and personal sacrifices mattered," Forst says. He hopes his story will help other police officers, including his troop mates, to take advantage of the programs now available for first responders and their families to deal with PTSD.

Above all, Forst remains practical about what police work entails, yet grateful for the many positive elements it brought to his life. "I don't miss the circus, but I sure miss the clowns."

—Helen Metella

R.G.
(Ronald)
KEEPING
Reg# 24838

KEEPING

C66/67 Troop
50th Year Reunion

IN MOST JOBS, there are repetitive days hardly worthy of memorializing. But even on the most ho-hum days, serving in the RCMP in the late 1960s through the first few years of the new millennium wasn't like most jobs. Although Ron Keeping spent his career in some of the most remote RCMP detachments in the country, in communities sprinkled across the Atlantic province of Newfoundland, he remembers the minutiae with such keen detail and in a voice so authentic, it paints a lively scene. Even when a Newfoundlander's yarn-spinning is awash in universal truisms, it always contains a surprise, or several, and Keeping's memories of his life in the RCMP certainly do.

"I applied for the RCMP at the age of 18, and soon afterward received a call for an interview. I lived in an isolated community in Newfoundland and I had to travel to St. John's, NL, for the interview, which entailed a week-long return trip.

"I managed to get through the interview with the personnel interviewer telling me he was recommending me as suitable for engagement in the Force. The only drawback was that I looked too young, and he was deferring my application for two years at which time I would be re-interviewed. This was in 1964.

"Two years later, in May 1966, I received another letter from the RCMP Staffing and Personnel Branch for a follow-up interview. I travelled to St. John's again and this time I was advised that I would now be accepted, pending results of a final medical examination. All medical and dental requirements were conducted at this time, and I returned home awaiting further word from the recruiting office. It was shortly after this that I received word that I would be travelling to Regina for recruit training. This meant that I had to travel to St. John's for a third time to be officially sworn in on June 9, 1966. I was to depart for Regina the following day by Air Canada. This was my very first airplane trip. I had anticipated that there might be another recruit travelling to Regina at the same time but unfortunately I was the only one.

"I have a vague recollection of my arrival at the Regina airport. There was someone there to meet me, but I can't recall if it was a duty driver or someone else. I do recall arriving at the training facility, which was not a very welcoming sight with all those stark-looking buildings and no familiar faces. We were assigned to four-man barrack rooms where two of the members were from a senior troop. They were responsible on a one-on-one basis to orient each recruit until such time as you became familiar with what was expected of you, and you were familiar enough with the procedures to function without supervision.

"The first few days of training included getting fitted for kit, which included a lot of articles of clothing and you wondered what they were all for. Soon, everyday routine became easier and a sense of esprit de corps developed among fellow troop members. Soon, they became like family as we were all experiencing the same feelings—homesickness, apprehension about whether or not you would survive to the last day of training, and other areas of stress that you found yourself under on a daily basis. In that sense, we all had something in common—or at least most of us did. A few had previous military exposure, and I suspect [they] found the adjustment from civilian to a regimented life-style somewhat easier.

"One in particular was Pete Albertson. Pete was from BC and had served in the Navy prior to joining the Force. He was selected as our right marker [the Troop's overseer, who helped maintain discipline] and did an excellent job in keeping our troop on an even keel. Transition from a private to a military way of life was difficult for most of us. Everything had to be done on time and there rarely seemed enough hours in the day to do all that was required of you. From polishing boots to washing and ironing clothes, re-writing notes from each day's class, studying the Criminal Code and preparing for an upcoming exam, it often felt like you were under constant pressure.

"I joined the Force as a non-swimmer and a non-driver. I did not have a driver's licence prior to joining the Force. I had never owned a motor vehicle, nor did I have access to one. I did manage to obtain some driving experience from various friends who owned a vehicle, but not enough to make me a qualified driver. The NCO in charge of the detachment where I submitted my application inquired with the Staffing and Personnel Branch on this matter and he was advised to take me for a test run. If he felt that I was capable of obtaining a licence with additional experience, then he could issue a certificate in this regard and that would be acceptable. In retrospect, I was probably further ahead by joining the Force without any driving experience—at least I had no bad habits to break. And you know what they say: 'There are three

Derk Doornbos and Jerry Forst were assigned as duty drivers to help Ron Keeping and other troop mates who needed assistance learning how to drive. The two police cars in front of the Mess Hall at "Depot" were used as driver trainer cars.

ways to do things—the right way, the wrong way and the RCMP way.'

"As for my swimming ability, that simply did not exist. I had had a bad experience the summer before joining the Force; I nearly drowned when a canoe in which I was travelling overturned, throwing me into the ocean. My now brother-in-law, who was also in the canoe, managed to drag me to shore. This was no confidence builder on the day I climbed the steps to the 30-foot diving board and looked down into the deep end of the pool. It was a do-or-die situation, and I knew there was no option.

"To make matters even tenser, if that was possible, George Piccott was ahead of me for the jump. Like me, George was also a non-swimmer and probably more scared of water than I was. Every member of C Troop, I am sure, won't forget George's free-fall off the end of the diving board, seconds before he was to be pushed by the instructor. The sound of George's blood-curdling yell and belly-flop as he struck water in the pool still remains with me to this day. I did have the presence of mind, however, to enter feet first, thereby eliminating any subsequent injury [belly-burn]. The journey from the diving board to the pool seemed an eternity, and I must have struck bottom in the 12-foot end of the pool. I remember surfacing with a bamboo pole sticking in my face, and the instructor holding the other end. In my state of panic, I made a grab for the pole, and the instructor said, 'Here, you can have it all if you want it.' He let go of the pole and there I was floundering around in the middle of the pool, trying desperately to reach the nearest side.

"Somehow or another, I survived this ordeal. I remember swimming classes the following day, when we only had to jump off the edge of the pool into the deep end. I thought to myself, 'This is so simple compared to yesterday.' When it was my turn to jump, I did so without hesitation and somewhat relaxed. And lo and behold, I floated like a cork and was able to swim the full length of the pool. I finished training with a Bronze Medallion, and in looking back at the situation, I feel that my initial fear of water and my inability to relax were the only reasons why I could not swim. Once these issues had been overcome, after my first leap from the diving board, then everything fell into place.

"In addition to all the regular stress levels associated with training, there was one other personal issue that I had to contend with. On the day I left home to join the Force, my mother was admitted to hospital with what was thought at first to be pneumonia. Shortly after arriving in Regina, I called to inquire how she was doing and was advised by my sister that she had been re-diagnosed as having lung cancer, and there was nothing they could do for her. Apparently, the disease had advanced to a critical level and she was not expected to survive long. She passed away on August 18 at the age of 57, just nine weeks into my training program. I will never forget the tremendous support I received from each and every member of C Troop throughout this ordeal. They were well aware of my situation and always gave me words of encouragement. I did not go home to attend my mother's funeral. My older brother called and suggested that it was better for me that I not. After just little more than two months into training, it would take at least two weeks for the return trip and it might be difficult to resume training after such a long period of absence.

"Looking back, it was probably the logical thing to do. After a break from the rigours of training, I don't think I would have been too eager to get back at it, not to mention the catch-up that I would have had to do. I might also mention that the Training Officer called me to his office to offer his condolences on behalf of the Force and asked if there was anything they could do. He told me that I would be excused from training for a couple of days until I felt up to the task, but it was up to me to continue to participate in whatever areas I wished.

"Halfway through the training program, things started to become more routine, and I was able to concentrate more on reaching my goal of graduation. I didn't have to worry about swimming anymore or my lack of driving experience. I was able to keep up with the other members in the driving program, and although I knew I would not get the required amount of city driving that I would need to become a proficient driver, this did not bother me; I knew it would all come with experience after I graduated. As for other areas of training, I was pretty much on par with other members of the Troop, or at least I felt so. I managed to pass the entire administrative portion, including all exams. I was paraded before the Sergeant Major on one occasion only, and that was on a day when we had a towel inspection before swimming class. When I opened up my towel, there was a boot print on

Ron Keeping in his pit, entertaining his fellow Troop mates with Maritime songs.

one side where someone had obviously stepped on it in the change room. I think I know who it was, but I just left it at that. The dirty spot appeared to be shoe polish, and there was only one member I knew who polished the soles of his boots an inch in from the outside. Anyhow, I held the towel up with the dirty spot on the inside towards me, thinking it would pass, but alas came the order, 'Turn it around.' The next command, 'See me in the Sergeant Major's office in the morning.' Three days' extra duties did not seem to fit the crime, especially when it was not of my own making. I felt that with just one appearance before the Sergeant Major, I had done extremely well, as we all know of members who were paraded many times.

"I recall one incident in particular when Mike Hampel came to me one day and said he would like to talk to me about something. I was curious as to what was bothering him because, as we all knew, Mike was a straightforward individual, hard-working and not one to complain. He said, 'Ron, I've made my mind up that I'm going to quit.'

"I just couldn't believe what he was saying, and I said, 'Why would you want to quit with just two more months to go?' He said that the training was getting to him; he didn't think he could stand it any longer, and the only solution was to quit. Mike and I had been rather close throughout training, and I believe he confided in me and wanted to know what I thought about what he was planning. I said, 'Mike, you can't possibly quit at this stage;

you would never forgive yourself if you got through four months of training and didn't finish the other two.' I said, 'You have to lighten up a bit, you are taking this thing too seriously. The instructors are trying to do everything possible to break you, but you have to show them who's in charge.'

"I reminded him of the stress I had been under for my first couple of months—which he already knew, of course—and I said, 'If I can get through this, you can too.' I said, 'You're just next door to your home province, you are familiar with the surroundings, the flatness and miles of nothing but prairie, whereas I am thousands of miles from my home and family. I miss the ocean, the mountains, the rivers and lakes. There are days when I would pay just to see the ocean and smell the salt air. You don't have to contend with this longing and feel as if you are living on another planet.'

"We had quite a long talk, and I said, 'I'll make a deal with you, Mike. If I quit, you can too. Agreed?' He said, 'OK.' I had noticed prior to this that Mike was looking depressed some days and appeared to be somewhat withdrawn. I thought that he was letting it get the best of him. Anyway, Mike continued on with training, he never mentioned quitting again, and continued on to graduate with the rest of us. On the day of graduation, he came to me and said, 'Thanks, Ron. I'm here today because of you and I shall always refer to you as Ol' Reliable Ron.'

"November 16, 1966, was probably the happiest day of our lives for the whole troop. Graduation Day had arrived at last, and we would all be heading to our postings forthwith. I was transferred to 'H' Division, Nova Scotia. At the time, Air Canada was on strike, which required travel across Canada by rail. I, and other members who were travelling east of Ontario, boarded the train in Regina the following day, in full Review Order, for the long

Celebrating graduation, November 16, 1966. Left to right: John Seniuk, René Charbonneau, Ron Keeping, Tony Antoniuk, Ernie Otway and Bruce Lyman.

journey eastward. I vividly recall the many goodbyes to each and every troop mate. After six long months of living together as one, we had finally become individuals, and the breakup of our troop had its bittersweet moments. It was great to be free at last from the rigours of training, but on the other hand, we were saying goodbye to close friends we might never see again. Now, 53 years after leaving "Depot," this feeling of closeness still remains, which was evident during our fiftieth troop reunion at Regina, in 2016.

"My first posting was at Windsor, NS, a medium-sized Sergeants' Detachment. I stayed in barracks, along with three other single members. The detachment was located on Main Street, on the top level of a furniture store. It was rather small and cramped, but several months after my arrival, we moved into a new detachment building with much more space and more private than the older building.

"I spent nearly four years at this posting. There, I encountered all the routine matters that you would normally expect from a detachment of this size. There was no such thing as overtime in those days, and you were expected to work around the clock if it was necessary, especially being single and living on-site.

"It was at this posting that I had my first PC [patrol car] accident. I went to work that morning at the usual time of 8:00 a.m. I worked through the day shift until 5:00 p.m., and then continued on into the evening and night shift. There was always a lot to do, and working extra hours provided the opportunity to get caught up. I recall finishing work the next morning at 3:00 a.m.—some 18 hours without rest. I had just gotten into bed when the telephone rang, I answered it as I was expected to do, and the call required an immediate response to the small community of Stanley, some 30-minutes' drive away.

"The incident there involved something taking place at a small airport in the community. I answered the call, took whatever action was required, and headed back to the detachment. I did not make an arrest, although I had considered it (thankfully, I didn't), but I had a number of exhibits that I had seized and placed in the back seat. The road back was very winding and [there was] no traffic present. Somewhere along this highway, the PC left the road, struck a culvert, flew across an intersecting road and landed upside down some 200 feet from where I left the highway. I had no recollection of the incident before or after, so my only conclusion was that I had fallen asleep behind the wheel. The vehicle was a six-month-old unmarked PC, and my first thought was that this would be the end of my career. I escaped unscathed from the accident, but examination at the hospital revealed that I had injured my wrist. It was a small price to pay for what might have been a different end result.

"The investigation was conducted by the Section NCO. One of the things he asked me was how long I had been working on the day in question, to which I replied, 'About 18 hours, not including the time responding to the call.' His reply was, 'I can understand why you would fall asleep after working that long.' He said, 'There will be no fault assigned to you for this accident. I will see that in future the NCO in charge will ensure that members of the detachment are not subjected to such unreasonable hours without proper rest.' That was the end of the incident, but a follow-up report from headquarters indicated that I would not be held accountable for loss of the PC, and no assessment would be made against me in this regard.

"While I was in Windsor, the Force came out with an experimental policy of sending members back to their home province. Several members applied, and my application was approved. I was transferred to Harbour Grace, 'B' Division, NL. I spent the rest of my career at various postings throughout Newfoundland."

For many RCMP members, providing security for VIPs, especially if they were assigned to rub shoulders for a considerable period of time, is a tale to dine out on for the rest of their lives. Indeed, Keeping has one of those memories from his posting in Newfoundland.

"One particular time in 1983, when Prince Charles and Lady Diana made an official tour of Canada, I was delegated as part of the security detail, which included various drills and driving manoeuvres for several weeks before their arrival in the province. Some might call it a highlight of their career, but I just felt honoured when I was selected as one of two official drivers for the Newfoundland portion of the trip.

"I was assigned to escort the royal couple in a Rolls-Royce convertible, my first and probably one-and-only time behind the wheel of a Rolls-Royce. I was accompanied by a member of the personal security team who travelled with the couple on their Canadian tour. He sat in the passenger seat next to me. I followed a planned route in the city of St. John's, NL, and he basically instructed me when to slow down or stop at any location the couple wished to explore or interact with individuals along the route. It lasted for approximately two hours. I was fortunate enough to record this event with a number of photographs."

But Keeping's brush with royalty isn't his best tale from his years as an RCMP member in the rugged, northeastern corner of North America. Not by a long shot.

"I should also relate a story from my posting at Grand Bank Detachment, when I was 27 years old, with about six years' service in the RCMP. It will serve to show how small a world we live in. The incident occurred on January 12, 1973. This was a two-man detachment and the Corporal in Charge had gone on holidays after the Christmas season was over. It was customary

Ron Keeping driving Prince Charles and Lady Diana during the Newfoundland portion of their Canadian tour in 1983.

that both of us stay around until after Christmas because it could become extremely busy.

"On the day in question, I decided that I would work an evening shift. Around 5:00 p.m., it started to snow, and I patrolled around the area until around 9:00 p.m., when the snow intensified and I decided to go back to the office to catch up on some paperwork, as it was too hazardous to stay on patrol any longer.

"Around 10:30 p.m., I received a call from a very concerned male from Fortune, NL, a small town about 15 minutes away. He advised that his son and eight other members of a wedding party had left Fortune around 5:00 p.m. to travel to the small community of Point May, where he was being married at the Roman Catholic Church. The plan was to get married and return to Fortune for the reception. They were travelling in three vehicles, with three individuals in each vehicle. The father had called the Department of Highways earlier, and the snowplow operator said he would take a drive towards Point May to see if he could locate them. [Point May was located some 24 kilometres from Fortune, and the gravel road was narrow and winding. A large portion of the road was exposed to the Atlantic Ocean and was noted for being treacherous, due to high winds with zero visibility when snowing.]

"The snowplow operator advised the father later that he had attempted to travel towards Point May, but he drove off the road because of poor visibility and had had to leave the plow and walk back to Fortune on foot. He had only travelled for about a kilometre when the visibility was reduced to zero, and he had been fortunate enough to make it back to safety.

"This was the only plow assigned to that area. I called the Department of Highways' depot to inquire if they could offer any assistance in locating the missing persons, and the person in charge advised that all plows had been pulled off the highways and he would not risk sending a plow operator out under the current conditions.

"This left me in a precarious situation, as now there was nowhere else to seek assistance. There was no way, however, that I was going to let nine people perish without some sort of rescue attempt. Then a thought came to me. One of the crew members of the patrol boat, *Acadian*, had purchased a snowmobile earlier that fall. To my knowledge, it was the only one in the detachment area.

"I called Constable Fowler, the member in question, explained the situation and asked him if I could borrow his snowmobile to attempt a rescue, and that I would like him to come along with me, as well. He readily agreed and came to the office.

"His snowmobile was on a trailer. We had no hitch on any of our PCs, and therefore had to hitch it up to his 1972 Javelin and tow it to Fortune. We took some blankets from the office, put them in plastic garbage bags, plus a couple of pairs of snowshoes and lashed them to the snowmobile. We had to siphon gas from the PC into the snowmobile, along with an extra five-gallon container as there was nowhere to buy gasoline.

"The drive from the detachment to Fortune was difficult; the snow had built up on the road in places, and one particular time when Fowler hit the brake, the trailer jack-knifed and slammed into the rear fender of his vehicle, causing considerable damage. We continued on as far as we could, but decided to pull into an empty garage parking lot and continue on by snowmobile from there.

"We had no idea where or if we would locate the vehicles in question. I drove the snowmobile because I was very familiar with the road to Point May, having travelled it numerous times. Visibility for most of the way was practically zero. At times, it became necessary to stop completely and wait for the visibility to clear. Winds were around 40 MPH, and the temperature I would estimate around -25°C with wind chill. In no way would it be possible for a human to survive for long under those conditions.

"It was around 11:00 p.m. before we began our journey down the Point May highway. These people had already been on the road for some six hours and were no doubt feeling the effects of the storm. The road itself was a secondary road, barely wide enough for two vehicles to pass. One side of the highway followed a steep upward incline, while the other featured a drop of 20 to 30 feet or more for the whole distance. It was imperative that we stay to the right because if we went over the incline to the left, the results would have been tragic for both of us.

"After driving nearly an hour, we noticed a huge pile of snow ahead of us through some lulls in the drifting. I decided I would have to try to get around it; it was impossible to go over. It was then that I noticed the glimmer of a red light showing through this heap of snow. We had finally located all three vehicles. They were stopped one right behind the other, completely buried in snow. We had to use our snowshoes as shovels to dig them out.

"We finally were able to open the doors of two of the vehicles and found the occupants still OK. All nine people were in two vehicles; the third had stalled and could not be restarted, possibly because snow had drifted around the distributor cap and spark plug wires. There were five male individuals and four females, the youngest of whom was 13 years of age. It was obvious that they were starting to feel the effects of hypothermia and/or asphyxiation. They were shivering profusely, and some had gotten wet trying to free the vehicles earlier in the evening. They were all lightly clad, as they were all prepared to leave their vehicles, walk into church for the ceremony, then get back into their vehicles and drive home. They certainly had not been prepared for this eventuality. Now the problem arose: how to transport nine people to safety with one snowmobile over a distance of 16 kilometres?

Well, obviously, it had to be done one at a time.

"We determined which ones appeared to be in the worst condition and transported them in that order. None of them would have survived much longer and certainly not until the storm abated at 10:00 a.m. the following morning. Each of us took turns driving back to Fortune with a passenger on the back, while the other remained with the stranded party.

"The member who stayed behind removed his storm coat and put it on the passenger on the back of the snowmobile, then wrapped the lower portion of their body with the blankets we had taken from the office. Then, when the member returned from one trip, we reversed roles and the other member made the trip, which took nearly an hour. We were both wearing Arctic Ski-Doo suits inside our storm coats, so we were OK for a good while without the use of our storm coats.

"This rescue continued for some eight hours until the last of the nine people had been delivered to Fortune. We had each made five return trips to Fortune over that period. Miraculously, we encountered no major problems during the entire procedure.

"The father of the groom was ecstatic when we finally arrived with the last person. He thanked us profusely and insisted that his wife make us breakfast, which she did.

"It had been a long, tiresome night, but knowing that you were instrumental in saving the lives of nine individuals under nearly impossible circumstances was very fulfilling. I forgot to tell my wife what was happening earlier that evening. She had no idea where I was or why I hadn't come home after my shift. It was not until the next morning when she tuned in to the local radio station that she discovered the reason.

"Later that morning, we were inundated with calls from news media all over when the story was made public. I had to relate the story to CBC St. John's, Halifax and Toronto that morning before I had a chance to get some rest. Our headquarters at St. John's called and requested a message follow-up, as they too were receiving calls from news outlets around the country. A reply back from St. John's Headquarters later that day simply said, "A commendable job under extreme circumstances." Constable Fowler later submitted a request asking the Force to pay for repairs to his vehicle. The reply: "You did not receive prior approval for use of your private vehicle, therefore we are unable to authorize repairs at public expense." Amazing. We did later receive a commendation from Bombardier of Montreal [the manufacturers of Ski-Doos], in recognition of our actions in saving human lives. They stated that they would be using this story later to promote use of their snowmobiles in rescue operation situations.

Ron Keeping and his partner used a snowmobile similar to the RCMP snowmobile displayed at the Heritage Centre, Regina, to save the lives of the wedding party.

"I had to relate that story in order to tell this one:

"On January 1, 2016, we were staying in Zephyrhills, Florida, as we do every winter. On the way from a New Year's Eve party at the local clubhouse, we passed a neighbour just two doors down from us. As we were passing, he called out and asked us over for a nightcap. We accepted, and joined him and his wife and several other people sitting on the patio. He introduced a couple who were visiting from Toronto, and during some small talk he indicated that the lady was living in Ontario, but had grown up in Newfoundland.

"I told her that I grew up in Newfoundland as well and that I had worked there for most of my life. I asked her where she was from originally, and she replied Fortune, NL, to which I replied, 'Oh, I know that area very well; I was stationed at Grand Bank as an RCMP officer in the 1970s, and Fortune was in our detachment area.' I said, 'What was your maiden name, as likely I may know your parents.' She told me, and I said, 'I recall an incident while stationed in Grand Bank where we rescued nine people in a wedding party from certain death in a blinding snowstorm and their surnames were the same as yours.'

"The look on her face was indescribable. She said, 'Oh ... my ... God! You're the RCMP officer who saved my life!' She said, 'Your name is Ron Keeping,' and I said, 'Yes.' She said, 'I have never forgotten your name, and I will certainly never forget that night. We thought there was no way possible we could be rescued, and we were resigned to the fact that we were all doomed to die.'

"She said, 'I have told the story a thousand times, and I know my husband is tired of hearing it.' She came over, gave me a big hug and a kiss, and said, 'I never, ever, thought I would meet and thank the person who gave me my life.' She was so blown away by this that she told the story to everyone she talked to in the park the next day. Her first name is Ellen, and she was 13 years old when the incident occurred. When I met her the next time, she was 56 years old and I was 70. She is currently living in Ottawa.

"Over the span of my career, I had the opportunity to serve on both small and larger detachments. I found that each had its pros and cons, but smaller detachments were definitely my favourite. On a smaller detachment, you were almost always the first responder, you got to form a stronger bond with the community and, in most instances, crime was easier to solve. You became a part of everything that happened. You were required to investigate everything from fatal motor vehicle accidents, drownings and serious assaults to any number of things that you would encounter in a larger area. You attended autopsies, performed Crown prosecution duties, performed breathalyser tests, lectured at schools, attended parades, and believe it or not, administered drivers' written and road tests on behalf of the Department of Highways. There was little or no need for informants because the whole detachment area became a source of information once you developed a climate of trust within the community.

"In one particular community, Point May, it was nearly impossible to get anyone to speak to you. You would certainly get no information from anyone, even from a simple inquiry as to where a certain individual lived in the community. We felt that there must be something we could do to improve our image. Point May is just seven miles from the French Islands of St. Pierre et Miquelon. Smuggling French liquor to the island of Newfoundland had developed into a huge business over the years, and the RCMP were considered a hindrance to the free flow of liquor and, hence, profit.

"We thought maybe we would begin with the younger citizens and get a foot in the door. There were virtually no extracurricular activities for any of the kids in the community. We approached the school and asked if they would agree to us setting up a Cub Scout troop after hours. They readily agreed, and slowly but surely our edging into the community began.

"We were soon able to meet with some of the parents personally, and they began to feel that we were showing interest in the betterment of their lives. We had never known, nor had it ever been shown over the years, that there were many people in the community who were deadly opposed to the smuggling trade.

"It soon became apparent, through our contacts and many visits to the school, that some were willing to share information with us. And share they did. Over a two-year period, we made more seizures of contraband liquor in the Point May area than had ever been recorded for the whole time of the detachment's existence.

"We soon started to see that those involved in smuggling had begun to feel that they were in the minority; they could no longer depend on their fellow citizens to clam up. One female informant in particular would call my wife at home during the night if she couldn't reach me at the office, and pass information to her to pass on to me, on some activity that required immediate action. Some wives eventually turned informant against their husbands, which goes to show just how opposed they were to these activities. I understand that today the commercial smuggling trade has all but disappeared, thanks to community co-operation and our efforts to develop a rapport that resulted in a major turnaround in our relationship with the majority of citizens who cared about the reputation of their community.

"There are so many changes from when I was a member of the Force to today. For example, no matter what you were exposed to—and as most members know, these experiences were often not very pleasant—there was no such thing as professional counselling. I never knew such a thing existed, which of course it didn't. You just did what you had to do and moved on to the next case. I never knew of any member who felt it was necessary to stay off the job to recover from a first-responder situation, but then again, it was probably customary for members not to show their inner feelings about anything. But as we all know, regardless of our image, we are still human beings who experience the same emotions as everyone else. Thankfully, today there is help for members who would otherwise suffer in silence.

"Looking back over my career, I am proud to say that I was a loyal, dedicated member. Even though there were mistakes made and situations that might have been handled differently by others, I still feel that I made a worthwhile contribution to the Force and am none the worse for my experiences. I feel that a sense of humour, no matter the situation, is conducive to a good working relationship, both inside and outside the Force. There were many situations that gave you a reason to smile—be it from other members, the situation itself or from a character you were dealing with. Those are the ones that create the best memories, and those are the ones that I best remember today."

—*Ron Keeping and*
Helen Metella

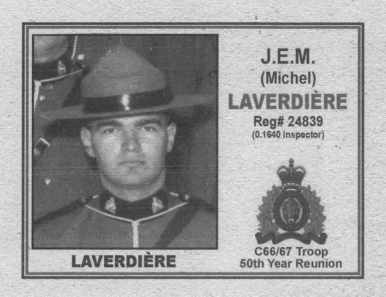

J.E.M.
(Michel)
LAVERDIÈRE
Reg# 24839
(0.1640 Inspector)

C66/67 Troop
50th Year Reunion

LAVERDIÈRE

AT AGE 20, Michel Laverdière craved a career that offered travel, meeting people, excitement—especially since he loathed the two years he'd just spent working as an accounting clerk in Quebec City. Over the next 30 years, the RCMP delivered all the adventure he'd hoped for, beginning with the first daunting episode. Laverdière arrived at RCMP Academy "Depot" Division in Regina speaking only French, and for the first three months was immersed in the mysteries of both police training and the English language. After Passout, his first posting placed him in Montreal's "C" Division, where he once again found himself in the thick of demanding scenarios that required him to adapt rapidly and nimbly. In quick succession, his job took him to Expo 67 and to John Lennon and Yoko Ono's high-profile "bed-in," followed by a five-year stint investigating the earliest international drug-trafficking rings in Canada, and then to the launch of the RCMP's Air Surveillance Division.

"In addition to our regular duties at 'C' Division [in the General Investigation Section], we were all assigned security duties during the six months of Expo 67. I was assigned to the airport security group, which consisted of providing security for arriving heads of state at Montreal International airport. This was a great experience for the young member that I was. Some of the work was exciting, while certain aspects were tedious and involved both work in uniform as well as in civilian

Left to right: Michel Laverdière, Carmen Brown and Peter Albertson, at "Depot," 1966.

clothes. Some of those airplanes had to be watched 24 hours a day. That was boring, watching Russian planes, watching Cuban planes, making sure nothing goes in. One of the VIPs was Idi Amin, the president of Uganda. He was a butcher, a vicious dictator. VIPs were not supposed to be armed while in Canada. This guy came in, in uniform, gun on his belt, a handgun with a long barrel that stuck out of his tunic. And nobody wanted to take it away from him."

Two of the renowned celebrities Laverdière met a couple of years later, after he'd transferred to the drug section, were far less intimidating. In May 1969, John Lennon and his new wife, Yoko Ono, had already celebrated their honeymoon in Amsterdam with a week-long "bed-in for peace," to which they invited the media. But they were prevented from doing a second "bed-in" in New York City because of John's recent conviction for cannabis possession. So, the duo set up at the Queen Elizabeth Hotel in

Montreal, where Laverdière's encounter with them was documented in a storied photo.

"That was one of the few 'undercover' jobs I did during my life in the drug section. John had been arrested in England for smoking pot, and when they came to Montreal, the RCMP wanted to know if there were drugs in their room. They said, 'You're going to do that job. Go look around and report to us.' So, I walk out thinking, 'How the hell am I going to get into that room?' As I left the office, I met one of the newspaper photographers I knew. He said, 'Grab a camera and we'll go as journalists.' So, that's what we did. Everything was above board. There was no marijuana. I would have smelled it [if they'd been smoking]. The photo [with John and Yoko] was taken by the buddy I went to the room with. He gave me that photo. It was lost for quite a few years—I had stuck it into a magazine someplace—until my eldest

John Lennon and Yoko Ono with Constable Michel Laverdière RCMP Drug Squad Montreal (sitting next to the bed, holding his glasses), in room 1742 of the Queen Elizabeth Hotel in Montreal, May 1969. Lennon and Yoko Ono spent eight days and nights in the room to promote peace and protest the Vietnam War and the Nigerian civil war.

daughter found it and said, 'What the hell is this?' Eventually I had it framed."

A fun memory, certainly, but what if there had been pot? Had he given a thought to what he would have done, faced with busting two of the world's most famous people? Laverdière just chuckles. "My job was to report it. That's it. Anything else, that was above my pay grade."

While still a junior member in the General Investigation Section, Laverdière had served subpoenas, summonses and arrest warrants under federal jurisdiction. Moving to the Immigration and Passport Section, his work was primarily arresting and prosecuting illegal immigrants, most of them ship-jumpers from Greece or American draft dodgers. Those draft dodgers figured prominently at his next posting, too, in the Montreal Drug Section, where new and sometimes disturbing work awaited.

"I didn't know anything about drugs, had never seen marijuana in my life. I don't think they ever mentioned the word 'marijuana' at 'Depot.' It was not a big problem in Canada yet. But the softer drugs were coming, mostly from down south, with all the draft dodgers moving to Canada. The draft dodgers are the ones that really started small trafficking of marijuana and hashish in Canada, in order to have some income to stay here illegally. And the conditions they would live in, you wouldn't believe it. One time, I was looking for somebody, and we went into an old part of town, to an apartment building. On the first floor there was a suite with quite a few people living in there, and they had raised all their beds about three feet off the ground because they had too many dogs on the first floor, and the dogs would do their thing on the floor. In one room, there was a baby on the floor, all dirty, sleeping with the dogs. You couldn't believe it. To me, it was an education on what happens when your main reason for living is to do drugs. While you see so much, that's what you do for work. That's not you. You live in different conditions. You go home. You don't think about it. You don't talk about it. I never talked much about work with my family, about what happened at work. That's the only way."

The drug trade soon exploded in size and net worth, once Montreal's mafia became involved through its European contacts. It was the dawn of an ugly era that persists today, as international drug traffickers became entwined with organized crime, and the trade was entrenched in Canada.

"Montreal became an entry port for heroin that was distributed all across the country, all the way to Vancouver and also to New York City. It came in by air and by port. The Italian mafia in Montreal was mostly in contact with the mafia in Italy and France. Marseille used to be the biggest place in the world that transformed opium to heroin, and the local mafia had the contacts there. We're talking about major drug traffickers and importers, organized crime. We were not dealing with angels. We were dealing with the worst of the worst as far as gangsters were concerned, with lots of money involved, millions and millions of dollars. I was part of a lot of major investigations, but it's not like it is in the movies. It's not the work of one or two people, but the work of teams. It involved following people, looking after the telephone conversations. All of it had to be done in a discreet manner. You had to watch yourself and not leave any traces. I was not one of the guys who would go undercover. We had supervising to do; we had to keep [the others] safe, help them along the way.

"I was seconded to the National Crime Investigation Unit for approximately a year and a half as organized crime was closely related to drug trafficking on the international level. One day, while attempting to arrest an individual who had just delivered

1.5 pounds of heroin to our undercover agent, I was forced to use my firearm and I wounded him. I successfully completed the arrest and the perpetrator was later convicted and sentenced to 14 years in jail. The incident affected me for some time. In those days, members who experienced traumatic or violent events did not have access to psychological support or treatment. For about a week, I hardly slept because I realized I could have killed him. Even though I'd been in the Army Reserves, killing somebody is not something to be taken lightly. It affected me. That's the only time I took that work home with me."

After getting married and accepting a promotion as a Criminal Investigation Branch Reader-Analyst because it promised a less disruptive lifestyle, Laverdière remembered everything he detested about working at a desk job. He had a hobby he had been perfecting, though—getting all his flying qualifications—and he put that to work. "During my time as a Reader-Analyst, I was occasionally tasked to fly aerial surveillance on major criminal investigations. I would always look forward to these surveillance jobs. They allowed me to get out of the office and eventually helped me realize that I wanted to fly for a living. In 1975, the Force introduced aerial surveillance to the three Special 'O' sections—Montreal, Toronto and Vancouver. I was selected by the Air Services Directorate to begin this program in 'C' Division. Three years later, I was asked to start a new Air Services Section in Montreal, which included another pilot and one additional transport aircraft. I did all kinds of surveillance. It's a lot easier to do it in the aircraft when you're working on a major drug investigation, or customs and excise. When there is 300 kilos of hashish leaving the airport to go to a destination, you sure didn't want to lose it. The Montreal Police Department had been using helicopters for several years, but helicopters are sometimes limited in the time they can stay in the air, and their speed was not good enough. Airplanes could stay in the air five to six hours, and if the target was travelling 60, 70 MPH in a car, we had airplanes that could follow. People on the ground could not keep up with the target, but we could keep them in sight at all times.

"We did a lot of work out in the country, surveillance on boot-leggers who built large stills for making booze. In the '60s and '70s, it was a big thing in the province of Quebec. They were supplying bars and there was a lot of money to be made. They were the toughest people to follow, though, and they were usually out in the boondocks. I remember working a couple of weeks following these fuel trucks that were going to large stills making hundreds of gallons a day. The fuel trucks would get close to the still and turn their lights off. Nobody could follow a truck without lights, but we were able to see them with surveillance equipment in the air. We found the location of the still, and the next day the police arrested them. We had a pilot and the observer. The observer was doing the communication, the actual surveillance. I was responsible to fly the plane, to keep aware of what was happening on the ground at all times and talk to air control. Over the city of Montreal, flying was kind of delicate. We had a major airport to contend with, and you had to stay out of the way. One time, we were doing surveillance at night and coming back to my airport on the south side of Montreal when we ran into a heavy snow shower. So, we had to do an instrument approach with minimum visibility. It was OK, we made it, but the next day, on the same job, 20 minutes after taking off, my vacuum pump, which operates the instruments, quit. No problem, we had visual conditions. But if that pump had quit the night before, with very poor visibility, it would have been a big problem, to say the least."

September 2, 1995, at Whitehorse Airport. Inspector Laverdière and Staff Sergeant Bob Bemrose flew RCMP Commissioner Phil Murray to Whitehorse from Ottawa to celebrate the 100th anniversary of the RCMP in the Yukon. Sergeant Rick Aberson (far left) is the Whitehorse Air Section member standing next to the C-FMPL, the Whitehorse Air Section Twin Otter.

Laverdière went on to fly for the RCMP in the Yukon, and then as part of the busy Thompson Air Section in Manitoba before he circled back to Montreal. Commissioned in 1992, he transferred to HQ Air Services Directorate, first as the Air Services Training Officer, and later as the Air Services Safety Officer. He participated in setting up the Air Services Safety Program and also assisted in the development of new aerial surveillance equipment. After taking a five-month leave to acquire airliner flying experience with Air Transat, he retired from the RCMP and spent 15 more years as a commercial pilot. But he views his wide-ranging career in the RCMP as not only playing to his strengths but shaping him as a person. "Doing all those things, with the responsibilities it entails, you learn how to conduct yourself, how to judge the people you are dealing with. It makes you grow up. You learn fast what life is all about. You live in an orderly society, a law-abiding society, where you think not just about yourself but about everyone else around you, and to be satisfied with your life. I am a person who, under stress, I get thinking quite fast, just like [you do] in aviation. I would always try to find a solution that would minimize the damages. What's the best I could do under the circumstances? I don't have a tendency to run away from the problem. The only problem I had was with routine. I always liked to be in the middle of the action."

—Helen Metella

D.M.
(Dave)
LEBLANC
Reg# 24825
(0.1623 Inspector)

LEBLANC

C66/67 Troop
50th Year Reunion

DAVE LEBLANC'S KNACK for creating bridges between the RCMP and Canada's First Nations communities was well-established by the time he received his Cree spirit name, but the story of that naming ceremony underscores how at ease he was with Indigenous culture and how much respect he received throughout his policing career in return.

The ceremony occurred while LeBlanc was attending a First Nations "bear camp" in the wilderness of northern Manitoba. The event required that he fast, consuming neither food nor water, for four days and then take part in a sweat lodge ceremony where he was to receive his spirit name from an Elder.

He survived the physically challenging fast, but while it was occurring, "I was not aware that a black bear had come into the camp and was observed going up to the big centre tipi and placing its paws near the doorway," says LeBlanc. "Then it went to the sweat lodge and did the same. It also did the same at my tent in the main camp."

During the subsequent sweat, eight women and LeBlanc were scheduled to receive their spirit name, but only the women did. The naming Elder told LeBlanc he had simply not received a name for him. This baffled his sponsoring Elder, but LeBlanc shrugged it off, and because he was famished, he turned his attention to the feast that followed. While eating was underway, the naming Elder suddenly called upon him and declared he had now been given LeBlanc's spirit name. "He explained about the bear coming into camp, and said that this was in my honour. He also said the name did not come with the others for the same reason [because it was a name of honour]. My name, translated, is Most Sacred Warrior Bear, which I am told is a powerful name. My clan is the otter clan because of my work ethic and fun-loving nature." A look at LeBlanc's remarkable history with the Force verifies each of the Elder's interpretations.

LeBlanc is indeed a hard-working warrior of policing. His official career with the RCMP lasted 36 years, but since retiring in 2002, he has performed numerous high-profile roles for its Veterans' Association, for a total of more than five decades of devoted service to the Force. He retired high in the ranks, as an RCMP Superintendent, yet his experiences emphasize the fundamental traits necessary to police such a large, diverse country as Canada, at any level of law enforcement. The threads running through his tale are patience, open-mindedness and a belief that being a member of a community demands active participation in it.

LeBlanc was already well acquainted with that last characteristic when he joined the RCMP at 19. He'd grown up on Cape Breton Island, the eldest of seven, in a town where people lived just above the poverty line, and everyone felt responsible for raising the community's children. "If you were walking down the road and you did something, people knew you were Jean and

David LeBlanc played a major role in C Troop winning the summer of 1966 "Depot" fitness challenge.

Charlie's son, and before you even got home someone would be asking, 'What were you doing throwing those rocks?'" he says.

Impromptu kitchen parties where everyone is welcome, the food is shared, and the music is lively are as natural to LeBlanc as breathing. His career-long interest in Canada's Indigenous communities derived from his sense that First Nations celebrations stem from the same human instinct as those East Coast gatherings—if you share celebrations with your neighbours, you'll grow closer to one another.

When his second posting after "Depot" found him in Fort Qu'Appelle, SK, a town nudged up against four First Nations communities, he rejected the prevailing local belief that "the Indigenous people were the drunks that came to town." Instead, he attended the summer's powwows, and even joined participants in the dancing. That turned heads, he says. People didn't expect to see a policeman acting as though such behaviour was no big deal.

"You need to visit people where they exist," says LeBlanc. "If somebody is wearing a turban, you need to find out what it's about. You don't have to join in, but you have to understand, ask questions."

Understanding Indigenous culture was a learning curve for LeBlanc, and it started in Fort Qu'Appelle, where he was introduced to the pain that residential schools were wreaking on communities. One of his duties as an RCMP member was to return "delinquent" students who had run away from school back to their reserve. "Not only for me, but for the other guys, it just didn't feel right, even though people told us, 'No, that's how they get their education.'"

His empathy for the circumstances in which First Nations found themselves prompted him to speak up whenever prejudices about "the drunken Indians" were voiced—there, or in his postings to Kipling, SK, and, much later, Thompson, MB. "I'd counter with, 'Hold on. We have roughly 5,000 Indigenous people living around Thompson, and out of that about 80 to 85 are habitual drunks. How many non-Indigenous people do you think are intoxicated in Thompson every night?' If they said, 'Well, not that many,' I'd say, 'Yeah, because they're at home; they're not visible. You don't know how many domestic violence incidents there are. But the police do.'"

His perspective was appreciated, sometimes in dramatic fashion. In the middle of the very first sweat lodge he attended, an Indigenous man began to cry. In a loud voice he declared that he could no longer hate his brother. "It's totally black inside—they describe it like being in the womb—very spiritual," says LeBlanc. "And you go through four sessions of water being thrown on heated rocks, so I was concentrating on not burning up, but he was going through a very traumatic spiritual understanding. Afterwards, the Elder told me I had to talk to this person. When I asked why, he said that I [LeBlanc] was the brother [the man] no longer hated. He had just served several years incarcerated for an armed robbery, and he hated police officers.

"I ended up talking to him, and he said that by me sharing his healing lodge with him, he no longer hated police officers. We became friends and kept in touch. To this day, we refer to each other as 'brother.'"

During the first 25 years of his career, LeBlanc spent considerable time deployed to small rural detachments in Saskatchewan and Manitoba, starting with Moosomin and including Kipling, Fort Qu'Appelle, Melfort, Gull Lake, Big River and Gimli, with a couple of transfers to Regina woven in when he worked highway patrol, plainclothes duties and the Regina Drug Section. Throughout, he steadily increased his skills by training in everything from breath-test and radar technology to arson investigation. The small communities educated him, too, as his years there were hardly uneventful. LeBlanc observed the full complement of murders, accidents and tragedies.

In Moosomin, as a brand-new Force member, he was the policeman who took a phone call from a male who said, "I just shot my dad and if you get here in five minutes, I will give myself up." As the junior Constable, he guarded the prisoner while the others conducted the investigation. A few days later, he answered a related call. The man's lawyer, who was also evidently suffering from mental health issues, had committed suicide.

In Kipling, a frightened young girl who gave birth surreptitiously to a baby that didn't survive placed it in the town dump, creating a mystery for the RCMP to solve. During the same posting, one spring LeBlanc was sent on a manhunt to Prince Albert, searching for a man who had killed two RCMP officers the previous autumn and then gone to ground. "We weren't sure he was still alive. The dog man recovered his body. He had encamped under the knoll of a tree, and if our members had gotten close, he could have been in position to take down a whole bunch of us. But the military had brought in a vehicle and men to help us, and we think he ended up killing himself."

Encountering so many heavy matters at a relatively young age demanded reliable coping mechanisms. Many police officers debriefed over a bottle late at night, but LeBlanc was a non-drinker, so practical jokes were also a typical release among him and his colleagues.

One day in Kipling, LeBlanc's wife, Joyce, broke her leg and several RCMP members arrived at the hospital with a floral arrangement. Within it, they had concealed one of many artificial legs the detachment staff had received as part of some found-but-never-claimed property that had been turned in to their office. Joyce, who had met LeBlanc while she was working the canteen at "Depot," was familiar with RCMP recruits' shenanigans, so when

Dave LeBlanc and his future wife, Joyce, on November 16, 1966, at the Passout dance of C Troop. Joyce worked at "Depot," where she met Dave during training.

the leg fell out, she laughed. But when LeBlanc and his colleagues hung some of the other artificial legs from the ceiling of the detachment's cells, and sent a visiting Non-Commissioned Officer ahead to inspect the area, that victim of their jesting almost had a coronary.

More effective than pranks, perhaps, was LeBlanc's practice of immersing himself in most of the sports and community activities available wherever they lived, often as a volunteer. He coached baseball, softball, and hockey, joined Lions Clubs and the Rotary, volunteered as drill instructor for a Kiwanis youth marching band in Regina, commanded the Air Cadet Squadron in Melfort, SK, and pretty much everywhere he curled and played golf. As he moved into supervisory roles, LeBlanc made sure the police officers he was responsible for always formed teams to play the community's teams. It was a form of self-preservation, he says, because it meant he wasn't solely interacting with criminals. "At the end of a terrible policing day, if you were coaching a local hockey team, it took you away from it."

Knowing all the parents of those he was coaching, picking up what they were discussing about goings-on in town, and being aware of who was who in the community helped him solve crimes, too.

In Big River, SK, when an arsonist set fire to the high school, a young, intoxicated man was soon arrested nearby. Although his hair was singed, he would not co-operate with questioners. LeBlanc had a talk with him. "I simply appealed to his conscience and asked how his mother, a local town councillor and respected woman, was going to feel about what happened." Left to mull that over, minutes later the young man confessed, and a multimillion-dollar arson was solved in less than 12 hours.

His calm but friendly approach quite often proved a useful tool, says Joyce. "Dave has this authority persona around him, but he can also pull out the 'I'm just a good old boy' with a sympathetic look to his body and face. He doesn't have to say much, but it works." Adds LeBlanc: "It's not a role, it's a philosophy. I think that's why it's successful."

However, encountering such a wide cross-section of people did produce situations that made LeBlanc give his head a shake, sympathetically or not. In Moosomin, an elderly justice of the peace the RCMP would contact at home whenever they apprehended out-of-town speeders [so they could collect the fine immediately], had an important question for LeBlanc after one such visit. "What do I do with the money?" he asked, opening a filing cabinet. He had accumulated 10 or 15 years' worth of cash from fines because no one had ever asked him for the money.

During LeBlanc's second deployment to the Regina Highway Patrol, when the speed limit was 60 MPH, he stopped a vehicle that his radar reported was travelling at more than 130 MPH. As LeBlanc started explaining to the driver through his rolled-down window why he was being stopped, the driver's wife stirred from her nap in the passenger seat. "That was as far as I got before she reached over and slapped him hard across the face and said she'd warned him before falling asleep not to go fast," says LeBlanc. "It was obvious the rest of their trip to Calgary was not going to go well."

From highway patrol, LeBlanc was promoted and transferred to the Regina Subdivision Drug Section, a challenging post for a non-drinker, since a lot of surveillance was done in bars. His cover story to whoever eyed him suspiciously was often, "'I've had a bad night with the wife, so I'm just going to sit here and relax.' In one case, a bike gang member ended up sitting at a table with me, and I told him that story and added that 'normally people think I'm a narc.' The guy said, 'No, that's the narc over there,' and he pointed to the guy I was protecting."

During this posting, Joyce gained a deeper insight into the tricky situations her husband's duties involved because, after getting married and having children, she was again employed by the Force. Her job was in Special Investigations, monitoring wiretaps that members had placed. While most of it was serious stuff, there were moments of hilarity. One night, she and another woman were on duty, monitoring an electronic surveillance bug in a bar. Joyce recalls that the local "hooligan mobsters" had occupied the same table all night, chatting mundanely. "I'm listening to it and all of a sudden I hear they're making arrangements for a hit," says Joyce. "I called the other monitor over to listen and she said, 'My God, we've got to call the member whose case it was.' When this

David LeBlanc while working as an undercover Drug Squad officer in Saskatchewan.

guy came in, he was so excited, but here were two women rolling on the floor we were laughing so hard. In between the time we made the phone call and he came in, we realized that the TV was on in the bar. I think it was *Kojak* that was on. That's where they were 'arranging a hit.'"

After a couple of years working both undercover and other drug investigations, LeBlanc discovered he was allergic to "of all things, marijuana." He was transferred and promoted, becoming the Non-Commissioned Officer in Charge of the Melfort Detachment, where there was more drug trafficking to police. A subsequent promotion to Sergeant took him to Gull Lake, SK, followed by Big River. In that posting, he was recommended for the promotion track that would lead eventually to positions as Inspector and then Superintendent.

But first he transferred to the Community Aboriginal Services Section in Regina, where he developed still more special skills while travelling the province to promote the Force within Indigenous communities and with various levels of government. His role was to be the Commanding Officer's speechwriter and right-hand man, but by listening and observing he was also amassing information about First Nations' relationships with the RCMP that strengthened his effectiveness in the Force overall.

"In one community, a kid came up to me and said, 'Did you bring my dad back today?' because the only experience he had of the police was of them arresting one of his relatives." In another place, LeBlanc noticed that children's drawings of police officers were only from the shoulders up. He realized that was because the police never left their cars while visiting that reserve.

Understanding how important it was to listen during interactions with First Nations members became invaluable to LeBlanc at later postings, including one to Gimli, MB. In an adjoining area to his detachment, Indigenous people had blocked Highway 6, the only highway running north from Winnipeg through the heart of Manitoba, because of a dispute with Manitoba Hydro. LeBlanc was called into a provincial government cabinet meeting with the ministers responsible for highways, hydro and justice to provide insight. "I did a lot of listening and learned they were getting a lot of bad advice from their assistants on how to handle Indigenous people."

LeBlanc bluntly told them that while the RCMP could certainly shut the protest down immediately, that would likely open the door to years of ongoing protests. He pointed out that an election for Chief and Council was imminent, and that the Chief was being backed into a corner by the provincial politicians who were trying to end the dispute by force. LeBlanc suggested the government announce that it would allow a roadblock, but negotiate in private with the Chief about how long it would last. Then they could meet at a neutral location for further discussion.

The plan worked and both sides saved face, simply by LeBlanc listening for what was really at stake. It wasn't rocket science, he says, but something much easier to come by. "In all the courses I've taught, I tell people that you can't teach common sense. You either have it or you don't."

LeBlanc wasn't afraid to play the heavy, however, when his common sense suggested it would be effective. During a later posting to Thompson, where he'd been promoted to Superintendent, a local Chief proposed a band council resolution demanding that all the RCMP officers be removed from their reserve. LeBlanc recognized this as a political strategy by the Chief, who was up for re-election and wanted to appear assertive to his voters. So, LeBlanc decided it was a good time to give his members a mental health break. He withdrew every member who was serving the community, and gave them a weekend of rest and relaxation. However, he told the Chief that he had won—the RCMP was "out of there." "By the end of the weekend [when the RCMP crew returned from their holiday], you never saw anybody so happy to see the police again," says LeBlanc.

When LeBlanc began supervising RCMP officers as an Inspector, he also started training other members in how to handle conflict. During his career, he taught scores of other courses, too, including training in traffic, drugs and multicultural and cross-cultural awareness. He was involved in developing the Alternative Dispute Resolution policy and training for the Manitoba Division, and delivered Interest-Based Negotiating to all employees.

As he moved through the ranks, he also shouldered responsibilities that carried new elements of stress. As most people do, he remembers where he was when 9/11 occurred—conducting a tribunal on an RCMP Act infraction at the training academy. By the beginning of the following year, he'd already decided to retire when quadruple bypass surgery made the decision final.

Yet by later in 2002, he had joined the RCMP Veterans' Association, and by 2005, he was serving as vice-president for Manitoba's vets. He's since served on the national board as a director, vice-president and president, and co-chaired the committee reviewing the Canada Not-for-Profit Corporations Act, which reorganized the association.

As president of the board, he has been a member of various committees that represented RCMP veterans' interests to the federal government, including the Veterans Affairs Advisory Council, Veterans Affairs Ombudsman Advisory Council, Veterans Affairs Minister's Family Committee and numerous RCMP committees.

Additionally, during his retirement he obtained his private investigator's licence and has conducted workplace conflict workshops and consultations. "My years with the Mounted Police made me the person I am today," says LeBlanc. "Throughout my whole career I've always tried to see the good side of people and situations—the humour as opposed to the dark side."

—*Helen Metella*

R.B.
(Bruce)
LYMAN
Reg# 24822

LYMAN

C66/67 Troop
50th Year Reunion

MOST CANADIANS IMMEDIATELY recognize that RCMP–GRC is the English-French acronym for Royal Canadian Mounted Police–Gendarmerie royale du Canada. But in Bruce Lyman's mischievous parlance, GRC stands for "Gravel Road Cop," the self-deprecating way he sometimes refers to his career with the Force because so much of it involved patrolling rural highways and back roads. Yet as snapshots of his 31 years with the RCMP are coaxed from Lyman's memory, over and over scenes pop up that are stamped "a moving and authentic Canadian experience"—the kind most Canadians only dream of having, whether it was patrolling by Ski-Doo and boat in a pristine and inspiring northern Manitoba setting, or seeing hockey transform a troubled community.

Lyman's father had built a dry cleaning factory in Moncton, NB, and Lyman was employed by the family business as a truck driver and salesman for a couple of years. But in the mid-1960s, polyester fabric and its magical wash-and-wear properties essentially killed the business. Lyman needed a new job, and fast. A friend was already in the RCMP, and it sounded to Lyman like a stable profession.

Driving from the Atlantic provinces to Canada's geographic middle to start RCMP training, Lyman promptly fell in love with the scenery. "All of Canada was a real experience, but when I got to the Prairies, I was sort of awestruck," he says. "I really thought they were beautiful, the openness and everything. Whenever I went back to New Brunswick, I felt closed in because there's so much bush, you can't see. But here, if you stood on a sardine can, you could watch your dog run away for three days."

His first posting after training at "Depot" was to Brandon, MB, where his overwhelming affection for his new surroundings was evident in the first week. "They showed me around for not much time, and then gave me a police car to go and patrol," says Lyman. "What do I do? It's my first time out on my own, and I really didn't want to stop anybody. I went for a drive west on Highway 1, and I looked up and saw a hawk circling in the sky. I'd never seen anything like this before, and all of a sudden he [the hawk] dives straight down. My eyes follow him down, and then I look up and I'm on the wrong side of the road! I damn near went into the ditch."

After his short training stint in Brandon, learning the rudiments of general policing and studying the *Highway Traffic Act*, Lyman was transferred to Manitou, a tiny agricultural town southwest of Winnipeg, on a highway that runs parallel to the nearby US border.

There was little real crime in the community, says Lyman, who recalls scheduling a dentist appointment directly after testifying in court on an impaired driving charge in nearby Morden, thinking nothing would interfere. That day, quite unexpectedly, he

The detachment office in Manitou, Manitoba. The office and cells were on the main floor, while the living quarters were on the second floor.

was called back to the stand and arrived with a mouth frozen from wisdom teeth extraction, making it hard to speak clearly to the judge.

Yet in this sleepy detachment he learned his first indispensable lesson in policing in small prairie towns. "The Corporal and I would work six days a week, nine to five, which was mostly PR and some paperwork, and we went for coffee. As much as people make fun of policemen and coffee, that's where we did most of our work. People didn't want to be seen coming to the [RCMP] office, so we'd go have coffee, shut our mouths and listen. Farmers like to gossip, and a lot of it is based on the truth. We'd glean a little information that way. And if somebody really wanted to tell you something, we'd see them hanging around and we were the last guys to leave the coffee shop."

Unmarried RCMP members were moved to new postings every six months in those days, so before long Lyman was in Virden, MB, working highway patrol on the Trans-Canada Highway about halfway between Winnipeg and Regina. Driver interactions were generally similar, he says—motorists feigning ignorance when he politely asked whether they knew why they'd been pulled over—but one incident sticks out in his mind. Naturally, it featured a stereotypically Canadian quirk. "There was one guy driving a brand-new Cadillac who came through over the speed limit, so we stopped him, and he was livid. 'Just because I'm driving a fancy car, you guys have been picking on me!' he said. He'd come from Vancouver and this was the tenth or eleventh time he'd been stopped. He just ranted. We didn't say anything, just gave him a ticket, and he got to where he was going. But on the way back, he stopped at the detachment and asked for us. I was living in the barracks then—the detachment was a house with the office downstairs and barracks above—so I came down. And he apologized. "I said, 'Thank you, but why are you apologizing?' He said, 'Because I was going to teach you guys a lesson, so I took the car to a dealership and told them to check the speedometer. It was 15 percent out.' Fifteen percent. That was within tolerance in those days."

Approaching policing with patented Canadian politeness was generally the best way to sidestep unnecessary friction on the job, says Lyman. In Brandon, his next detachment, he learned this while escorting a prisoner who had just been convicted of writing fraudulent cheques, from court to jail. "We were in my two-door patrol car with no shield, no protection at all, and he was a real con artist. He just couldn't help himself. We got close to Portage la Prairie, and he said, 'You know, you have to provide me with lunch,' and he gave me a long song and dance as to why I should. I said, 'OK,' and we went to a hotel and got him lunch. I didn't have him in handcuffs; we just walked into the hotel and no one thought anything. I paid for his lunch. Now, in his mind, he had won. He came back out and sat in the car, no problem. Later, I put it on my expense account. So, I won."

Lyman's subsequent transfer to Rossburn did not have "easygoing" and "auspicious" written all over it, however. Most members were loath to go to the town situated near the southwestern edges of Riding Mountain National Park, near the large reserve now known as the Waywayseecappo First Nation. They considered it a featureless and rough outpost. Indeed, the reserve was "where all the work came from," says Lyman. "There was a lot of

drinking, and drugs were starting to come in, marijuana and cocaine. It was a very violent reserve, and the violence was against
their own, which was foreign to me ... the only industry on the
reserve was the band office, and basically, there was nothing to
do there. I remember one night there were two cars full of people
driving and drinking. I was patrolling the reserve, and so they
turned off their lights so they couldn't be seen. But they couldn't
see each other, and they collided head on. It was sad there. I
blame it on them learning some real bad ways from us. You're
fighting a culture. But when I returned nine years later, they had
discovered hockey and built an arena. One of the guys I used to
pick up for being drunk daily—we had a room reserved just for
him—when I saw him, I said, 'You're not drinking?' He said, 'Oh,
no, there's a hockey game tonight, and I have to go.' They had a
good Chief there, and he turned it around. He gave them hockey
and purpose." In fact, the team has grown in stature since and is
now a Junior "A" member of the Manitoba Junior Hockey League.

Lyman was part of another defining Canadian moment, albeit
one that was devastating to the country's collective consciousness,
when he was subsequently posted to The Pas for a month in 1971.
He and his partner had been called in from Thompson as part
of a massive RCMP contingent deployed to The Pas following the
murder of Helen Betty Osborne. The 19-year-old Cree woman
was kidnapped off a main street in town by a group of young
white males who beat her and then murdered her with abject
brutality. The case, which was not solved for another 16 years,
opened the entire country's eyes to the shameful degree of racism
that was and is directed toward Indigenous people.

Lyman and his partner's assignment was to keep watch at a
position on the highway for a week, as leads were investigated
and possible suspects' whereabouts were tracked. "It is one case

that really bothered me," says Lyman. "We knew within a day who it was. We had the backing of the community. These guys were known—my wife was related to one of them—but the investigators had to shut it down. The break didn't come until we could get a warrant for wiretaps [years later]. Then, one of the investigators put a story in the paper stating that a new direction had been found and they were getting close. One suspect was still in The Pas and the rest were spread out across the country, and that's when the phone calls started going out. That's when they got the information."

While Lyman's recounting leaves no doubt he is still outraged, almost five decades later, by how long the Indigenous community had to wait for justice, there is one piece of information he picked up while in The Pas that makes him smile on behalf of the local Indigenous community and its reserve. "The Chief and Council there were very smart people and they had gravel on their land, so I think in the 1950s, when they built the highway, they had the only gravel. There's a stretch of road on that highway called The Bog because it has no bottom. It's a bad piece of ground."

He explains that its permafrost would thaw somewhat each year and so The Bog needed an annual refill of gravel. "At the time, the price of gravel was set at something ridiculous [very low] so the people running the reserve said, 'OK, we'll sell it for that, but we have a fee for your trucks to come on our land.' So, they had a toll and they made money. They had good leadership and these guys were smarter than a lot of municipal politicians. Not long after that they built a shopping centre [with their profits]."

Lyman's next move was to Thompson Highway Patrol. Back during his first stint in Rossburn, he had met a schoolteacher named Connie Shoemaker, and the two of them married during his time in Thompson. Connie, who hailed from Grandview, a

Bruce and Connie Lyman were married in Grandview, Manitoba, in July 1970. Connie passed away on June 20, 2015.

community a bit north of Rossburn, took it in stride when her marriage meant she was suddenly living in a town filled with men from the nearby Inco nickel mine. "I remember I took her to the theatre and it was packed, but with maybe five women," says Lyman. "I'm sure she wasn't thrilled about it, but she never complained."

Meanwhile, Lyman was himself adapting to another peculiarly Canadian feature of Thompson's environment. "We used to drive the highway everyday and there'd be this big bump by a tree, so you'd know to slow down because otherwise you were going to be airborne. But the semi-trucks would come and move that bump because it was a bog underneath and the permafrost had thawed out. If you hit that bump when you were going fast, you'd not only be airborne, you'd scrape the bottom of the car. If you hit the oil pan, you were toast."

The Thompson RCMP members improvised a solution by bolting a steel "skid plate" frame under their cars' engines, a practical but still "loosey-goosey" fix considering they had to chase numerous speeders and intoxicated drivers at high speed along that highway. "I remember one time looking back and there were sparks coming out from under the car," says Lyman.

The same highway played a key role in another memorable, possibly quintessential, northern Canadian scene. "We had two mines south of us and they had billets for their single workers," says Lyman. "On payday, they'd pool all their money and give it to somebody to go buy beer at the vendor. Which is legal. Unless you pop a beer on the way back—and they always did. And guess what? I'd take all their beer. Then you'd go to the dump and take a shotgun and blow up all their beer cases, which was faster than opening up every bottle and pouring it out."

Lest anyone remain in mourning for all that perfectly good Canadian booze gone to waste, Lyman offers a bit of solace that was introduced by a wise Staff Sergeant who would visit the detachment periodically and check the inventory of seized goods. "At one point in my career there, you used to take any liquor that was not opened to the personal care homes and have it signed for by the manager, and they would dole it out to the residents that wanted it. I was only going to break it, so I thought that was nice."

Lyman and Connie's daughter was born in Thompson in 1971, and in 1972, the family moved to Swan River, a pretty community of predominantly Ukrainian and Métis residents near the Saskatchewan border. There, Lyman's two sons were born, and the family mostly enjoyed the area's tremendous natural beauty. "I remember having no money and because we had no money, we didn't have a big social life," he says. A trip to Winnipeg was eight hours, or two days' travel there and back, so that treat was infrequent.

While policing involved mostly routine matters and occasionally helping out conservation officers (who weren't authorized to carry firearms) to enforce poaching infractions, the rural area's tucked-away location tempted a few criminals with more ambitious schemes. "We had a couple of big fraud cases—insurance fraud," says Lyman. "They used to raise a lot of racehorses out there, and I think maybe someone was passing off ordinary horses as thoroughbreds. Although I didn't get to know the ins

RCMP police vehicles assigned to isolated detachments such as Island Lake, like the GMC Crew Cab shown here, could only be sent for servicing by ice road or barge once a year. When members had no vehicles they were left to their best resources to patrol their detachment area.

and outs of the case, I got to patrol the periphery whenever they [plainclothes officers from Winnipeg] wanted to set up surveillance, or if someone was coming."

After returning to Rossburn for a couple of years, where he became a senior Constable, Lyman's next transfer produced another promotion and some of the most purely Canadian experiences of his life. But the move was to a detachment so remote that the location didn't have an accessible high school. So, his wife and sons stayed behind in Rossburn and only joined him in the summers.

Island Lake is located on the east side of northern Manitoba, north of where the province's border takes an elbow bend on its way to Hudson Bay. The detachment there was responsible for four nearby reserves totalling about 1,500 people, in what was "absolutely the most gorgeous country of Manitoba," says Lyman. "All the white people lived on the island. My patrol was by Ski-Doo and boat, and we had ice roads in the winter. We had a Hudson's Bay store there, which stocked vegetables, milk and meat. They would fly in the fresh stuff and truck in the nonperishables in the winter, but it was very expensive because it cost 50¢ a pound to fly anything in, and they still had to make a profit."

Lyman's duties in the two years he was posted there mainly involved helping the band Constables on the dry reserves. He investigated the inevitable smuggling of liquor, some sudden deaths and a drowning. But it was a routine responsibility one late winter night that almost cost him his own life. "I remember going out on the Ski-Doo to help arrest some drunk. I went out in the middle of night and put him in the cells, and then I went back home the short way. I hit a small lake, but the ice had gone down because of the weight of the snow, so there was water on top of the ice. Once I got in it, it was too late. I just had to go as fast as I could to get across. When I finally got off the lake, the drawstrings of my mukluks had formed balls of ice on them about the size of softballs. The lake was deep, and if I'd frozen [the engine] in the middle of it, nobody would have known. Nobody would have known I hadn't taken the normal route. I don't know if I slept at all that night. I don't think I told my wife about that one. I think it would have worried her too much."

The stunningly beautiful scenery of Island Lake provided Lyman and his family several one-of-a-kind Canadian experiences during the summers, including waterskiing on pristine waters surrounded by cliffs, and hitching sightseeing rides with a Manitoba Hydro employee who regularly checked lines and towers in an area known for its astonishing waterfalls.

Another singular scene he describes manages to draw a vivid picture of a little-known RCMP duty, capture this country's complicated history in an anecdote, and also shed light on the often overlooked, gentle humour of Indigenous

Bruce Lyman patrolling in his summer transportation at Island Lake Detachment, 1984. As soon as winter hit, Ski-Doos became the winter transportation.

people. "We were giving out Treaty money," says Lyman, referring to the annual payments made to Indigenous people to fulfil treaty agreements made more than 200 years ago, and promised for all time (although the payments are not indexed to inflation). "I was in Red Serge and sitting with the band councillors. The amount that was written in the Treaty is $5 and a box of .22 shells. I was sitting with the Councillor who is the money man on the reserve and who I thought was a very good and smart man. We're just sitting there talking, and he looks at me and says, 'You white men, you really screwed things up.' I said, 'Oh, what do you mean?' He said, 'Before you came, us Natives ran the country and there were no taxes.'"

With so many distinctively Canadian experiences already tucked under his belt, it almost stands to reason that Lyman's last couple of assignments were in everyday scenery where people more typically expect to spot a Mountie. He spent two years on highway patrol in Stonewell, a bedroom community north of Winnipeg, and when that unit was closed, he was transferred to Winnipeg's airport. "It was the most boring job in the world," he says with candour. Yet he observed moments there that make a person's Canadian pride take a bow, too. "We had the [Winnipeg] Jets then, so there were hockey teams that used to come through. Tie Domi [a legendary penalty-drawing tough guy who played, at the time, for the Maple Leafs] was there quite a bit. His plane loaded in the north end of the airport, so he'd go to the south end and walk through the whole airport and speak to all the kids. He was one of the nicest people on Earth."

Since retiring in 1997, Lyman settled in his wife's hometown of Grandview, where he has kept busy into his 70s, delivering rural mail, stopping and talking daily with people along his route. Small-town Manitoba agrees with him as much now as it did throughout his RCMP career. "They all have their own culture; they're all different. But I sort of like the fact that you know most people in town." That familiarity is likely even more comforting since Connie passed away in 2015.

As for his policing career: "I thought it was a good career. It was something different everyday, and I thought I was doing something good."

—Helen Metella

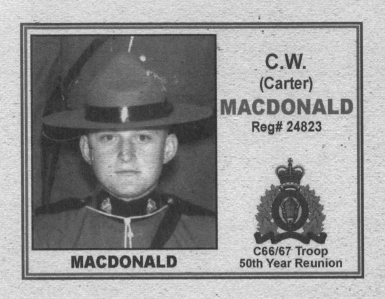

C.W.
(Carter)
MACDONALD
Reg# 24823

C66/67 Troop
50th Year Reunion

MACDONALD

CARTER MACDONALD ALMOST missed getting into the RCMP, but once he did, he made the most of every opportunity, from graduating at the top of his class to parlaying his skills into high-ranking positions with Canada's spy agency 18 years later. "That's one of the reasons I had such a diverse career," says MacDonald. "I was never afraid to try something new when it was offered."

MacDonald was 22 and the veteran of many a dead-end job when he first tried to apply to join the Force. He had already been a drummer in a band, a bookkeeper, a boat worker and a sign painter. He had just come off a midnight shift where he had laboured with a team of workers cleaning a broken blast furnace at the Sydney Steel Plant in Cape Breton when he entered the RCMP Subdivision office in Sydney, Cape Breton, hoping to obtain an application form to join the RCMP.

"When the blast furnaces go down, you had people working 30 minutes on and 30 minutes off because the residual heat in the furnace and the bricks was something you couldn't put up with for a prolonged time frame," says MacDonald. "You're lowering a chain that cleans out the flues of the furnace, causing plumes of hot dust to rise. That leaves a person caked with dust, somewhat weakened from the heat, and your back gets all itchy." To say the least, his appearance was dishevelled when he met the crusty Sergeant at the RCMP Subdivision office. Due to having alopecia, an ailment that had rendered him bald since childhood but which had abated enough by his early teens to let an irregular strip of hair grow down the middle of his head, he also looked somewhat unusual.

"It wasn't a very professional way to present myself," he admits, "but I was just looking for the application form." The Sergeant, meanwhile, seemed to be looking for a way to squelch this wannabe recruit. He measured MacDonald's height and pronounced him less than the regulation cut-off height of 5'8". Dejected,

MacDonald's experience in a band served him well at "Depot," where he, Dave LeBlanc and Bob Bossence were affectionately nicknamed "band scoffers" by members of C Troop. Being in the band allowed them to miss cleaning the stables and grooming the horses. It also meant they could sleep in while their troop mates marched off to perform their stable duties.

MacDonald was back to contemplating a future in which even the dreadful job at the steel plant was in jeopardy.

It was a tough reality for a young man who already knew something about the concept. His family had moved around on several occasions due to the poor economic conditions in Cape Breton. Eventually he, his parents and his five younger siblings moved to his father's family farm, owned by a kind and understanding uncle. At the time, there were no other viable options for the family.

Luckily, the adult MacDonald had a champion—an RCMP Corporal named Gus Matheson with whom he had, ironically, played basketball. At an event in the Bras d'Or Yacht Club in Baddeck, where MacDonald was playing in a band, the Corporal learned of MacDonald's unsuccessful visit to the Sydney Subdivision office and he invited him to the detachment in Baddeck the following day so that he could be re-measured. Gus insisted that MacDonald stand up tall, and measured him at 5'8¼". He said that he would vouch for the accuracy of this measurement to the original RCMP Subdivision office. MacDonald was subsequently accepted and headed off to RCMP Training Academy "Depot" Division, where he was surprised to meet "two other members of C Troop who were shorter than I was!" MacDonald enjoyed his training experience in "Depot" in Regina. The camaraderie with his fellow troop mates and the discipline needed to function as a cohesive group provided him with valuable lessons that would serve him well later in life.

His first assignment after graduation was in Ottawa and consisted mainly of routine duties, such as answering inquiries and taking radio calls from Traffic Division. MacDonald soon traded in the duties of a front desk/dispatcher in Protective Subdivision by stepping up when a unique position was offered to him doing racetrack supervision duties in Ottawa, and, later in Kingston and Belleville. "I was trained on how to calculate the parimutuel betting system," says Carter. "There were two of us who would go to the track, one of whom sat with the officials who reviewed the film tapes of the individual races to confirm if there were any infractions—occasionally one rider might foul another and there would be a complaint to be investigated. Officials wanted to have somebody in law enforcement there when these issues were decided."

Mike Hampel (left) and Carter MacDonald (right) entertain the Troop with either a square dance or a jig.

The other officer would work behind the scenes, monitoring the betting. "Where I liked to work was with

George Piccott (left) practices his police holds on Carter MacDonald (right).

the people calculating how much money was bet and how the amounts dedicated to various areas were put aside," says MacDonald. "In Ontario, nine percent of the total money wagered would go to the track, six percent to the province, and 0.5 percent to the Department of Agriculture, the federal department responsible for ensuring this supervision of the proper dispersal of the monies wagered." The remaining 84.5 percent of the monies wagered were returned to the public in the form of winnings.

Rotating through the two different tracks in Kingston and Belleville, the job took four days a week, and on the other day, MacDonald worked on general detachment duties in Kingston, which included patrols of the St. Lawrence Seaway on the Marine Division boat, checking duck hunters to ensure they had federal licences, and other duties as required.

Despite the novelty of this work—"my math skills improved tremendously and to this day I credit my ability to be able to calculate things in my head to that constant practice at the tracks for two seasons"—there were more intriguing paths in store for MacDonald back in Ottawa. In 1969, the *Report of the Royal Commission on Security* (the *Mackenzie Report*), recommended two things that would benefit RCMP rank-and-file members: French-language training and a university degree.

MacDonald, who had always been a history buff, liked both ideas. He began taking French-language classes at Algonquin College and university courses at Carleton University, later earning some credits by studying at the University of Ottawa in French. His interest in learning French came to the attention of his superiors and ultimately changed the direction of his career via full-time language training in a federal government training centre. But first, current affairs had a few things to teach him.

On October 5, 1970, a cell of the Front de Libération du Québec (FLQ), a group agitating for Québec's independence from Canada, kidnapped British trade commissioner James Cross in Montreal and demanded money, the release of prisoners, and safe passage to Cuba. A few days later, another cell kidnapped Pierre Laporte, a senior provincial minster responsible for Immigration, Manpower and Labour. The October Crisis, as it came to be known, caused Prime Minister Pierre Trudeau to implement the *War Measures Act* on October 16, limiting Canadians' civil liberties in peacetime for the first time. A day later, Laporte was found dead (believed to have been executed; it was not until 2010 that it was revealed he had actually been killed accidentally during a struggle with his captors). Before the worst of the drama unfolded, the RCMP quickly created a security detail for the prime minister and other prominent cabinet ministers who, surprisingly, did not have one at the time. MacDonald was one of those selected for the job of providing close security for the prime minister. "Many people portray him as aloof and arrogant, but my experience with the man was the polar opposite," says MacDonald. "I found him easy to speak with, open and reservedly friendly in our interactions."

One of his first assignments occurred at Harrington Lake, the official retreat for Canada's prime ministers in the Gatineau Hills. On a rainy day, MacDonald and his partner arrived for a 3:00 p.m. shift start to learn that Trudeau and a guest had taken a boat to explore the lake and the surrounding woods. The RCMP detail was instructed to leave Trudeau alone, but to take another boat and find him if he was needed. About an hour later, Mitchell Sharp, the minister of External Affairs, called to say that he urgently needed to speak with the prime minister. Given the serious nature of the phone call, MacDonald and his partner headed out to locate the prime minister. It had begun to rain and MacDonald's partner borrowed the raincoat from the uniformed RCMP officer who was on duty at the entrance gate to the property. Mac-Donald did not have a raincoat, so he used an umbrella he had brought with him.

They quickly spotted Trudeau's boat but not its occupants, who had evidently gone for a walk in the woods. Shout-outs received no reply, so MacDonald's partner fired two shots in the air from his .38 calibre, short-barrelled revolver. Still nothing.

MacDonald suggested they move to the centre of the lake to avoid any echo rebounding off the surrounding hills, and he then fired two shots into the air with his .38. Trudeau and his guest then emerged from the woods, and the prime minister was told of the urgent call from Mitchell Sharp. Trudeau invited the RCMP officers to follow his boat back to the residence.

"I later learned that the PM's guest was Margaret Sinclair, soon to become Margaret Trudeau, wife of the prime minister," says MacDonald. The evening ended memorably for MacDonald, because he and his partner ended up sharing tea and conversation with Trudeau in the kitchen. Years later, when University of Waterloo history professor John English published the book *Just Watch Me: The Life of Pierre Elliott Trudeau, 1968–2000*, and MacDonald read an excerpt from its second volume in *Maclean's* magazine in 2009, the tale had changed somewhat dramatically. English wrote that Trudeau and Sinclair, who were unaccustomed to the security, "misbehaved by trekking into the forest one rainy day at Harrington Lake to escape watchful eyes. They got lost, the security forces panicked, and when the pair finally emerged in a clearing, they heard gunshots. There, in the middle of the lake, was an 'absolutely bald policeman' holding an umbrella in one hand and shooting a rifle in the air with the other to guide them home." MacDonald scoffs: "My tiny snub-nose .38 was certainly not a rifle. I can only suppose Margaret mistook my umbrella for a rifle." The incident had also been misrepresented earlier, when the CBC TV miniseries titled *Trudeau,* starring Colm Feore, was released in 2002. "There's a scene where he's walking through the woods, and this male-pattern baldness Mountie sporting a checkered shirt appears shooting a rifle in the air," says MacDonald. "I fully believe that was intended to be a representation of the same event."

MacDonald was also on duty and nearby during two of the October Crisis's more historic moments. On October 13, his detail escorted Trudeau's car to Parliament Hill, where there was a heavily armed military presence and reporters wanting to know how far he would go. "That's the night when the reporters asked him what he'd do, and he said, 'Just watch me,'" says MacDonald.

A few days later, on October 17, they provided an escort on the same route to Centre Block, because Laporte's body had been found in the trunk of a car adjacent to an airport outside of Montreal. "We really had to come of age as a country as a consequence of the actions of the FLQ," says MacDonald. "Before the October Crisis, a person could drive [his or her] own personal car to Parliament Hill, park it on the driveway and go right into the building."

An assignment that MacDonald held a few years later drove that home. The 1976 Summer Olympics in Montreal were the first after the 1972 Olympics in Munich, where 11 Israeli athletes and a West German police officer were kidnapped and later killed by a Palestinian terrorist group. Following some full-time French-language training, MacDonald had been transferred to a group called the Olympic Secretariat, created to help ensure security arrangements for the planned 1976 summer games. In addition to various duties within the Olympic Secretariat, MacDonald helped co-ordinate the activities of a team of security experts who travelled across the country, holding security training at major border crossings and international airports.

The experience of helping to lay the defences against a threat such as the one that had occurred in Munich strengthened his interest in the foreign-service aspect of policing. "I realized that things happening on other sides of the world could be visited on a place like Germany, and it was not a stretch to think it could happen in Canada."

After the Olympics, the now-bilingual MacDonald was posted to Paris, where he handled visa control duties for France, but also for Spain, Portugal, and occasionally Morocco and Algeria. The job entailed criminal and security background checks on people who wanted to immigrate to Canada, with interviews of applicants who aroused suspicion or who fit a specific profile, such as country of origin. It bolstered his ability to size up people effectively through interviews, but one incident also reinforced his lifelong habit of taking every opportunity to improve his skills.

The embassy in Paris had started to see a number of people from Sri Lanka applying to immigrate to Canada. MacDonald's review of the background materials he had on that country revealed they were out of date. So, when he got wind of the fact that the RCMP liaison officer from New Delhi was travelling through Paris, MacDonald invited him to meet so he could pick the latter's brain. As they chatted, MacDonald jotted down the names of current revolutionary groups active in Sri Lanka on the back of a form he normally used for visa interviews. The next day, while interviewing a male Sri Lankan who was not revealing any red flags under standard questioning, MacDonald turned the form over and began going through the list of names the liaison officer from New Delhi had cited.

The applicant's eyes grew big. Under further questioning, he soon started spilling everything he had done with one particular group that was known to have committed acts of terrorism in both Sri Lanka and in Canada (in the case of Canada, this included bank robberies to get funding for the group's activities in Sri Lanka). He also admitted to other acts of intimidation and violence. "He obviously thought I knew about him, because I made a point of referring to the back of the form several times during the interview, and I could see that he was openly nervous because he believed I had telling information on the back of 'his' form," says MacDonald. "It was fortuitous." It was also an indication of where MacDonald's career was headed—definitely deeper into security work.

While living in Paris was exciting, the job created challenges for his young family, which included his wife Elizabeth (a former RCMP civilian employee he had met in Ottawa). Eventually, the family of four became a family of five when their youngest daughter was born in Paris. "Carter was away one week of every six, and something often happened when he wasn't there," says Elizabeth. "I had a miscarriage. Our house was broken into. Our son John needed stitches on his lip after falling. I did manage a bit of a fender-bender at the Étoile, the roundabout that circles the Arc de Triomphe. My French was hard to understand and the fellow in the other car did not speak any English, so I started to cry. He then decided it was easier if he just let me go!"

From Paris, they were transferred to Lima, Peru. The family spent six weeks of Spanish-language training in Guatemala, en route to Lima. "We were fortunate to find a wonderful Guatemalan woman to act as the nanny for our six-week-old daughter, Meredith," says Elizabeth. "We met

Carter and Elizabeth MacDonald were married on July 1, 1972, in Ottawa, Ontario.

215

a few people during our language training, some of whom are lifelong friends."

Once in Lima, MacDonald again handled visa control duties in Peru and Chile, and also assisted with investigations of Canadians who went to Peru with the intention of buying drugs. "At the time, Peru was the second-largest supplier, after Colombia, of cocaine coming into Canada," says MacDonald.

Although MacDonald was not on the frontlines, there was always the fear that "someone would try to get to me through my children. It was recommended that you hire a domestic [servant] so that you always had somebody at home, because [the criminals] will keep an eye on residences."

One quite concerning incident occurred when MacDonald and his wife went to a port outside of Lima to pick up their automobile, which had been shipped from Paris. MacDonald had previously been advised to take one of the locally engaged embassy employees along with him because of potential complications related to getting Peruvian customs officials to release the vehicle. This included bringing some cash in Peruvian currency to pay "inducements" to various officials to expedite the process.

The embassy employee was named Carlos and he was successful in getting the vehicle released, along with the required forms needed to get the vehicle licensed in Peru. On the trip back to Lima, however, their newly liberated car had a flat tire on a particularly remote stretch of the highway. The wheel nuts had become corroded by salt water because the vehicle had been stored above deck on the ship that delivered it to Peru. Neither MacDonald nor Carlos was able to remove the flat tire.

While their struggle was underway, Carlos noticed that "one vehicle kept passing us in both directions," says Elizabeth. On the third pass, the car carrying several young men stopped. The driver rolled down his window, "asking questions regarding who we were, what the nature of our situation was, etc.," says Mac-Donald. "Their questions did not seem to be leading to an offer of assistance, rather they appeared to be inquiries designed to test our relative vulnerability. When Carlos was speaking to the young men, he had the wheel wrench in his hands and he held it in a manner that suggested that he would use it to defend himself." Carlos also made it clear to the young men that MacDonald was a police officer, and that they needed to move on, remembers Elizabeth. "Fortunately, they did."

Happily, a truck driver soon stopped to help change the tire, and the MacDonalds returned safely to Lima. But "it occurred to me and Carter that we probably should not have gone together to pick up the car, leaving our children in the care of a friend from the embassy," says Elizabeth. "We were fortunate that night, and it was an experience I would never wish to repeat."

After a year in Peru, MacDonald was transferred back to Paris to work with the RCMP's counterparts in the French intelligence field. It was stimulating work, and another reminder that by taking the initiative to learn more skills—in particular by having learned French—his career was continuing on an upward trajectory. "Absolutely I don't think I would have attained the rank I attained without it," he says.

In 1984, while he was still in Paris, the Canadian Security Intelligence Service (CSIS) was created and, because he was already in the RCMP's Security Service, MacDonald was automatically transferred to what is often referred to as Canada's spy agency. While he had the opportunity to rejoin the RCMP after two years, by that time MacDonald had spent 15 of his 18 years of service in security and intelligence work. Moreover, had he returned to the RCMP, he would have been subject to posting anywhere in Canada, including remote detachments.

MacDonald opted to remain with CSIS and was put in charge of the CSIS office in Paris. During one of his weekly visits to the offices of the Police Nationale, he received a message asking that he urgently return to the Canadian Embassy. There he was informed about the Air India disaster, the largest loss of life by a terrorist act in Canadian history. It was a shocking reminder that the need for vigilance in monitoring such threats to the security of Canadians was the top priority for the newly formed CSIS.

Upon his return to Canada, MacDonald became the manager of technical services for the Quebec region and later the manager of an operational branch.

While he is still bound by the *Official Secrets Act* to not reveal most of what he was involved with during those positions, Mac-Donald does say he was helping guard against threats that even the most sophisticated Canadians may not believe exist. In one case handled by the Atlantic Region prior to MacDonald's arrival, which had previously gone to trial and so can be discussed, the agency's surveillance discovered a sleeper agent living in Antigonish, NS. "It was a case of a family of Hungarian immigrants. The father had married a woman from Cape Breton, who had serious mental health problems, and she ended up shooting her husband. Their two sons, who were born in Canada, went to live with family in their father's native country and were brought up in Hungary. During this period of time, at least one of them was recruited by Hungarian or Soviet Intelligence and became a sleeper agent and was sent back to Canada. The operation happened in Newfoundland, and the judge who heard the case said, 'I can't believe my ears. This stuff doesn't happen here.'"

Another element of the CSIS era that MacDonald can talk

about underscores his willingness to always try something new, in service of progress. While he was working in Montreal as the manager of technical services for Quebec, a group of his technicians approached him with an idea for an operation that would require a lot of operational support. Read: people and equipment. He liked the idea and pitched it to the operational area it most closely concerned. He was turned down. He then took it to three successive levels of senior management and was turned down by each, although the last one told MacDonald that if he was so passionate about the idea, he was welcome to undertake it with his own personnel, only three of whom were intelligence officers.

MacDonald accepted the challenge. "After one week, the operation was showing some promise; after two weeks we had much more encouraging results. Soon it was decided that the prime minister and cabinet needed to be briefed on the success of the operation." Although one of the senior managers who had turned him down did the briefing in Ottawa, "this did not wound my pride. I took satisfaction from the fact that I listened to people who reported to me and I found their proposal to be very worthy of consideration." Someone else must have seen it that way too, because MacDonald was later promoted to director general of Training and Development for CSIS.

In his last position, as director general for Atlantic Region headquartered in Halifax, MacDonald was only three or four rungs shy of the agency's top leadership position. He took advantage of that role to give interviews to the media to help inform the public about CSIS's mandate and the legislation's definition of legitimate threats to the security of Canada. He also spoke about the oversight mechanisms designed to ensure that CSIS respected the limits of its mandate because he believes passionately in accountability. "As a federal agency we need to show that we are above board," he says. "People and threats to the security of the country need to be identified and neutralized, but in order to be representative of the kind of country we are, which is one of the world's great democracies, we need to be open and accountable."

MacDonald retired from CSIS in 1995, but continued to work, first at Saint Mary's University in Halifax and then at Camosun College in Victoria, in security, transportation management, occupational safety and emergency preparedness. From 2007 to 2019, he was the student ombudsman at Camosun, a position he very much enjoyed until his retirement at age 75.

"Coming from where I was born and brought up in Cape Breton, where life was at times very joyous but economically not very easy, one of the things I vowed to myself was that I'd try to provide well for my family. Having a career with the RCMP and all the opportunities it offers allowed me to do that," MacDonald says. "It was an absolute gift to have the career I had, along with the opportunity to travel to so many places in the world. I feel fulfilled."

—*Helen Metella*

J.R.
(Ross)
MORTLOCK
Reg# 24842

MORTLOCK

C66/67 Troop
50th Year Reunion

ROSS MORTLOCK'S FATHER was right on both counts when he reacted to Ross's declaration that he was going to join the RCMP with, "At the very least, it'll make a man of you."

How could it not mature a 19-year-old to be assigned, on just his second shift, to the midnight-to-morning suicide watch at Edmonton's gloomy RCMP barracks, guarding a man barely older than himself who had just murdered a police officer? Or not long after that, to be first on the scene at a head-on car accident while on his way to a different task, dealing with bodies, first aid and traffic control—in the dark, without a radio or emergency lights and on his own?

Even though, during his six months at "Depot" he had learned traffic control and accident investigation, "You had the fundamentals but not the experience," says Mortlock.

Yet his dad was right about the first part of his remark, too. Seasoning as an adult is the least of what Mortlock's career with the RCMP provided him. Through postings in Edmonton and

Ross Mortlock (standing). Sitting to his left is René Charbonneau. The night before graduation, November 15, 1966, at the Westward Hotel, Regina.

Calgary, in a small Alberta town on the edge of a First Nations reserve, at highway patrol detachments in the Rocky Mountains and during several years with the RCMP Security Service, Mortlock's most enduring and meaningful memories are of the remarkable people who crossed his path, usually under atypical circumstances.

The sweetest of those stories involves Jean, to whom he has been married since 1971. They met while he was performing a task that many relatively new RCMP members got stuck with, one that was dreadfully boring but necessary—in this case, guarding the Bank of Canada in downtown Calgary. "It's the bank's bank," says Jean, who was a 19-year-old teller there. "You didn't have clients or customers, only other banks. There were Loomis trucks coming in constantly, people delivering money. We were counting cash—everything by hand then—looking for counterfeit cash, looking for accuracy. They issued bonds too, so we had high values of money. We easily had millions of dollars go in and out in a day; old money that had to be destroyed, new money that was going out. It would have been a prime target if anybody knew about it. But it was a very boring job for us, and it was boring for them, too [the RCMP guards]. They sat in this tiny cubicle and couldn't move."

According to Mortlock, that doesn't capture the worst of it. "You could not go to the bathroom; you couldn't abandon your post. You sat on a hard, elevated stool behind two-inch-thick bulletproof glass. We were issued a shotgun and three shells. No training on how to handle a shotgun, which is rather frightening when you think of it. Once, one of the chaps was putting the gun in the container [which held the gun inside the cubicle] and he blew a hole in the floor! Did I mention that we could not read, eat or drink, and we were there for a minimum of three or four hours?"

The monotony was abruptly broken one day, but that incident involves one of Mortlock's more mortifying moments as a young policeman. A motorcycle cop burst through the front doors of the bank at high alert, certain he was arriving to assist at a robbery-in-progress. In fact, a teller had accidentally tripped the silent alarm by setting an empty money bag on top of it. Mortlock hadn't noticed the alarm's red light blinking at knee level below his bulletproof glass as he performed endless, numbingly boring scans of the small, empty room.

His reward for all that tedium was meeting a fascinating young woman. "We were not to talk to the tellers, either," says Mortlock. "One of them [Jean] took pity on me and threw a couple of paper airplanes at me to relieve the boredom—both hers and mine, I think. We ended up going out. Three years later, I proposed."

It didn't happen quite that seamlessly, though. Jean quit the bank job after a few months, went on a month-long holiday in

Eastern Canada, and then entered university. The two lost touch. Meanwhile, Mortlock was consumed by the fortunes of an unmarried RCMP member, being transferred at short notice and often to remote detachments.

One such posting was to Gleichen, a town east of Calgary, where he was also responsible for policing the Blackfoot Indian Reserve, which bordered the town. It's where Treaty 7 was signed in 1873 between the Canadian government and the Blackfoot Nation, a confederation of the many First Nations that inhabit southern Alberta.

"It was a very interesting but sad place," says Mortlock, who was posted there for nine months. "The reserve was across the railway tracks and it was dry [no alcohol], but it wasn't dry in town, so there was an attraction. It was reported that many people had passed away, killed coming home from bars, hit by trains. We attended many house fires, broke up many fights. You were arresting people who were staggering drunk, falling down drunk, who weren't going to make it very far. This was during the later stages of when Canada was still utilizing residential schools, so we were primarily dealing with adults whose children had been taken away from them. Beautiful people, but a horrible set of circumstances."

Despite dreadful memories that unsettle him still—of three children lost in one fire, of his first not-well-handled [he says], home visit to notify a woman that her father had died—overall Mortlock recalls the post with affection because of the reserve's inspiring collection of kind and hard-working community leaders. "I met some really great people out there. There are a lot of fine, upstanding leaders." Among them were men such as the late Reverend Arthur Ayoungman Sr., a Siksika Elder and ordained priest who ranched there and served for 24 years on band council

Ross Mortlock, Banff Highway Patrol, 1970.

and community committees. Or women such as Arthur's daughter, Vivian Ayoungman, who was the first Indigenous person to graduate from the University of Calgary, later earning three graduate degrees in the United States. After Mortlock left Gleichen, she had a distinguished career as a teacher, principal, university instructor and college administrator at the Old Sun Community College, situated in what was her former residential school.

Mortlock's friendships and respectful interactions with the Indigenous community influenced him long after he left the RCMP, says Jean.

During his second career working in the oil patch, as a land man who negotiated for access to lands so his employer could drill for oil, he also helped broker jobs and training for Indigenous residents of reserves. "His experiences in Gleichen and later in Cochrane made him more understanding and much more willing to go that extra mile and get them into programs," Jean says. "I think it carried on throughout his life."

From Gleichen there was another sudden transfer, this time to the Banff Highway Patrol, where the then-two-lane highway through the national park was busy winter and summer with highway accidents.

In high summer, when tourist traffic increased significantly, the Force set up a satellite office 45 minutes west, in Lake Louise. There, the accommodation consisted of sleeping alongside two fellow officers in a rudimentary building the RCMP had claimed for its officers, an old one-room schoolhouse with a screened-off sleeping area where they set up beds.

"We were never off duty," Mortlock says of his time in both small towns, policing the long and remote stretches of road between Lake Louise and the BC border, and up Highway 93 [the Icefields Parkway] to Jasper, at a time when police radios weren't that reliable in the mountains. "A typical day saw us awake prior to 6:00 a.m. and on the road. Our night shift often went to 2:00 a.m. We frequently worked with partners because if something was going to go wrong, help was a long time in coming, and the member frequently had to bring his private car. There were vehicle accidents involving rocks, elk and other vehicles, rollovers, assisting stranded motorists, patrolling, and checking hitchhikers. Six days on duty and one day to do laundry. This was before overtime or time-off-in-lieu. We were single and deployable."

While completely consuming his life, this highway work was more stimulating than Mortlock's very first assignments driving Alberta's highways, which occurred directly after graduating from "Depot." His first postings had been to Edmonton and Calgary, and though he was in "the big city," his duties were entry-level drudgery. He often conducted prisoner transfers after sentencing, taking them from the Edmonton barracks to the Fort Saskatchewan Correctional Centre northeast of Edmonton, or while in

Calgary, transporting mentally disturbed patients north to what was then called the Alberta Mental Hospital in Ponoka, halfway between Red Deer and Edmonton.

Once, because Fort Saskatchewan's jail was full, he and two Special Constables drove a busload of prisoners from Edmonton to Calgary in conditions that weren't that different from all the other journeys—long and uncomfortable on multiple fronts. "It was July and there was no air conditioning, and for obvious reasons we could not open windows," says Mortlock. "You're herding 40 of these people. Do you talk to them, do you listen to their catcalls or do you ignore them? It was lonely, and it stunk."

In contrast, highway patrol work in the Rocky Mountains was never dull. One day, on duty near Banff, Mortlock was involved with an incident he still believes was his most effective moment as a law enforcement officer. In this instance, the notable character who crossed his path was not an impressive one, and Mortlock was able to foil him.

While headed west on the two-lane Trans-Canada Highway, against a thick line of holiday traffic, he spotted a large Chrysler speeding past the stream of traffic heading east but doing it on the right shoulder. Mortlock used the ditch to make a quick turnaround—a manoeuvre taught at "Depot"—and took off in pursuit. He travelled at about 90 MPH in the westbound lane facing oncoming traffic, pulling into the eastbound stream whenever the odd westbound car approached. That went on for 18 kilometres. "I didn't use the siren for fear of alerting the other drivers, who would have pulled over to the right and into the path of the Chrysler, and I did not try to gain on him for the same reason."

Instead, he radioed ahead and organized an improvised roadblock—a paddy wagon that blocked the entire line of traffic and allowed him to safely stop the speeding driver on the shoulder. "As I was talking to the driver and pulling out a case of beer and open bottles, many cars honked and expressed their gratitude. I still believe I removed a hazard from the highway that day. Unfortunately, I was unable to convict him of dangerous driving. Despite the fact that he was speeding and passing several hundred cars on the right, the judge only counted them as two offences, and you needed three transgressions to convict on dangerous driving. The illegal possession of open alcohol was irrelevant to the driving offence. I *was* able to convict on speeding, passing on the right and illegal possession of alcohol, but most importantly, I believe my actions averted a tragedy that day."

Yet even the sharp instincts police develop about likely problems can't prevent every tragedy. In Banff National Park, the RCMP often patrolled at the entrance gates, since it gave them a chance to safely execute routine spot checks of vehicle occupants who were paying admission. One summer afternoon, Mortlock and some colleagues checked a car full of people who triggered their "spidey sense." Although they smelled alcohol, "we had not witnessed any erratic driving, and at the time you could not demand a breath test without a reason to make a demand, so we let the vehicle go."

About 15 minutes later, their three RCMP patrol cars were racing to an accident in which that same vehicle had driven into a concrete bridge abutment. Bodies were lying inside and outside the car. Mortlock began administering mouth-to-mouth resuscitation to one male passenger—placing his lips directly over the victim's mouth because it was the era when first responders were not yet protected by plastic airway devices issued for this task. Very quickly, the man's gin-soaked breath caused Mortlock to stop and vomit in the ditch. "One of my partners took over until he too proceeded to follow my action in the ditch. We continued to administer mouth-to-mouth as best we were able. I don't remember the outcome. I have a feeling it was fatal and our efforts were in vain. I relive the taste of gin bile every time I think of it."

The public often doesn't realize that the RCMP does so much more than hand out tickets, says Mortlock. Many scenes they assist at haunt members for decades. While Mortlock was off-duty one day, a small airplane crashed into a downtown backyard in Banff. He helped remove the pilot from the plane and accompanied him via ambulance to the resort town's then-tiny hospital. While the emergency room doctor tried repeatedly to insert a breathing tube, he instructed Mortlock to hold down the pilot's wildly flailing hands. "The pilot continued to struggle against all attempts," Mortlock says, a sadness rising almost 50 years later that makes him choose his words economically. "I don't think the airway was inserted before the pilot died in my arms."

Mortlock's duties during deployment in the national park didn't always end so sorrowfully. The potential was always there, however.

While in the Lake Louise Detachment, he took a call from the young woman running the motel across the street who demanded he "Get over here, there's a bear in the unit." Since he and the other officers had kibitzed with the woman before, Mortlock scoffed when she told him the bear had ripped the door off a fridge. Then he looked out the window. "A black bear was exiting the unit—without baggage—and retreated to the rough side of the lodge toward the river." Chasing it off was a task made trickier by a clueless family of tourists who had sent their children toward the bear with a cookie to lure it toward them for a photo. Mortlock saved them from their idiocy by guiding the bear back into the forest with his patrol car.

A second bear encounter was even more intense. At the time, national parks had not yet introduced bear-proof garbage containers, and visitors' trash was merely collected in a few garbage dumps throughout the park. The sites naturally became such magnets for bears that people often drove to the dump to enjoy a close view of wildlife. That created a headache for park wardens, who had to keep animals and people apart.

Mortlock and his partner spotted a warden near the Johnston Canyon dump who had just hit a silvertip grizzly bear with a tranquilizing shot but needed help loading it into a culvert-style trap on wheels. Once the animal was inside, the warden would be able to fasten the pipe's steel end-gates and safely move it. "The bear he had laid down was about a two-year-old, a big 300- or 400-pound bear," says Mortlock. "His claws were about six inches long and were curved. They were very formidable and dangerous looking. When we tried to loop the rope around its neck, it bit down and held it in its teeth, and held it there until we dragged it the 300 or so yards to the culvert. It was not knocked out, it was just disoriented. The tranquilizer was wearing off and there was no question this thing was going to be a bit annoyed. We were able to drag the bear half into the trap. My partner and I bravely decided that one of us would haul the rope from the front of the culvert trap, while the other held the rifle in case things went bad. But we said to the park warden, 'We all have career choices, and you chose animals, so *that* end [the rear] is yours!'"

Wildlife wrangling mostly ended for Mortlock at his next detachment, but his job continued to introduce him to unusual people. In October 1971, Mortlock and Jean, who had become a couple again while she was studying in Calgary, were married, and they moved to his new post in Cochrane. During weekend highway patrol there, he spotted a car that an all-points bulletin had just advised him belonged to a suspect in a double homicide that had occurred that morning in Calgary. Stopping the driver, Mortlock matter-of-factly asked if "he had hurt anyone that day." The man admitted he had shot his father and stabbed his mother.

"As it turns out, it was not a double homicide," says Mortlock. "His mother survived and hired one of Calgary's best defence lawyers to de-

Jean and Ross Mortlock, October 16, 1971, Calgary, Alberta.

fend him. He was a young kid, about 17 or 18 years of age, and as I understand it, his father was very domineering and one Sunday morning the kid had had enough."

Mortlock met and was impressed with the famed defence lawyer during the subsequent trial—Milt Harradence, who later became a noted judge—but the young murderer was also somewhat memorable. "While in prison, he became an accomplished saxophonist," says Mortlock.

The Cochrane period contained some far less easy-to-dispatch events, however. One spring in nearby Ghost Lake—within the span of a few days—a boat capsized on a river that fed into the lake and then, on another evening, a small plane went into the lake and a canoe capsized. A violent storm postponed an immediate search for bodies, but over the next days, prisoners from Spy Hill Correctional Centre helped the RCMP drag the lake.

"All of the bodies were found in the lake," says Mortlock. "A total number of 12, but recovery was over two or three weeks."

Whether it was a reaction to such work, a long-cherished desire, or both, with Jean's encouragement Mortlock began attending university night school classes. Around the same time, he was transferred to the Calgary Detachment of the RCMP's Security Service (which later became part of CSIS). Like CSIS, its role was to investigate activities that might constitute a threat to Canada's security. While Mortlock can't reveal much about the work he did there, two assignments provide context about its breadth.

"It was during the Cold War, and there were lots of people trying to change our democratic way of life by violence or subversion," says Mortlock. "There was no WiFi then, and we used landlines for wiretaps. But it was suspected that, just as they did in World War II, spies during the Cold War might be using shortwave or 'ham' radio, and those all required huge towers. So we had to go around and look for ham radio towers in Calgary and report their positions—every road in a city of 400,000 people! The city was divided among four Constables, and we were each assigned a quadrant. My wife was with me, and a lot of it was done after hours."

"That was date night," says Jean, laughing.

Another assignment was on the clock, albeit undercover. Mortlock's unit had orders to follow a trade delegation's bus excursion as they visited Banff's Sulphur Mountain. When the group took the gondola up to the lookout, he was sent up too, to watch for any unusual contact made with people outside the delegation that might suggest it housed foreign agents. But bad luck struck. It was a miserably cold and windy autumn day, and Mortlock was the only other person at the summit. His presence was obvious.

"It was a huge parking lot, with one bus parked near the entrance and three plain cars [unmarked police vehicles] huddled some distance away, all of which was visible from the mountain lookout." Worse still, when they snapped a group photo, he was included. Him: six feet tall with short, police-regulation-length hair and a light jacket. Them: all a foot shorter, with different complexions and "groovy" 1970s clothes. "Not good," says Mortlock, who aborted the assignment. "I figured they guessed who I was and had a good laugh."

Mortlock's otherwise successful record with the Security Service produced the offer of a promotion and a transfer to Ottawa, but by this time life's big decisions were intervening. Jean was pregnant, housing was three times as expensive in Ottawa, and Mortlock was keen to finish his university studies. He resigned from the Force in January 1976, and after a short stint as a teacher, he forged a long and rewarding career working for Husky Oil. He started as part of a team that identified, acquired, explored, drilled, and produced oil and natural gas, and retired as the company's manager of mineral land, brokering deals between the company and landowners.

According to Jean, "He had a very good career and because of what he did do there was a lot of stability for our family. But I think at his heart he will always be an RCMP officer. It was a different type of work. Working at an office job is not the same as the adrenalin rush of highway patrol. Now that we're retired, those are the stories he tells."

—*Helen Metella*

GETTING ACCEPTED INTO the RCMP was no small feat for Bill Pertson. In fact, you could say it was literally a stretch.

As a teen, Pertson was intrigued by the notion of becoming a Mountie. His interest piqued when he became a civilian member in the Fingerprint Identification Section of the RCMP in Ottawa in 1962. His fascination with the Force grew, and after a couple of years, Pertson applied to become a regular member. "I thought it would be a wonderful service to provide to the public of Canada," he says. However, acceptance into the regular Force was a tall order. When the Winnipegger applied to the RCMP, officers had to be at least 5'8". The 25-year-old was an agonizing three-quarters of an inch too short to meet the Force's height requirement.

Demonstrating the same dogged determination he would later exhibit investigating homicides and other crimes, Pertson aimed to hit the target height. Religiously, he did a series of stretching exercises several times every day, for months. "I'd start first thing in the morning, and then I'd do a little bit of hanging upside down," he says. When he reapplied to the RCMP, he took his medical at an Ottawa hospital early in the morning. "I had learned from doing the exercises that a person is taller in the morning than they are later in the day," Pertson says. Good timing and stretching paid off. Measuring exactly 5′8″ inches, Pertson was accepted into the Force as a regular member.

The troop found training and the instructors tough. For some members, it was their first time away from home. They were lonely, homesick, and, at times, so overwhelmed they considered throwing in the towel. At the ripe old age of 26, Pertson was a father figure to many. "We'd sit and talk, which seemed to really help," Pertson says.

An introvert by nature, he didn't take part in dorm shenanigans, but Pertson was a sitting duck for some tomfoolery while napping. On one night of silliness, some tricksters tucked a *Playboy* magazine in the crook of Pertson's right arm while he was catching some "*zzzs.*" During an unheralded dorm inspection, the NCO discovered the verboten magazine,

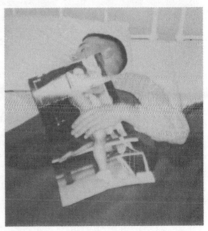

Bill Pertson soundly sleeping in barracks with a "friend."

woke Pertson and demanded to know where the illicit "reading material" had come from. Pertson could only plead innocence when no one confessed to the deed.

Despite the daily challenges at "Depot," Pertson never considered quitting. But, like the rest, he had his share of low moments. When he was feeling down, he turned to senior staff members

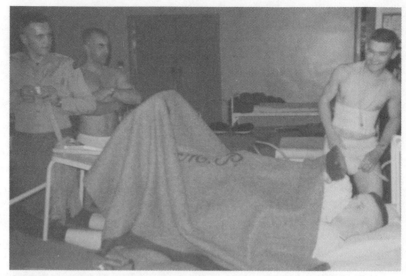

Bill Pertson was the subject of many pranks because he simply could not be awakened once he fell asleep. Here, Ken Scheske, David LeBlanc and George Piccott are caught red-handed by the hidden dorm cam in 1966.

and others. Together, they supported each other through the long days at "Depot" and eagerly awaited their first postings.

Pertson's first posting was supposed to be to a small town about 200 miles from Cranbrook, BC. But the night before he graduated, he was reassigned to Cranbrook because a member at the detachment was getting married, and the Force wanted him transferred. His first day on the job, Pertson was thrown into the thick of things—a murder investigation.

The rookie was assigned to find a hunting knife used in a homicide. "We searched for it for a week before it was finally found," Pertson says. However, "We could not send it to the lab because it was contaminated. It had been lying in the elements—snow and rain—so we couldn't use it for evidence." After all the effort made to locate the knife, it was a frustrating find.

Pertson was just settling in at Cranbrook's 15-member detachment when he had his first encounter with a deadly accident.

First on the scene, Pertson found a car flipped over in two feet of water. Of the five occupants in the vehicle, three had drowned and two survived. The loss of life often replays itself in the minds of officers long after they've left the scene, but in that era few talked about their emotional state after responding to traumas. One of the toughest parts of the job was seeing the aftermath of serious car collisions involving young people, Pertson says. "You never get numb to it."

Like anyone beginning a career in policing, the risks of the job weren't readily apparent to the rookie. In one case, Pertson took some heat from his higher-ups when he pulled over a vehicle while working alone. Later he was told he should have called for backup because the occupants were wanted criminals. Pertson walked away unscathed, but it was an important reminder that a routine stop can be dangerous, or even deadly, for officers.

While learning the ropes of policing in Cranbrook, Pertson met Valerie Manson and fell in love. The couple continued dating after Pertson left Cranbrook in 1967, and married the following year. Prior to the nuptials, Pertson was briefly posted at a two-man detachment in Midway, BC, where he was the newbie. "We did not have janitorial services, so it was up to the junior Constable to keep the barracks clean and shovel the snow in the driveway," Pertson says.

After a transfer to the three-man detachment in Fruitvale in 1968, Pertson was busy policing the community and the large surrounding rural area, often by himself. Life at home was also hectic when Pertson and Valerie's daughter, Lisa, was born on June 13, 1969. Often new parenthood brings challenges, but a year after Lisa's birth, Pertson experienced unspeakable sorrow. Valerie's depression had deepened, and she used his service revolver to kill herself. Pertson discovered her body in their home.

Discussing that horrific chapter of his life is painful. To this day, Pertson struggles to make sense of it. A man of few words, he says simply: "It was tough. You try your best to handle it and you talk to family members, friends and more senior members." But who could fully comprehend his grief? The mother of his child had ended her life with the gun he'd been issued to serve and protect. There were no support groups or mental health professionals to turn to for help. Suicide was talked about in hushed voices but rarely discussed openly. Survivors were solitary in their grief— no one to answer the reverberating question: "Why?" Pertson handled his grief by focusing on policing—a job where answers could usually be found if you dug deeply and long enough.

The RCMP recognized that Pertson needed support balancing policing and parenting a small child, so he was transferred to Lundar, MB. Pertson's sister lived in Winnipeg Beach and she was able to care for Lisa for a time.

While the transfer gave Pertson a fresh start, policing in Lundar was tougher than it had been in BC. "The general public were pretty hard to handle," Pertson says. "There was a lot of drinking going on and a fair bit of trouble from time to time." On the more positive side, it was in the line of duty in Lundar that he met Sharron Anne Willis, a young teacher in town. "She came to the police office to make a complaint," Pertson recalls. "She'd been receiving obscene phone calls." Pertson and Sharron got to know each other, started dating and eventually married. Over the years, Sharron's steadfast support would help Pertson deal with some of the demons of policing.

Before the couple married, Pertson was transferred to Teulon, a small town 60 kilometres north of Winnipeg, where the teen-aged Pertson had first started dreaming about being a Mountie. "It was ironic because I had taken my Grade 12 in Teulon and then I came back to police it," Pertson says. "It was better than Lundar."

Pertson was in Teulon for a few months when he was sent to Ottawa for an eight-week course in the Identification Section. The use of forensics in policing was relatively new and Pertson had been avidly reading about the use of scientific tests in crime detection. When he was accepted for training in the Identification Section, he was in his element. "It was very good, very interesting."

At the same time, Valerie's death continued to have a profound effect on him. Sharron encouraged Bill to talk about his feelings—something he found difficult to do. "Sharron was very understanding," Bill says of the woman who died in 2008. "Sharron helped me realize that work wasn't the only thing that counts."

While stationed in Ottawa, the couple became the proud parents of Jason on December 14, 1971. Then, less than two years later, the family pulled up roots and moved to Swift Current, SK, where Pertson became a member of the two-man Identification Section.

He responded to break-and-enters, homicides and fatal crashes in addition to patrolling, which included domestic dispute calls. "We didn't receive any training that I can remember related to domestic disputes," Pertson says. "You sort of had to play it by ear when it came to how you would deal with it … it was difficult."

Often officers were on patrol by themselves. In the Swift Current Detachment, they covered a huge area that stretched east halfway to Regina, west to Maple Creek, as far north as Kindersley and south to the US border.

Working in the Identification Section, Pertson took measurements, fingerprints and photos at scenes—all of the essential elements of an investigation that could be used in court. "It was fascinating," he says. "The reason I stayed in the Force for 37.5 years was because I found it very exciting. The use of DNA in investigations was just coming in before I retired."

One of the greatest challenges of Pertson's career occurred in Prince Rupert, BC, where he was posted from 1975 to 1978.

As a newly promoted Corporal, he worked on cracking 10 cases involving the disappearance or suspicious deaths of women along a 720-kilometre stretch of Highway 16 dubbed the "Highway of Tears." At least 18 women, most of them Indigenous, have disappeared or been murdered since 1969 on the infamous highway, which runs from Prince Rupert, on the northwest coast of British Columbia, to the central interior and Prince George. "As soon as we were called to a scene, we'd conduct an examination and look for all types of evidence, like blood or hair," Pertson says. "If there was a body, we'd look for marks." He left no stone unturned.

At the time, Pertson recalls there were debates about whether one individual, several individuals or a serial killer was at work. Officers were unable to substantiate who or how many were involved. "Back then in the late '70s, we were far removed from the DNA advances we have now," Pertson says. "We tried to do the best we could. Sometimes, we had suspects taken in for questioning, but there just wasn't enough evidence. It was, at times, quite frustrating." Pertson wasn't a man who liked leaving unfinished business. When he was transferred to Vernon, he could only hope more evidence would come forward and the cases would be solved.

He subsequently saw how powerful a single piece of DNA evidence can be after his son Jason joined the RCMP in 2001. Using a DNA sample that sex worker Ellie May Meyer had proactively submitted to the RCMP's Project KARE database, Jason was able to help solve not only Meyer's 2005 murder but also the murder of teenager Nina Courtepatte that occurred a few days later, in cases that were resolved five years apart. "I believe we both reflect back on these experiences as an opportunity to seek justice for, and be a voice for these women and their families," says Jason.

Pertson proudly presented his son with his badge in Regina on May 14, 2001, 35 years after receiving his own badge at "Depot."

During his eight-year tenure in Vernon, Pertson was promoted to Sergeant and continued his work in Identification. One of his cases involved assisting Bev Busson (later the Commissioner of the RCMP) and her husband. The duo was working on a murder case that involved a young woman employed by a car rental company. The young woman had been flagged down, kidnapped, and later shot in the back with a rifle near Revelstoke. In that case, there was closure. With the help of the Identification team, Busson and her husband solved the crime after an intensive investigation.

Two more transfers were in the cards for Pertson. He was NCO in Charge of the Yorkton Identification Section from 1986 until 1991, after which the Force moved him to Dauphin, MB. He retired in Dauphin as the NCO in Charge of the Identification Section on his sixtieth birthday in June 1999. It was a career that brought him a sense of accomplishment and pride. "When you worked in Ident and you could come to a conclusion, that was very rewarding," he says.

Pertson takes pride in his family's long history of serving in

Ernie Otway and Bill Pertson in their pit at "Depot" during the thirtieth anniversary gathering of C Troop, 1996.

the national police force. Back in the early 20th century, his uncle, Paul Pertson, was with the Royal North-West Mounted Police, the forerunner of the RCMP. He was among the officers who policed the 1919 riots of the Winnipeg General Strike, Canada's best-known general strike. Pertson's brother, another Paul, also served with the RCMP for 17 years. He spent his entire career in northern Canada.

"My Dad told me that his brother had decommissioned the last Mountie dog-sled team up there," says Jason, Pertson's son. "His brother left the Force because they wanted to transfer him out of the North." Pertson is very proud that Jason was sworn into the RCMP in 2001. "It's rewarding for someone in the family to follow a parent," Pertson says.

Recalling his long career with the Force, Pertson says the investigations were the highlight. "It was a very important part of police work and they were very stimulating. I enjoyed my career. It was very interesting and satisfying work. I got to meet some good members and people where I was stationed. I have no regrets."

—Pamela Cowan
and Helen Metella

R.P.M.
(Rick)
SAVILLE
Reg# 24833

SAVILLE

C66/67 Troop
50th Year Reunion

IF YOU COULD write the perfect plan for a career as a policeman, it might resemble the career that Rick Saville put together, both within the RCMP and beyond it. Essentially, absorb all the routine, skill-building stuff relatively quickly and without suffering any lasting trauma, then take on challenging and unusual work as part of the security service protecting your entire country from threats. Finally, re-deploy all your experience to a less dangerous job that will nonetheless keep you engrossed for almost as long as your active police work did.

"I got to do everything I wanted to do; I was well treated and I made certain decisions that worked out well," says Saville, whose working life was divided into two almost identical lengths of time—23 years with the RCMP and the Canadian Security Intelligence Service (CSIS), followed by 22.5 years enforcing public gaming policies and rules for the province of British Columbia.

Saville grew up in Ottawa, where the predominant impression of the RCMP was as guardians of Parliament Hill and patrollers

Members of C Troop celebrating after completing their final drill before graduation, which was filmed by the Swedish film board. Front row, left to right: Allison, Saville, Mortlock and Forst. Back row, left to right: Brown, Swift, Seniuk, Charbonneau, Laverdière, Bossence, Stagg and Coles.

of the National Parkways. He was inspired to sign up for training as a Mountie because he had an affable neighbour who was a member, and he was impressed by the young RCMP trainees he saw strolling near "N" Division, a few blocks from his childhood home. What they actually did was more of a mystery, says Saville. "When I signed up, I was probably on the shyer side. I was just 19, with not much exposure to the real world."

During his three-month orientation posting in Victoria, BC, he learned how much of police work was routine: he served summonses, executed warrants and escorted convicted prisoners to federal and provincial jails to serve their time. He also spent time performing escort and security duties in BC Supreme Court trials held at the Law Courts in Victoria. "That was kind of interesting, sitting through all of those cases. They were all serious charges, so it was a bit of an education."

He was assigned occasional weekends at the Shawinigan Lake

Detachment, a one-man operation where young officers were sent to take charge for a couple of days so that the member stationed there could have time off.

There was a brief bit of excitement on January 9, 1967, when Secretary of State Judy LaMarsh (the minister responsible for Canada's Centennial Commission) arrived in Victoria to launch the Confederation Train's cross-country journey. Saville was the youthful RCMP member who drove her and British Columbia's Lieutenant-Governor George Pearkes to the opening event and then to the Empress Hotel for lunch. For a 20-year-old, it was a formal task that taught him that people are just people. "It was kind of funny," says Saville. "I drive over to Government House, I park, I go to the door. It's this big mansion, and I'm wondering, 'What do I do?' I rang the bell and George Pearkes answered himself."

At several of his subsequent postings, beginning with his first in Nanaimo, Saville came to deeply appreciate the building blocks of the RCMP's founding reason to exist: to police Canada's thousands of small municipalities and rural areas that can't afford to support a stand-alone law enforcement organization.

That's where his best hands-on learning took place, albeit sometimes comically. Along with many break-and-enters, and a lot of bad cheques to investigate, in Nanaimo, Saville met the regular complement of drunks, including one who was one of his earliest arrests. "It was one of my first times in court, and the fellow was co-operative during the investigation, but he pleaded 'not guilty' at his court hearing. It was a simple impaired driving stop, but it was before the breathalyser was in use, so your physical evidence was important—what you observed, the details you collected. I was trying to use his exact words, and so spoke in exactly the sloppy drunk way that the accused did when he was answering my questions. I probably said something like, 'He told me, 'I saw you in the *rrrrear ver mirrorrr.*' Apparently I was quite funny, and he was convicted."

Saville's attention to detail made him an obvious candidate to be trained on the breathalyser when the opportunity arose in 1971. "You had to be so precise because of the challenges that could be made, the way you tested it and set it up and administered it. It was critical as an operator because the results might have been called into question and that could have implications for the whole system. I was very careful. I was never challenged in the operation." That's why he knew something was very odd when, after he pulled over an older male driver who was weaving all over the road, the breathalyser result declared that the man was sober.

"I knew it was accurate; there was no question about that," says Saville. "I don't know whether it was reaction to a medication—we just never knew—but I suspended his licence for the day and gave it back to him the next day. That was not something that was in my purview at all, but I wanted to make sure he didn't get into any trouble that day."

Nanaimo delivered some other firsts for the young Constable, including a heartbreaking scene that seems all too common in the careers of his Troop colleagues. "I was off duty on my way home," Saville says. "I came upon an accident. A little four-year-old boy had just been hit by a car and he was on the road, with his distraught mother nearby. He was hit very hard. I went over to see if there was any sign of life, and there wasn't. You just take it all in, but it was very sad." Thankfully, police and emergency crews arrived on the scene within a couple of minutes.

From Nanaimo, Saville transferred to Port Alice, a remote location at the northern tip of Vancouver Island, accessible at the time by ferry from Kelsey Bay to Beaver Cove, and then by road north toward Port McNeill, with the last leg comprised of a turn west that ended on an old logging road. The detachment area had a population of 1,500, mostly involved with the pulp mill and logging camp. Although a new town with new housing had been established, the RCMP office was in the old town site next to the mill, about four miles away.

Rick Saville was the last single member to live in the old Port Alice Detachment, which was located on northern Vancouver Island, from April 1969 until May 1970. It was considered an isolation posting. Saville's living quarters consisted of a bedroom and a bathroom with shower, sink, and toilet. The rest of the building was the general office and cell block.

"It was just me and the Corporal," says Saville. "He lived with his wife and a couple of kids in an old house designated as the married quarters. I had a bedroom off the police office, in the detachment: just a shower, toilet, sink and bedroom. You walked out into the main office. I was never late for work!"

There were few serious incidents to deal with besides car accidents and alcohol issues, says Saville. He was authorized to give driving tests and issue temporary driver's licences so that the residents of Port Alice could drive the 250 miles to Campbell River for formal testing. But the remoteness of the location meant he had little outside contact. "There was a cafeteria where I had a tab, and we did have two auxiliary RCMP officers who worked for BC Hydro and BC Tel. They'd come out on Friday or Saturday night and lend a hand. There was very little communication other than the land line, because the radio in the car would only communicate with the next detachment in Port Hardy once you were five miles out of town. We had a single side-band radio in the office, which allowed me to talk to Victoria and halfway across Canada, too, but not to Port Hardy."

The one break from the routine occurred every Friday night, when anyone charged with an offence that required a court appearance could enter a plea. Some would plead guilty in front of the lay magistrate and be sentenced. Others would plead not guilty and receive an adjournment in order for a trial date to be set before a travelling magistrate.

Despite the isolation of working in such a small place, when a transfer to Courtenay was offered about a year later, Saville told his supervisors he'd prefer a posting to another small site. A week later, he was advised that he was posted to Chemainus. He viewed the decision as a chance to take on a wider array of responsibilities and administrative duties.

Saville certainly learned the fine art of when to employ the most practical supervisory strategy during that posting, after one unnerving incident that took place in the nearby Ladysmith Detachment. Three youths, each about 17 years old, had been locked up in the Ladysmith cellblock pending their court case for petty crimes but had somehow escaped. "In those days, there were no permanent guards overnight, just a local citizen hired to come in to assist," says Saville. "On this occasion, these fellows tricked the guard into opening the cell and overpowered him. I got a call at my home in Chemainus about 1:00 a.m. I met the dog master north of Ladysmith and followed about 200 yards behind him along the train tracks into the darkness. A few hundred yards down the track, I come across the three escapees, but no dog master. I handcuffed the two biggest ones to each other and marched them in front of me, and took the small one by the arm. I knew they could have overpowered me if they'd wanted to. Fortunately, I ran into the dog master as he was backtracking. The escapees were returned to their cells, but the incident was never reported," says Saville. "Losing a prisoner was kind of a major thing—nobody wanted to be involved with that!"

While Saville's decision to learn more of the advanced ropes justified his move to Chemainus, the universe apparently saw it as the perfect opportunity to have him cross paths with Noreen, the nurse he'd marry within a year of arriving. "She wasn't supposed to be there, either," says Saville. "She'd just graduated from St. Joseph's Hospital in Victoria and had no intention of applying to Chemainus, but she hadn't yet received any responses to the applications she'd put out. Her dad said, 'Have you tried Chemainus?' and when she said, 'No,' he said, 'Get in the car.' She went in, met the matron on Friday and started work on Monday."

Naturally, RCMP members who dropped by the hospital in the line of duty quickly discovered whether there were new nurses in town, so it wasn't long before she and Saville met and fell in love. The couple settled into a stretch of the east coast of Vancouver Island overlooking the Strait of Georgia's Gulf Islands that residents often refer to as "God's country," and felt fortunate to find a cute little house to rent for $90 a month.

Almost immediately, Noreen discovered one major downside of having a husband frequently away on patrol—he was often out of immediate reach when she needed him. "I get a call on my radio saying, 'Your wife called, would you go and see her?'" says Saville. "She'd walked out on the back porch to put some clothes in the washing machine and came face to face with a rat. She ran into the house and the rat ran into the basement. That was the beginning of rat-trapping season. I trapped 16 rats our first winter in that house."

Rick Saville transferred to the RCMP Security Service in 1973, and in 1984 to the newly created Canadian Security Intelligence Service (CSIS). He continued in the same line of work until he retired in 1989.

During their first year of marriage, they were both so enmeshed in respective shift work that they never had a weekend off together unless they booked a holiday. "That's what first got me started thinking about my career path," says Saville, who transferred to the RCMP's Security Service in Vancouver in 1973, eager for more predictable working hours. A roommate from his Nanaimo posting had enticed him by reporting that the work was interesting, weekends were usually free and it was a plainclothes job. With his eldest child on the way, that sounded perfect to Saville.

His first tasks were conducting security clearances for all the federal ministries. Although he provided security when the Queen and Prince Philip visited Victoria in 1982, he was already working on counter-espionage files in the late 1970s, keeping tabs on visitors to Canada from the Soviet Bloc and from the People's Republic of China, and working closely with the FBI in Seattle. "It was a bit of cloak and dagger," says Saville. "It was a very important job because you learn that there are people who are trying to undermine or influence the way we live." He's still bound by confidentiality laws to not reveal exactly what he did for four years in Vancouver and seven years in Victoria with the Security Service, or for another five years when it became CSIS.

Yet even his general descriptions suggest it was fascinating work. "We'd do surveillance on Soviet Bloc officials coming to Victoria, mainly doing paperwork, reports, targeting sources to get information for us—live sources, people in the community. To develop sources, you might become aware of someone who was, say, visiting a Soviet ship, often for a legitimate reason, perhaps just to practise the language. You'd have a little chat with them if they were willing to talk to you. The aim of this was to determine if any espionage operations were being directed toward Canadians. One of the more interesting times, we put in several months of work dealing with a defector. We spent several weeks debriefing this fellow in an apartment hotel in Victoria. When we determined that a member of the hotel staff understood the language he was speaking, we had to relocate him without delay to another location."

Other interferences could be trickier to manoeuvre in this relatively quiet region of Canada. "On another occasion, we had an embassy official from an Eastern Bloc country under sur veillance. It was more difficult to conduct discreet surveillance in a remote place like Ucluelet, near Tofino. The target would stay at one hotel, and our team would stay at the other one. We had five cars; he had one. We could observe him using counter-surveillance measures in order to detect us, including driving into a dead-end street to see if one of our team would follow, as an example."

It was much easier, apparently, to keep his neighbours in the dark. Just recently, at an RCMP member's funeral, Saville ran into a friend who was surprised to discover that Saville had even been with the Force. "He worked in plain clothes; he worked downtown. I don't think most people thought he was a policeman," says Noreen. Saville is proud to have been a part of the RCMP and what it stood for, and enjoyed the camaraderie so much he has

Rick and Noreen Saville are members of the RCMP Veterans' Association and Rick serves on its executive.

remained active with its Veterans' Association. "But what it really did for me was it shaped my second career."

In 1984, Saville transferred to the newly created CSIS to continue working in the same line of work. In 1989, CSIS wanted to transfer him back to Vancouver, but Saville's family was settled in Victoria. Instead, he retired and became a licensing officer in the licensing division of the BC Public Gaming Branch. He was soon leading the section that determined eligibility and administered licensing of all charitable or religious organizations that applied to run raffles, bingos and charitable casinos. Seven years later, as gaming was due to expand in the province, he joined the Gaming Audit and Investigation Office. "The Office was responsible for investigating the eligibility of organizations for licensing, and conducted due diligence to ensure the appropriate use of gaming funds. I was also assigned to duties with the Gaming Policy Secretariat, tasked with setting up a new regulatory regime for government-run casinos in the province."

In 2001, there was a reorganization of government gaming agencies into the newly formed Gaming Policy and Enforcement Branch, a better-resourced body to oversee an expanding gaming industry. With this change, Saville led the Registration and Certification Division that was responsible for conducting background investigations into companies and persons connected to the gaming industry, including gaming equipment suppliers, bingo, casino and racetrack operators, and all gaming personnel. When he retired in 2012, Saville was the division's executive director and registrar.

One of the benefits of working in gaming was the opportunity Saville had to participate over a period of more than 15 years with colleagues from Canadian and American gaming jurisdictions in the North American Gaming Regulators Association (NAGRA). The interaction with these jurisdictions was instrumental in developing best practices for the regulation of the gaming industry in British Columbia. As his level of involvement increased, Saville was the NAGRA director for Canada. A few years later, he was honoured to be president of the organization when the annual conference was hosted in Vancouver in 2010.

He's never regretted his move into a second career but says, "I think it's fair to say that I missed the RCMP. Although one tends to look at the past with rose-coloured glasses, there are some serious or tragic incidents that are etched in my memory that I would like to forget. But I was, above all, very lucky, and I am very proud to have been part of that organization, and what it stands for."

—*Helen Metella*

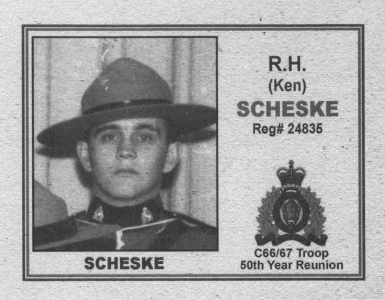

R.H.
(Ken)
SCHESKE
Reg# 24835

SCHESKE

C66/67 Troop
50th Year Reunion

KEN SCHESKE GREW up on a small family farm near Southey, SK. His father hoped that he would one day take over, and Ken, like other farm boys, worked the land and tended to the animals from a very young age. In his words, "I started driving a tractor and doing field work when I was about 12 years old, but that wasn't for me. I wanted to see the world. My way of doing that was joining the Force." And so on June 8, 1966, shortly after he turned 19, Ken and his parents drove to the RCMP "Depot" Division in Regina. His acceptance into training opened the door to the world beyond the farm on which he had been raised.

If the truth be told, Ken was a little deflated when he was deferred to the Regina Division. At the time, there were two RCMP training sites in Canada, one in Regina and the other in Ottawa. Naturally, he was hoping he would land in Ottawa, since Regina was only half an hour from home. "Being from Southey, why would I want to go to Regina? I joined the Force for the adventure." However, once at "Depot," Ken quickly settled in and began one of his life's great adventures. He would never look back.

Soon after arriving at the training academy, Ken and his troop mates received a stack of uniforms and boots and lined up to have their hair buzzed off. Ken chuckled when he thought about that first day: "The haircuts were quite the deal. I bet they put 32 of us through there in about 35 minutes—there was just no hair left, none at all. I had my hair cut just before I went because I wanted to look nice. What a waste of money!"

The process of turning the raw young recruits into professional police officers involved a rigorous training program, with certain levels of performance that all members were expected to meet, regardless of their individual skill levels when they arrived at "Depot." In some cases, it was—quite literally—"sink or swim." Not all the new recruits were swimmers when they signed up, but they were all treated equally in the pool. "We were all lined up there, and you had to jump in the deep end. Of course, for people who can swim that's no problem, but we had people who couldn't. We had one guy who hit the water, went to the bottom, came up and swam right to the other end and he was a non-swimmer." Another non-swimmer wasn't so lucky. He jumped into the pool, sank and had to be fished out with a pole. By the end of training, however, all troop members were competent swimmers.

The physical training component was particularly memorable for Ken because of the bruising he took. As he tells the story, he made a rookie mistake by informing the instructor he had a blue belt in judo. Consequently, Ken was a guinea pig for his fellow troop mates as they learned self-defence. "They beat the hell out of me, but I was young enough that I could take it. I did learn that you don't volunteer for things!"

One of Ken's great disappointments was that his troop couldn't ride the training horses at "Depot." Shortly before C Troop arrived, the RCMP announced that the horses would no longer be used operationally. "If we'd been in training three weeks earlier," he notes, "we would have ridden."

C Troop members did not ride but still had to clean the stables, groom the horses and take tourists on tours of the stables in Regina until September 1966, when the horses were auctioned or sent to the Musical Ride.

However, although they couldn't ride the horses, the recruits still had to muck out the stables—a dirty job done in double time. "That was lots of fun—especially early Saturday morning if you'd had a few drinks the night before," Ken says. "Marching through the stable doors, the smell just hit you." In that respect, Ken was a bit more fortunate than some of his fellows. He had grown up on a farm and was no stranger to cleaning barns. The city boys in the troop had to master the art of "mucking," with sometimes hilarious results. Piles of horse dung would be shovelled from the divides into the centre aisle. In their haste to finish the smelly job, however, some of the guys would run down the aisles with four-foot wide scrapers, and they'd slip and fall. "There was no time to brush yourself off because you had to get it done really fast," Ken says. "I don't think we were there more than 35 minutes and the place was spotless."

Ken's first posting after graduation was to the Vancouver Town Station. He made the trip to the BC coast with fellow troop mate Bob Bossence, in Ken's new 1967 Ford Mustang. Once there, Ken felt let down because he was doing "mundane" jobs, such as serving subpoenas, attending court, and transferring prisoners from the provincial jail, federal penitentiary and a mental health facility in Coquitlam that has since closed.

About four months later, Ken was transferred to North Vancouver, where "there was real police work." Working with 48 members and a Staff Sergeant, the rookie Constable learned the realities of policing. On one occasion, he and other officers were part of a massive manhunt. A suspect wanted for shooting and killing a person was tracked to a large, thickly wooded area in North Vancouver. "You couldn't see more than five or six feet in front of you," Ken says. "The guy in charge had us spaced in intervals to push the bush and find him." The officers knew the suspect was carrying a rifle, but at that time Mounties did not wear bulletproof vests or any type of body armour. As a result, fear was foremost in the officers' minds. "We thought, 'If we don't see him first, we're going to get shot!'" In the end, the suspect surrendered and no one was injured, but it was a harrowing experience.

While Ken was stationed in North Vancouver his father died, and he requested a compassionate transfer so he could be closer to home and help his mother with the farm. His request was approved and he was sent to Minnedosa, MB.

While at that detachment, he and other officers guarded Princess Anne when she toured Manitoba in 1970 to celebrate the province's entry into Confederation. Throughout the royal visit, Ken kept his boots and breeks on—even in bed—for an unusual reason. "From training until then, some of us had put on a little bit of weight," he says. "The boots were so tight that I thought if I took them off, I wouldn't get them on again in the morning. I was glad to get them off after a few days."

While in Minnedosa, Ken also became acquainted with some of the grimmest aspects of police work. One of the worst calls he responded to was a fatal collision between a car and train. Ken was the first officer to arrive at the horrific scene. "I'll never forget that one," he says. "A younger woman got hit at a level crossing between Minnedosa and Brandon. The thing that I remember, that was really quite terrible in my mind, was that her feet were in her shoes in the car, and the rest of her was thrown out." The horror of that crash still haunts Ken half a century later, and he wonders if police officers drink to cope with traumas such as traffic fatalities or men beating their wives. "Domestic violence calls were the worst because you never knew what to expect," he says grimly. "I never had an incident where I felt that I was in danger, but probably one of the worst was in Russell. We arrested the guy and he was in the back seat and he was violent." The officers ducked kicks and punches from their assailant and safely got him to the detachment cells.

Unlike today, no training scenarios were held at "Depot" to prepare officers for dealing with domestic abuse calls. "It was learn as you go," Ken says. "There was no counselling afterwards. There was nothing. The mentality was 'You're men; take it.'"

On highway patrol in Minnedosa, Ken and Corporal Charlie Fisher were running radar between Neepawa and Gladstone and made one stop that would have lasting consequences for Ken. Back in those days, officers set up a tripod on the edge of the road to clock the speed of drivers. While hiding in the bush, Charlie radioed Ken to tell him who to stop and their speed. As a result, "I flagged in this pretty young lady for doing 84 miles an hour in a 60-zone and gave her a speeding ticket," Ken says. Carol, the woman caught speeding, spotted a wedding band on Ken's hand and thought, "Why are all the good-looking guys married?" She later learned Ken wore his father's wedding ring on his right hand, but in the panic of getting a ticket, Carol didn't pay attention to which of his hands had the wedding band.

The interest was mutual, and while writing out the speeding ticket, Ken noted details from Carol's driver's licence, including her address in Gilbert Plains. He wanted to see her again, but couldn't track her down because Carol's address on her licence had not been updated. Later he discovered she was a public health nurse who had moved to Neepawa. Ken caught a fleeting glimpse of Carol leaving the Neepawa airport where Pierre Elliott Trudeau was campaigning in the lead up to the 1968 federal election. To his chagrin, however, Ken was doing traffic control and couldn't chase after her. But soon his luck changed.

On patrol between Neepawa and McCreary, Ken passed Carol driving in the opposite direction on the highway. He wheeled his cruiser around, activated the lights and siren, and was in hot pursuit of the beautiful young nurse with the lead foot. Carol was worried when she saw the cruiser's flashing lights in her rear-view mirror. "I thought I was getting another ticket and was worried I'd lose my job," she says. But instead of handing her a ticket, Ken asked her out for coffee.

Before accepting, Carol checked Ken's marital status. Learning he was single, she agreed to a date, but she didn't know what she was signing up for. Instead of going out for coffee, the couple went to an RCMP bush party, where members were drinking around a bonfire. "What a bunch of yahoos," she remembers thinking. "What have I got myself into?'" But the

Ken and Carol Scheske's wedding on June 7, 1969, in Neepawa, Manitoba. C Troop member John Seniuk (second from the end) was part of the wedding party.

bush party didn't derail the budding romance, and the couple married on June 7, 1969, in a Red Serge wedding in Neepawa. "I still tell our friends, it cost her $14.75 at the time—and it has been costing me dearly ever since," Ken says affectionately.

An RCMP colleague who was taking flying lessons in Brandon opened up new horizons for Ken. "When he got his licence, he took me for a ride," Ken says. "I'd never been in an airplane before, and that's all it took. One ride in an airplane, and I said, 'This is what I want to do for a living.'" After getting his private and commercial fixed-wing licences, Ken bought a plane to log more flying hours.

One hot summer day, he and Carol flew from Russell to Brandon to practise loops and rolls in the wild blue yonder. Heading towards Brandon, the plane fell out of the loop and started spinning to the ground. About 6,000 feet above the ground, Ken over-corrected and the plane spun the wrong way. There were some tense moments before he corrected the plane's flight and regained altitude. "I'm trying to maintain what a cool guy I am, and Carol looks over at me and asks, 'Aren't we heading back to Russell?' I was so happy to be straight and level again, I didn't realize I was going the wrong way!"

Hooked on flying, Ken applied to get into the RCMP's Air Division. At that time, applicants' names were put on a list, but they weren't told where they stood in the pecking order. "You never knew how long the list was and you never knew where you were on it," he says. "By the time you hit your twenty-eighth birthday, though, you were taken off the list automatically."

As time passed with no word about his application into the Air Division, Ken got antsy and sought advice from the Officer in Charge of the RCMP Subdivision in Brandon. "I asked him, 'What should I do? I want to get into the Air Division, but if I'm not in by the time I'm 28, I'm an old man.'" Recognizing Ken's love of flying, the officer encouraged him to follow his heart. Ultimately that meant Ken quit the Force after serving for four years and three months. Because he'd signed up for five years of duty, he had to "purchase" his way out of the RCMP, which meant paying the Force $200 to leave.

After his release from the RCMP, Ken tried his hand at running a crop-spraying business, and had four planes in the air spraying crops in Manitoba and Saskatchewan, but the venture was short-lived. He didn't enjoy working with chemicals, and the job didn't fulfill his ultimate dream of flying choppers, so he then trained to become a helicopter pilot in Penticton, BC. For the next 30 years, he flew just about every kind of helicopter built in the West, including the giant Sikorskys. He started by flying helicopters with Panarctic Drilling, a company that was exploring for oil offshore in the Arctic Islands.

One helicopter flight was nearly the death of him—a close call that rattles Ken to this day. The flight was in pitch darkness in the middle of the Arctic Ocean, north of Resolute Bay. It was the dead of winter. Just before he was scheduled to touch down, a layer of ice fog totally obscured visibility. "You're out in the middle of nowhere," Ken says. "The nearest helicopter was 1,100 miles away and it was -40°C. If we'd had an accident there, we would have frozen to death. We survived and didn't crash, but that was the closest I ever came. I didn't tell Carol about it for at least three years."

In 1973, he took his first overseas contract with Okanagan Helicopters. Again, he had many brushes with death. He and another pilot were responsible for flying two helicopters out of Kota Bharu in Malaysia. Times were tense as the Vietnam War was raging. The two pilots flew to two drilling ships just off the

coast of Cambodia to service the ships and shuttle their personnel back and forth. As they flew, the roar of guns and bombard-
ments were a constant reminder of danger. The two choppers
were kept under constant surveillance by gunboats below. "In
September 1974, we got chased out of there," Ken says. "We left
or the Khmer Rouge would have killed us all."

Danger lurked on the ground as well. In the jungle, Ken contracted malaria and subsequently suffered bouts of illness for four
or five years. The other helicopter pilot contracted a different type
of malaria, which ended his flying career.

Despite the close calls, flying helicopters was Ken's passport
to the world. His many missions took him from coast to coast in
Canada, to the high Arctic, the United States, Europe, the Middle
East, North Africa and New Zealand. In Europe, he fought fires
from the air and worked for the Gardia Civil, the federal law enforcement agency in Spain, during the 1992 Barcelona Summer
Olympics.

Ken had many contracts in Thailand and also flew in Burma,
now known as Myanmar. "It was a horrible place," he says. "The
military built a compound and the four helicopters that we were
flying in the offshore of the Indian Ocean were in the compound
and we lived in the compound—it was all walled and had machine gun bunkers in the corners with guards. They would lock
us in for the night—in the name of our 'safety.' They were so
paranoid about us being there that they didn't want us in town
fraternizing with anybody. It was like living in jail. The only time
you got out was when you fired the helicopter up and flew out
to the rig."

Carol was by his side during some postings. The couple's first
child, Michael, was born in Inuvik. Their second son, Daniel,
was "made in Thailand," but born in Prince George, as was their

Ken Scheske on the helideck of the White Dragon II semi-submersible drilling rig in the Sea of Siam 120 miles off the coast of Thailand.

daughter, Lindsay. When the family moved to Kelowna, Ken continued to fly internationally. "I flew in New Zealand offshore towards Antarctica," he says. "We had a drill ship south of the Campbell Islands and then the next stop after that was Antarctica. The seas down there were the worst I've ever seen. They were 50-foot high seas all the time." He did most of his flying with the Sikorsky S-61 helicopter, widely used for heavy utility industries such as oil and gas, and forestry. The huge helicopter is flown by a pilot and co-pilot and can hold 32 people. On one trip from the rig, one of the twin engines on the Sikorsky helicopter failed. "We came back with no incidents at all, but if we'd had to go in the water, we were dead."

When Ken worked in Abu Dhabi in the Middle East, he flew Bell 212 helicopters to offshore platforms and did installations in the Arabian Sea. He was there in the build up to and during the Gulf War. "It was touch and go a lot of times because of all the military stuff coming in and how careful you had to be," Ken

Ken Scheske logging on the west coast of British Columbia.

says. "I did that for two and a half years, off and on. I didn't particularly like flying in that part of the world, but it was very good money."

Back at the controls of the Sikorsky, he fought fires in the United States and did heli-logging on the west coast of Vancouver Island with Coulson Air Crane and Hayes Heli-Logging. Later he was the chief pilot for Helicopter Transport Services Canada's logging operation. During six years of heli-logging, he never had an accident, dented a machine or hurt anyone, but there were close calls. On two occasions, while flying in northern Saskatchewan and northern British Columbia, Ken was piloting a single-engine helicopter when the engine failed. Drawing on his vast experience, he was able to get the big bird to the ground safely without a scratch. "I had two engine failures in the S-61s and again, no problem, I got them back to the ground."

His closest call came with a Sikorsky-61 while he was logging on Vancouver Island, when a log was incorrectly hooked up to the chopper. "It fell off a cliff and gave us such a jolt that our main blades hit the tail rotor drive shaft," Ken says. "We got it down on a sand bar—which was close enough, thank goodness—because probably within 10 seconds the whole hind end of the aircraft would have come off."

Ken continued flying until 9/11 changed the world forever. At that time, he was "setting steel"—putting huge air conditioners on top of buildings, building ski lifts and moving oil rigs. "We were setting steel in northern Manitoba and 9/11 happened and everyone worldwide got grounded for three days," he says. "We sat it out in Thompson, and then I had three days left to finish the job. I finished the job and at that stage in my career, when I'd be going to work, I'd think, 'Man, I hope nothing mechanical happens that I can't handle.' I'd lost lots of friends in helicopter accidents, so when I got home I told Carol, 'I'm done.'"

Despite his love of flying, he regrets the time he spent away from his family—sometimes on jobs that lasted as long as three months. On the home front, Carol juggled caring for their three children and working part-time as a nurse. Since retiring at 54, Ken is making up for lost time. He and Carol enjoy spending time with their children and grandson, golfing, hiking in hills and mountains, and cycling all over the world. Ken has not piloted an aircraft since retiring. These days he prefers to sit in the back of a plane with a drink in his hand.

Retirement has given him time to reunite with the RCMP vets. He was surprised to be asked to join the Okanagan Division's board because he'd served as an RCMP officer for less than five years. However, Ken was told he brings a different perspective to the table. "All these guys have vast experience with the RCMP, but once you're in the Vets Association, you leave your old rank at the door … There's no Chief Superintendent, there's no Assistant Commissioner, there's no Constable—you're all the same."

Looking back at his storied career, Ken traces much of his success to the RCMP. "It shaped me as a man and gave me the confidence to accomplish whatever I set my mind to."

—*Pamela Cowan*

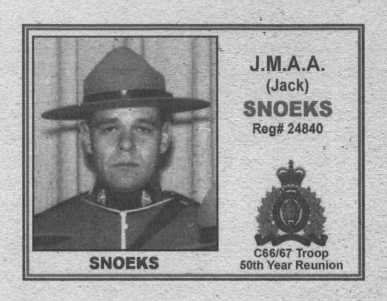

J.M.A.A.
(Jack)
SNOEKS
Reg# 24840

C66/67 Troop
50th Year Reunion

SNOEKS

"THE DOORS OF 1495 Saint Catherine Street were neither impressive nor imposing. As a matter of fact, they looked like they could have used a good sanding and a paint job. The most impressive thing about them was their neighbour, the Montreal Forum, home of the best hockey team in Canada. It was cold that day in November 1965, but I still remember the sign next to the door. A picture of a Mountie pointing at me, much like the proverbial 'Uncle Sam' [the flag-emblazoned caricature] who pointed out with the 'We want you' request during World War II. I don't remember if it was a 'We want you' or a 'Have we got an offer for you!' slogan, but it directed my feet to the RCMP recruiting office. It took six months of psychometric, dental, physical and a plethora of other exams to bring me to the point of being told, 'You have been chosen [one out of 40] to proceed to the training centre at "Depot" Division in Regina, SK.

"I had never thought of being a police officer, nor had I ever had any inclination towards any type of public service. I walked in looking for a job, not a career. I had heard that there was a distinct possibility that the job I was in would end in the next year. So, my walking in was as much of a lark as an actual foray into the job market. I was working as a lab technician for a packaging material company, which involved a lot of quality control and a fair amount of innovation. As well, I was working on my Bachelor of Science, going to university at night and working during the day. My interest in the RCMP would probably have waned had it not been for one word I noticed as I read the brochures lying around the waiting room: 'forensic.' I had been told I had to go through two years of recruit field training before I could 'direct my career' towards my field of choice. It would take me that long to interpret what the RCMP meant by that!

"One day, I got a call to pick up my train ticket and I was given a list of things I should bring with me. Later on I developed a list of the stuff I *should* have brought with me! I don't remember much of the day I headed for the train station, and even less of my trip across the country. I remember spending a lot of time either in the dome car or at a window to take in the sights of a country I had never seen. I had been as far as Niagara Falls, but everything past or around that was new. There were other recruits heading to Regina on the train, but I cannot recall any interaction we might have had. All I did know was that my emotions sat on my lap, and my apprehension grew with each mile of our westerly trip.

"At the train station in Regina, the others and I were met by a chauffeur who would drive us to 'Depot.' Arriving at 'Depot,' the stiff little recruits dashing from place to place in strict formations was an ominous sign of what was to come. I don't remember the greetings and welcome being extremely friendly. I started feeling like a 'one of' pretty quickly, and that loss of identity was frightening. That first day is a blur. I think there was just too much emotional reaction to realize what was happening to me. (It took a couple of weeks to recognize that it was happening to 'us.' At the time it was all about 'me.') It was all so strange. Momma's boy had suddenly lost his well-established support system. I was no longer an individual but rather part of a group that was being trained to become a support for the community. Of course, I didn't realize it at the time.

"No matter where you go in a pre-established organization there always seems to be an initiation rite. Thankfully there was. no hazing at this point of the 'get to know' process, but someone still tried to get me to go to the Saddler's Office and get measured for my stirrups. Yes, a city boy will fall for that type of 'gotcha' fun, but as I was a lab tech, they couldn't sell me on finding the polka dot paint for our barracks. It was all in good fun and, looking back, it broke some of the ice for a lot of us. I wasn't the only recruit with doubts, and that would become more obvious later on as we coalesced into a troop. It didn't take too long for the BMOC (big men on campus) guys in our troop to realize that they couldn't carry our training time alone. Depending on each other was a major lesson, and for some it was a hard thing to swallow without losing face.

"There is an expression: 'The outside of a horse is good for the inside of a man.' Thus, losing the equestrian part of our training was a disappointment. Still, having to take care of the horses we would not be riding was a bigger disappointment. Let me state right here that opening the barn doors first thing in the morning after a night on the town was often a gut-wrenching experience. Also, do not get caught disciplining a horse that just tried to hoof you to death. Especially if it is the Ride Master's horse! I spent quite a few days trying to get out of stallion grooming.

"Even getting on the back of the 'shit-scraper,' or pulling it, was a pleasure compared to the Force grooming experience. Some definitions here are in order: the 'shit-scraper' was a piece of thick plywood attached to a horizontal handle that was held by several recruits while other recruits pulled ropes attached to the 'blade'. It was fast and didn't stop for the unwary. Step backwards out of a horse stall while the scraper was passing, and you ended up in the pile at the end of the run. In the case of 'horse-troughing', a watering trough was attached to the wall and ran the length of the hallway behind the horse stalls. If a person did not co-operate with the rest of the troop, the trough was filled to the top and he would be put in one end and speeded by ropes to the other end while being submerged. Another favourite was 'manure burial', whereby a recruit who had a troop discipline problem would be taken to the back of the barn where a six-foot hole had been dug. He would be forced to stand in the hole while it was filled with horse manure up to his neck. A water hose would then complete the filling process. The recruit would be left there for about a half-hour to contemplate his relationship with his troop. Although I have often witnessed and been part of the scraper speedway, I have only been told about these disciplinarian processes from former recruits.

"Discipline is part of any military training. At 'Depot' this meant: short haircuts; *no* white socks; jacket and slacks for Church Parade, if not in uniform; bed sheets are to bounce a quarter; gym shorts are to have a crease; articles placed on a bed cover are to be set in one way only; your service revolver has a serial number, remember it (in my case, c533072); all kit not being worn has a proper place; the list goes on. Leaving 'Depot' required permission; getting back into 'Depot' required permission. The parade square was a spectacle of pride. Senior troops led the field with sharp manoeuvres and the sound of one boot

C Troop's top track team. Front row, left to right: Snoeks and LeBlanc. Back row, left to right: MacDonald, Stagg, Seniuk and Swift.

fall. The troops behind them had various proficiencies in marching and decorum. The sound of their stop rarely ended on one boot fall. Then, when a troop got in trouble (and it could be for *anything*), they got to brass polish every fire extinguisher in 'Depot,' or pick up all the rocks in a field and put them in a pile. The next day you might see another troop re-distributing them back in the field. The idea was not to punish us but rather to force us to work together in a common goal. It worked. The more we did in hard times, the more we would do in all times. We were never in it alone, and the thought that we might not have somebody to cover our backs was not a consideration.

"Classes were numerous. Someone told me that we did 64 different subjects in our six months. I'm not sure if that included swimming and Phys. Ed. but most of it was interesting. 'Hi guys. Today we are going to learn about tear gas. What I want you to do is walk into that small bunker wearing your gas masks; I will lob in a CN gas grenade and allow you to see how the mask protects you from burning eyes and breathing distress. Then I'm going to tell you to take off the masks to see what an effect the gas has. The first one who runs out of the bunker loses.' This was followed by the second part of gas training. 'I'm glad it's a kind of windless day today. I want you to all hold hands and form a circle. There are no gas masks today and we are using CS gas so you can appreciate what it does. For those of you who don't know, CS gas causes heavy eye irritation, difficult breathing, and it makes you sick to your stomach immediately. I am going to toss in a grenade and you will rotate in the circle (in case there is a breeze) holding hands. First one to let go loses.' Our troop was determined and there were many emptied stomachs as we held hands. Eventually one let go as his stomach couldn't handle it any longer. Absolutely sickening but a great learning experience!

"Not all learning was gut-wrenching. There was Model Detachment, where the trainers tried to imitate what we might run into as part of our police experience. We found out that a lot of police work involves writing. The reports, statements, observations and site plans all had to be constructed to reflect what might have to be presented in court. At the same time, our instructors had to get us ready for confrontations with various aspects of the public. To say our instructors belittled us would be an understatement. They swore at us in absolutely profane terms. They tried to intimidate us. They cajoled and browbeat us until we had a hard time concentrating on the investigation we were doing. They tried to build in an inherent protection against the abuse we might suffer in the field. They instilled the primary goal of getting to the truth and the facts of the case, no matter the divergence. I hated my instructors for the longest time. I thought they were pigs who had no concern of our feelings. It took me a long time to realize how much they cared about our ability to cope. Emotions were raw at times, but even that was a learning experience. Later on in my career I experienced the suicides of several work partners and saw where those coping skills could have come into play.

"We spent a lot of time on Criminal Law. Another eye-opener for me was the difference between 'justice' and the 'law.' I, like so many of my peers, always thought the terms were synonymous. As we discussed case law that had been established in the courts during various trials, I came to see the not-too-subtle difference between what may be right and what is lawful. I was being taught to uphold the laws of the land. If there is a question of justice, it might be better determined by the court system.

"If it sounds like our 'Depot' existence was all negative, it wasn't. Each day, usually after supper, members of the troop returned to their human form rather than their uniform. Our nights were filled with a lot of homework, and more importantly, a lot of camaraderie. I didn't know or hadn't realized that some of our members had other lives in the streets of Regina. Girlfriends had followed some to Regina, and other members formed strong relationships with local girls. There was also a lady named Marilyn who appeared to have a bad case of 'scarlet fever' and made herself available for dates with many members of many troops going through training. And then of course there was support from each other. I was an introvert and kept pretty much to myself, but many of my closest friends in the troop were wonderfully extroverted and I have always credited them with creating the heart of our troop. Off-colour jokes, family stories, relationship secrets, songs and an arm around my shoulders spelled relief for a lot of my anxieties and worries. I had many doubts that I would be able to finish training. This whole world was so alien. Often it seemed surreal, as if I were an observer watching these talented people do what I often couldn't fathom. My troop mates were so much better than me. They came from diverse and interesting backgrounds, while my life was so simple and regulated. I was in awe. It would take me weeks and weeks to establish enough self-worth to make me feel deserving of their friendship. They were exceptional in my eyes.

"There were some equalizers where I felt I had as much chance as they did. One of those was firearms training. Anybody can blast away at a paper target a few yards away ... or so it seems until you are actually in front of one! I have come to learn that the length of a barrel and the accuracy of its sights have a lot to do with getting the bullet in that black area of the paper. Learning how to breathe while aiming a rifle while lying on a supported incline and slowly squeezing the trigger is a lot different than doing a run up at a target and stopping every few yards to fire your snub-nose revolver. I was amazed how large the target got as I ran toward it. I was even more amazed by how inaccurate I became the closer I got. Watching TV 'cops and robbers' shows is often more like comedy than reality. Amazing shooting while flying through the air, not worrying how you land as other people shoot at you, is something created in movie scripts. The only other descriptor would have to be 'fluke.' Usually when you arrived at the range, you would shoot off two rounds and then use the empty shell casings as ear sound protectors by leaving them inserted in your ears for the shoot duration. The instructors had regular earmuff-type sound protectors. Stupidities did occur on the range. The occasional bullet was fired into the ground not far from toes, not always your own.

"Then there was driver training. This usually consisted of a recruit driver with the instructor in the front seat and two or three more terrified recruits in the back. This was not the CAA-approved driver testing one would expect on applying for your first licence. This was more like NASCAR on Kentucky blue grass. How fast can you 'take the ditch' and come out of it without wiping out the other cars on the road? How safely and how fast can you manoeuvre through pounding rain while pursuing a subject? Occasionally we even got to drive the speed limit!

"'Can you swim?' That is a leading and revealing question if you are standing at the side of the 'Depot' swimming pool! If you said you could, you got to jump in and swim to the other side. That much I could do, but not much more. I had drowned twice in my youth where I had to be resuscitated. I had water fright. Now, if you were a non-swimmer, you got to go to the deep end of the pool and jump in feet first. If I was scared when I swam my length, the non-swimmers were terrified when their heads went under water. The instructor carried a 16-foot bamboo pole, and quite a few of the terrified recruits tried to climb up it to get out of the water. If you think that was cruel and unusual punishment, the non-swimmers were then 'allowed' to go to the mezzanine above the pool and jump in from there. When you are standing on the edge of the mezzanine, you see one of two things: the top of the water or the bottom of the pool. The swimmers got to jump or dive off. The non-swimmers got to step out into air. My heart went out to them as they sputtered and coughed to the surface and tried to climb the bamboo pole once again. It must have been one of the most terrifying days of their lives. But there were no non-swimmers in our troop at the end of training. Although we had a lot of swimming technique training, we also had a lot of water rescue training. One of us would play victim, spluttering and flailing at the deep end of the pool, and another got to play rescuer. As a victim, it was your job to fight off a potential rescue due to your state of being terrified. The rescuer's job was to calm the victim sufficiently to assist him in getting to shore. The instructor made sure the victim did not make that an easy exercise. Slowly we learned what worked for us. If we had a particularly good day in the pool, they allowed us to play 'murder ball.' Essentially it was water polo without the rules. Having the ball usually meant you got dunked, sunk or had your bathing suit tied around your ankles while trying to score. It was a lot of fun and actually taught us a lot of defensive skills that were utilized in our rescue scenarios.

"Training would not be complete without a mention of the 'Fat Boys Club.' Almost all of us got a chance to participate in this attempt to bring us to our absolute minimum weight and maximum muscle mass. For anyone unable to challenge the problem of an expanding waistline, or who had problems keeping up with the overall fitness of the troop, after-hours participation in the 'Fat Boys Club' was mandatory. All kidding aside, some of us needed the extra gym time. I never got to be the 6'2" guy with the 32" waist, but they did get me down to 34".

"I guess my fondest memories revolve around the hallway of our dorm. Having your 'pit' area spotless and absolutely organized was the motivator to do everything possibly disorganized, unkempt or dirty in the hallway. There were guys ironing their shirts, spit-shining their boots, de-linting with tape rollers and studying or doing their class notes. And there was buffoonery throughout the processes. Pillow fights, sneak attacks and pile-ons were just part of letting off steam from the constant pressure of having to be 'perfect.' There were letters home and letters from home. There were long telephone calls at the pay phone, and the guys who had instruments brought them out and played. Humour was the medicine for all ills. Laughter was a mainstay of being part of the melee. There were good times to be had and we had them.

"On Sunday there was Church Parade where members would march into town according to their religious leanings. Those who were affiliated to some of the less popular religions were left to go to the church of their choosing. I was suddenly a member of the apostolic faith and my church was at Smitty's Pancake House. I noticed that many other 'Christian' denominations attended the same church.

"Of course, attending that church required a vehicle. The 'Depot' parking lot was littered with fine examples of vintage cars. Many of those cars had been owned by a myriad of troops and probably had a lot more stories to tell than we did. They were the only way to get to Regina Beach and the Trianon Ballroom. Many had seen speeding tickets trying to get back before 'Depot' curfew, and our baby even ended up being an ambulance to the hospital.

"Early on, as did almost all policemen, we learned that rural policing often means waiting long hours for a response to trouble. There are not enough detachments, Mounties or police cars to service all the complaints quickly. A solitary police officer is forced to use a lot of discretion when something criminal or physically dangerous happens in the 'boonies,' so having a bunch of recruits come upon an accident scene with fatalities teaches great lessons: taking care of the injured, handling road traffic, and taking notes and pictures of the scene took priority over getting a 'real' policeman there. We were first responders before that term became popular. Likewise, at a drowning at Regina Beach, a dragline had to be formed to try and find the body. When that was successful, it was still necessary to try mouth-to-mouth in an attempt to resuscitate. Failure was another life lesson. Life is not a script. It is what it is, and you have to learn to accept that you will not always be successful.

"The lessons of C Troop continued over a hot summer and cold autumn. It was a time of coming of age, of maturing, of learning. All of us looked forward to graduating and finding out where in Canada we would be posted. I was hoping for British Columbia as my teenage travels had taken me there. It wouldn't turn out that way, but I did get the chance to re-encounter the beauty of BC later in life. We all knew that BC took more graduates than any other province. It had the largest provincial contract in Canada. With all this floating in my head, I enjoyed our graduation. Many troop members had family from far and wide come to celebrate grad. The girlfriends I had not previously met came out of the woodwork or arrived by plane. I had no family or friends come from home but I did have my girlfriend from Regina with me. She was a wonderfully supportive young lady I judged to be too good for me. It was a case of ships passing in the night. The party was an orgy of dancing and drinking. At the end, we ended up taking a $200 taxi ride back to 'Depot' ($20 for the trip and the rest for the cleanup). One member of the troop was a non-drinker until grad. There he was weaned on rum and Coke at the start and was drinking straight dark rum at the end. Not a pretty sight in the morning.

"The next Monday we were called up as a troop and read our marching orders. As expected, many would be heading to BC. The French language members were sent back to Quebec, and I was with them because my French was tolerable and 'C' Division had a critical shortage of members. I was disappointed, as I'd had my hopes set for BC, Alberta or Saskatchewan. Going back home to the apron strings I had left was not part of my plan. I had to go; I was not allowed to marry; I was not allowed to live common-law; and saying 'no' to the transfer would be career-ending. It was an untenable situation, but I chose to go, hoping my girlfriend would follow once I was settled.

"Within days I was on the train heading back east. My compensation was that some of my troop mates' relatives were on the train with me. Party time! It was a great time getting home and for once I wished it didn't have to end so quickly.

"I was a third class Constable entering field training in an area of federal policing that had been only lightly covered in training. There was a lot to learn while re-acclimatizing myself to 'big city life.' My first three months were spent in Montreal Protective, where I felt like a security guard looking after the 'C' Division headquarters building. Again, it was something I had not envisioned or expected as part of my life of 'action' as a police officer. Apparently most of the new recruits get a tour of this before being placed in a squad. General Investigative Services (GIS) was my next placement, and I enjoyed it much more: Interpol enquiries, FBI liaison, interprovincial cases, NNOK (notification of next of kin), missing persons enquiries, prime minister and foreign dignitaries protection services, investigations not pertaining to specialties such as drugs, immigration, customs, commercial crime and other major federal duties. My life was suddenly busy and meaningful. I also got a chance to work with other squads if they were short of men. Please remember that these were the days before bulletproof vests and good communication systems. We were not TV policemen in baseball caps saying GRC/RCMP with little flip mikes and a backup ERT team. Most of our work was in plain clothes without formal identification and little or no contact with other members of our assault team. There were times we had advance knowledge of weapons on the premises but those times were rare. Takedowns were usually done about 3:00 a.m. to lessen the chance of a co-ordinated counteroffensive. Tasers hadn't been invented, and handcuff poly ties were non-existent. Police work was more precarious and had a different danger level. We all considered these problems to be part of the job.

"I then got a chance to join the Drug Squad. That's where the trouble began, I think. There was too much work and too much court preparation. Although I could hold my own as an investigator, the squad moved me to the background so I would have limited need to testify in court. Everyone realized my French language skills were not good enough to take me through a cross-examination in court. I was a liability. As a result, I was then transferred to Special 'O,' the Surveillance Squad, which operated in English. Surveillance techniques were an eye-opener because it was the art of seeing without being seen. It was a different type of police work. I worked on behalf of many investigative arms. I might follow a drug courier to a meeting place, follow 'mafia' members to find their safe houses, follow financiers to establish contacts and 'drops,' or follow international criminals to help determine their lodging, associates and possible crimes in planning or progress. We also assisted in covering Special 'I,' as they conducted surreptitious entries and electronic surveillance equipment installations. We helped build specialized surveillance vehicles. It was exciting and there were many late nights when we 'burned' in excess of 100 traffic red lights to get ahead or keep up with a subject. We developed a lot of intelligence for various squads who were working on major cases.

"However, my language impediment became a stumbling block when threat of Quebec separation became a political reality. I believe the Division decided to go all French to appease the political pressure of the day. Quebec legislation brought in 'language in the workplace,' and my days were numbered. I was called into Staffing and told I had to leave the province if I wanted to keep a career in the Force. I was asked where I'd like to go and I told them 'anywhere in Canada except Newfoundland or Toronto.' They informed me that there were openings in PEI, and I could expect to change from federal to contract policing. That night my wife and I sat down to look for motels for our house-hunting trip. The next morning Staffing called to let me know I was transferred to Toronto. I was not pleased.

"My wife and I had been looking at fully detached, three-bedroom bungalows around Montreal for $13,000. We arrived in Toronto to find two-bedroom townhouses at $32,000. Again, I was not pleased. A new job, a pregnant wife and a one-year-old daughter was not a happy accounting with a fixed salary. At least the work was familiar: Drug Squad. Our Jarvis Street HQ sat in the middle of the 'red light' district of Toronto. A lot of our work was literally around the corner. Many of the hookers were drug-addicted and the 'johns' came down for the women and easy access to drugs. Once I was established in the squad, I was approached to work in the Court Liaison section. Court Liaison was a quasi-administrative unit that arranged for court appearances and witnesses, and helped

Jack and Johanna Snoeks, plus their daughters Ann and Kyra. Their son Christopher was born after this photo was taken.

to prepare evidence with the investigators. It wasn't 'police' work per se, but it was extremely interesting and gave me a far greater insight into all kinds of police investigations. Court Liaison also acted as the prosecutor on Airport Vehicle Control Regulations (AVCR). Each week I had the opportunity of acting as Crown counsel and preparing all the evidence. We could only process about 35 cases per week, but there were about 120 infractions per week. Obviously we were building a backlog! As I mentioned earlier, part of my lab technician work involved innovation. I analyzed the situation and realized the backlog was caused by our inability to type the necessary court and summons documents as fast as infractions were being issued. I met with the judges who sat on the court and asked them if I could change the format of the court documents. I developed various 'masks' with strategically located holes that would allow the info on the violation ticket to show through and be photocopied to become part of the 'information' that went before the judge. Our throughput changed from 35/week to 620/day. No additional staff was required to clear the backlog and AVCR ceased to be a problem.

"Sometimes your reputation precedes you and people exaggerate your accomplishments. My ability to solve throughput problems came to the attention of our Records Manager, who was continually swamped with files to update and had to maintain a huge quantity of index cards to search those files. We had clerks putting reports on the correct files and cataloguing everything. In back rooms and in the basement there were areas where there were hundreds of filing cabinets of files that were dormant and 'cold-cased.' It wasn't a paper empire, it was a paper quagmire. I was asked to join the section and work on the problem. If computers had been available back then, my job would have been a lark.

"It took over a year and a lot of design work and flow charting to address the many redundant procedures occurring in the office. My biggest problem was the 'it has always been done this way' mentality of both the system and the crew. Changes were made to the point where we had almost a 300 percent increase in both throughput and accuracy. The ideas were sent to the Branch in Ottawa.

"Coincidentally, our third child was born and unfortunately he was born with Down syndrome. As neither my wife nor I had any type of family support system in Toronto, I asked for a transfer back to Montreal. Although I had been taking French courses at OISE (Ontario Institute for Studies in Education), my proficiency was still not 'fully' bilingual, so the Force transferred us to Ottawa where we would be a couple of hours' drive from my extended family.

"I was quickly promoted into a Sergeant's position in HQ Records Section. Now, Records has a reputation that the misfits and incompetents are hidden there. I was aware of possibly having that cape thrown on my shoulders. Nobody realized I was a volunteer for that type of work—I was good at it. I realized that my unfulfilled desire to get into forensics should have led me to the realization that I was probably better backing up policemen with the information they needed than being a policeman myself.

"I guess I should explain that little anomaly. At two years in the field and having acquired the rank of first class Constable, I had the opportunity for a staffing interview. The Staffing Officer noted my interest in forensics and asked me two things: One, had I done anything in the past two years to increase my proficiency in chemistry or taken courses to stay up on current trends? Two, did I still want to head in that direction and what were my plans to achieve that target? The first question was pretty easy: nothing.

The official reception for the Canadian contingent in Den Hague during the 35th anniversary of the Liberation of Holland. Left to right: Sergeant Ziggy Segstro, Mrs. McKinnon, Minister of Defense for Canada Allan McKinnon, Princess Margriet of Holland and her husband, Pieter van Vollenhoven, Corporal Jack Snoeks, 1980.

I had been so busy learning my police role that I hadn't had the time nor made the effort to advance myself toward my initial goal. I had been mulling the second question for several months. Did I really want to handle test tubes, gas chromatographs and infrared spectrometers for the rest of my life? The interest wasn't there anymore. I enjoyed working in the field. I knew I could handle the scientific aspect of forensic science, but I was unwilling to give up what I now had. Dreams and reality are often at odds and this was absolute proof.

"I finished my career in Records. I had a good Sergeant who just about ran the day-to-day operation of the main office by himself. I had a Corporal who took good care of our sub-records offices around the city, and I had a fantastic crew of dedicated

Jack and Johanna Snoeks at the Senior NCO Mess, Ottawa, on Jack's retirement from the RCMP on June 9, 1990, with 24 years and 3 days of service.

public servants who worked with me rather than for me. The only thing I didn't have was job satisfaction. Innovation was frustrating at best. The fact that the Records Branch was so close to the operation often led to conflicts that would not have occurred had I been managing a Division Records office. I welcomed computerization and helped design some of the software that would make the operation more efficient and cost-effective. I redesigned some of the legacy systems to accommodate integration with our automated systems. However, Branch encroachment on plans and designs corrupted the work I was doing. My last two years were an exercise in tedium. I longed to leave until I left.

"Now what? I was 45 and retired. I had always wanted that transfer to BC. My two girls were no longer at home and my son was doing quite well at home. I had my final move coming to me, so the three of us headed to a small city called Cranbrook in the East Kootenays of BC.

"After several months, I was reflective enough to realize that I was too young to retire. I decided to start a business of my own as a marriage mediator. It was a brand-new field and the courses for it weren't particularly expensive or long. At the same time, I joined the board of directors of the E.K. Mental Health Association (EKMHA). They welcomed me with open arms as I had sat on the board of the Prescott/Russell Community Living Association. As all this was going on, the lawyers of Cranbrook began to realize that marriage mediation could be a lucrative pastime and slowly squeezed me out of the way. My voluntary position at EKMHA started getting busy as we made forays to merge with the Canadian Mental Health Association. I became the negotiator, and eventually joined the administration and contracts of both organizations. The new combined board approached me to become the executive director of the operation. I stayed in that position about three years.

"About that time, our children started having children of their own and we contemplated a move back east. Our son, Chris, had been in high school and community college attending special courses while we lived there. He had met a young lady who also had Down syndrome, and they decided to get married. When they had been married for several months, my wife and I told Chris we were going back east, and offered to take him and his bride with us. After a few days, he and Cora told us they wanted to stay because Cora had family there.

"The two of us returned to Ottawa and started looking for a place to live. I worked at several different jobs over the next few years, but one day I was stuck in rush-hour traffic and I decided that I'd had enough. When I got to the office, I called my wife and asked her to start looking for a house outside of Ottawa because I was retiring for good. We settled in the city of Cornwall, which is halfway between our children and grandchildren. I sometimes renovate houses and we have tried being landlords. I have done some work for the RCMP in a consulting capacity and as the co-ordinator for HQ PROS training.

"I have been very fortunate in my life. I've had a loving and supportive wife for over 50 years. My two daughters and my son have generated nothing but love and pride in the wonderful adults they have become. My three granddaughters are growing into fine adults who are getting close to starting another generation. I thank the RCMP for giving me the opportunity of raising my family in relative safety and comfort. In exchange they have had my loyalty, honesty, devotion to the public I served, and the integrity of giving them more than a day's work for a day's pay.

"One of my regrets in life is not being able to spend more quality time with the 31 guys who shared my transition to adulthood. I owe them a debt of thanks for taking me into their lives and sharing their own journey with me. They will always hold a special place in my heart."

— *Jack Snoeks*

J.E.C.
(Ernie)
STAGG
Reg# 24852

C66/67 Troop
50th Year Reunion

STAGG

"IT'S UNCERTAIN WHETHER it was an aptitude test in high school that indicated I would be suited to become a farmer or a policeman, or the fact that my father was a member of the Calgary City Police that prompted me to apply to the RCMP. In any event, at age 18 I set the ball in motion. There was paperwork to be completed, a written examination, interviews and a physical examination. I was told I would be contacted.

"I was fortunate to have been hired immediately after graduating high school by an oilfield natural gas well testing company. I had been working for the company for almost a year. I was on a well site in an area north of Calgary when my boss arrived on-site. He told me that my application to the RCMP had been approved. I needed to be on a train to Regina that was leaving Calgary two days later. My boss was there to drive me back to Calgary. On the drive back, he asked me to consider staying with the company. They had planned to sponsor me in oilfield-related training at Southern Alberta Institute of Technology. I was tempted but

C Troop in the 32-man dorm, September 1966. The Troop awaits dorm inspection that will determine if they have the weekend off or if they are confined to barracks. Ron Beaucaire (left front), Ernie Stagg (right front), and Jack Snoeks (at ease next to Stagg).

decided to pursue a career with the Mounties. I looked forward to riding a horse.

"There were a few of us on that train to Regina, none knowing what was in store for us. I wondered if I had made the right choice, but I was already on the train. The following six months were challenging but went by very quickly. The closest we got to

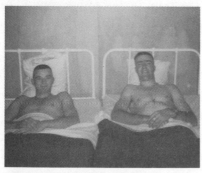

Pit partners Ernie Stagg (left) and Bob Swift (right) waiting for lights out in the 32-man dorm, 1966.

equitation training was cleaning the stables and stalls of 80-some horses!

I arrived at my first posting, Surrey, BC, with a troop mate, and checked in at the main office in Cloverdale. My troop mate was told he would be staying, and I was told, 'You are going to Whalley.' I

thought this must be the detachment Commander. I soon learned that Whalley was a sub-office of Surrey Detachment in North Surrey—the more densely populated area of Surrey.

"I worked with the Senior Constable for a short time, and was introduced to the routine

Constable Ernie Stagg typing complaints. Constable Norm Leibel is talking on the detachment complaint line, White Rock, BC, 1967.

aspects of policing. I considered this the start of my career with the Force. I was transferred several times in my service. I was posted to White Rock Detachment after my initial six months at Surrey. Transfers to Port Coquitlam, Coquitlam, back to Surrey, Chetwynd, Tumbler Ridge and Sparwood followed during 22 years with the Force.

"I will always remember my first solo break-and-enter and theft investigation. I discovered the break-and-enter in the early morning hours while checking property during the graveyard shift. A service station had been entered through a smashed window. In squeezing through the opening, the culprit lost his wallet full of identification! Fingerprint evidence collected by our Identification Section confirmed our suspect. Unfortunately all cases are not solved as easily.

"Nightly property checks were a tedious but necessary part of policing. I was checking property in Port Coquitlam late one night and discovered a restaurant had been entered through a side window. The restaurant was on the ground floor of a two-storey building in a remote area of the city. I could see movement in the dark. As I was alone on shift, I asked for cover from our neighboring detachment in Maillardville. Circling the building on foot several times, I was concerned that the culprit would exit and escape. I was getting somewhat tired by this, and there was no cover. I didn't think climbing through the jagged glass was in my best interest, so I decided to shoulder the door since it appeared quite flimsy. I realized why the intruder went through the window, as I nearly dislocated my shoulder! Then I heard a voice from the second-floor balcony. 'Do you want the key?' he asked quietly, and he dropped it to me. I sure felt silly, but I managed to find and arrest the culprit in the kitchen. Within weeks he was serving time in Oakalla Prison Farm.

"The judicial process was more expedient then. In the early days, detachments had court liaison personnel or sections that handled the court documents and processes. Often, ad hoc prosecutors presented the cases. These incidents were not always that easy to resolve. We had a rash of residential and commercial break-ins in Port Coquitlam and Ranch Park in Coquitlam. Through routine patrols of the city, I was able to identify a group of six young adults who I felt were responsible. I took it upon myself to work a little 'voluntary overtime' and started following them around the downtown area of Port Coquitlam at night, in my personal vehicle and on foot.

"The group often split up. Some of them walked up into Ranch Park, which was in the Maillardville Detachment area. I stayed with the group in the downtown area. Several days into this endeavour, I followed one of the fellows into a back alley. He pried open a window to a sporting goods store and tried to crawl in. I caught him halfway through the window and arrested him. He eventually implicated the others who had been involved in numerous break-and-enters and thefts in Coquitlam and Port Moody as well. These individuals had used proceeds of their endeavours to support drug habits.

"As I look back on my career in the Force, I realize that I gained a great deal of satisfaction from bringing incidents and investigations to a successful conclusion. Whether resolving serious criminal investigations, robberies, homicides, armed and barricaded persons, motor vehicle accident investigations or disputes, it was rewarding. I was fortunate to have been posted where it was always busy. The 22 years flew past!

"During those years, I was witness to the construction of an entire town—Tumbler Ridge, BC. It was built in the southeast corner of Chetwynd Detachment area, approximately 95 kilometres away, via a new hard-surface highway that was finished in about two years. The influx of workers resulted in a tremendous increase in police workload.

"Routine police work increased dramatically. Assaults occurred regularly, and reports of thefts of tools and equipment were common. There were reports of heavy equipment (loaders, bulldozers and other Caterpillar equipment) stolen, as well. Initially, Chetwynd Detachment members were responsible for attending, but eventually the Dawson Creek Detachment took a lead role with Chetwynd Detachment providing assistance. The Force provided an on-site trailer to serve as an office and short-term accommodation at the town site while a permanent detachment building was constructed.

"I enjoyed the Peace Country for all it had to offer and decided to make a future home in this area. While I was there, an opportunity arose to acquire land on a lease-development basis. There was an auction of leases by BC Lands Branch in the Hudson's Hope area, north of the detachment. I had no farming experience but decided to enter the auction. I was successful on the 'bonus bid' for a 250-acre parcel. The lease required that 25 percent of the land had to be developed to seed bed over a period of 10 years.

"Armed with a dream and a shovel, I set out to make Hunker-Down Buffalo Ranch a reality. I used my vacation at Chetwynd to start developing the property and building a log cabin on-site, using the logs from the property. A new neighbour and I purchased some equipment together, and we started clearing our respective land parcels. Eventually, I was transferred to Sparwood Detachment, in the lower southeast corner of the province near Crowsnest Pass, and was unable to continue clearing. As it also became apparent that any future postings to the north would not be forthcoming, I answered a job posting with the city of Whitehorse, Legislative Services Division. I was successful, and I retired from the Force.

"It took six more years to develop the land in accordance with the lease-purchase agreement, and I finally obtained title. It was now time to leave the city and work full-time at the 'ranch.' The Peace Country Bison Association presented a course in buffalo (bison) farming, which I attended. I became very interested in buffalo and thought that was a good fit for the ranch.

"My wife, daughter and I moved into the cabin. My wife, Lin, liked to describe it as having a 16′ × 26′ living room, a 16′ × 26′ kitchen and 16′ × 26′ master bedroom—these measurements all referring to the same room. There was also a loft, and running water was a plastic 45-gallon drum with a tap. Needless to say, a house was a priority. There was not a dull moment for our family. Within two years, the log house was built, fences were erected and a corral with buffalo-handling equipment was constructed using planks from a neighbour's sawmill.

"We started with five buffalo cows purchased from a local producer and soon the herd grew to 20, selected from other herds and buffalo auctions. It wasn't all fun. We had a bad windstorm that uprooted a number of large aspen trees, and the trees crushed the high-tension wire fence that was holding the herd in the pasture. The buffalo took advantage of this situation and left our property. The BC Game Farming Policy stated that any farmed buffalo found on Crown land became the property of the Crown. Imagine how we felt with $100,000 worth of buffalo on the loose—the ranch was surrounded by Crown land! Fortunately, after a few days' search they were tracked to a neighbour's unfenced parcel. We learned that you can chase a buffalo anywhere it wants to go. Eventually, we managed to herd them back to our pasture.

Ernie Stagg traded his RCMP badge with a buffalo head on it to raise real buffalo at Hudson's Hope, BC.

"As breeding stock prices began to decline, we started a buffalo meat business—Peace

Ernie Stagg takes time to scratch his buffalo's nose.

Country Buffalo Products—and began to market our federally inspected meat. We had a cube van with freezers filled with product that Lin set up at a number of shopping centres. Rain or shine, heat or cold, Lin set off to sell product. One winter day at -30°C, she was heard to tell one of her customers, 'It's so cold, I would be warmer in one of those freezers.'

"It was a great experience developing the ranch. Buffalo are extremely intelligent. We soon had over 200 pets. I believe the herd considered me their leader. I was able to step into the corral containing up to 200 head in order to sort and identify each, and I was never threatened. I did, however, have to be fast on my feet.

"Raising buffalo was an experience I will never forget. It was not a lucrative business, as it turned out, but the lifestyle was amazing. It was also fitting that a retired RCMP member was raising buffalo, since the Force has had a buffalo head on its badge since the days of the North-West Mounted Police, its founding police force. Mark Gaillard, the RCMP Veterans' Association historian, says that when the NWMP's second permanent Commissioner, James Macleod, led his members into the area of the Canadian West now known as Alberta, he was so impressed by the herds of bison (or buffalo) on the Prairies that he later suggested . that a buffalo head was a worthy symbol for his Force's badge.

"I had two other jobs while we were developing the ranch. I . was a loss control specialist doing risk assessments for commercial operations and residential properties throughout BC and part of northern Alberta, and I worked as a coroner's agent, investigating sudden deaths in the Hudson's Hope, Fort St. John and Dawson Creek areas. I continued as a loss control specialist, conducting inspections, after the ranch was sold in 2007 due to health concerns. It's still in operation, and I assisted the new owners in handling the buffalo as they had no background in animal husbandry. After the ranch, we resided in Whitehorse, Cranbrook and Mackenzie, and I did inspections from those locations. I also worked in a lumberyard and as a licensed property manager in Mackenzie, BC. I retired in 2015 and moved to southern BC.

—*Ernie Stagg*

R.D.
(Robert)
SWIFT
Reg# 24834

C66/67 Troop
50th Year Reunion

SWIFT

IT'S A GOOD thing Bob Swift grew up as the class clown, always happy to ease tension with a laugh, because his work as a small town RCMP Constable often involved situations that were simultaneously stressful and ridiculous.

Relatively early in Swift's career, he was posted to Lac La Biche, a hamlet on the historic fur trade route about 225 kilometres north of Edmonton, where he was part of a seven-member RCMP team that policed the town, the rural agricultural area and three reserves. "We had a cell block that held four prisoners, and I think we had 28 in there at one time during Pow Wow Days, when there were a lot of drunks, a lot of raising hell," he says. In fact, over the course of that weekend, he figures they locked up more than 60 people in a rapidly moving scene that quickly devolved into a farce. "We were throwing guys out of cells that were still absolutely drunk to put in the more serious offenders. But the worst part was smelling the shoes. Imagine a pile of 28 pairs of rotten, stinking shoes. All of them had been throwing up all

C Troop marching on the parade square before field day, July 1966. Lead: John Seniuk. Second row, left to right: Bob Swift, Jack Snoeks, and Ernie Stagg.

over them, and half of them had been drinking shaving lotion. For the whole weekend. It was funny, but the smell was terrible!"

Swift had a clear idea of what the backbreaking alternative to this job could have been, however. Raised in North Kamloops, BC, before joining the RCMP at 19 he'd worked a couple of summers alongside his father, a sawmill crane operator who lifted logs off rail cars and dumped them in the river. In contrast, the RCMP promised challenging, everchanging work, something he certainly experienced even though he spent his entire 28-year career deployed to small and medium-sized detachments across Alberta. "I never had any huge, big cases that made a difference to the world," he says, self-effacingly.

And yet the record suggests he did. Day in and day out, Swift called on instinct and sturdy training at critical points in the lives of people living in rural, often isolated and sometimes harsh circumstances. More than once, his police work made an essential difference to their world.

During his time in Lac La Biche, one of his calls was to a tiny community another 30 kilometres northwest, following up on a report that a family was neglecting their children. He and a partner entered a shabby house to find a completely blind grandmother in charge of four or five children whose heads were full of lice. The parents' location was unknown. There was not a shred of food around either, Swift remembers. The officers loaded everyone into a car to transport them to the welfare authorities, but at the door something made Swift take one more glance around. "There was a blanket. I thought it was a wall tapestry, but it was just a blanket held by a few nails ... and something moved behind it. It was a two- or three-month-old baby. It was alive. It was lousy like the rest of the kids and hadn't been changed. The only thing it had in there was a half-sized baby bottle with tea and milk that had gone mouldy. It moved at exactly the right time to be noticed, otherwise I would have left it there."

In a less dramatic incident while posted to the Lac La Biche Detachment that could also have ended dreadfully, Swift took a shortcut down an infrequently used back road on his way into Plamondon, AB, and returned the enthusiastic wave of a man who was changing a flat tire. Retracing his route at least 45 minutes later, Swift noticed the car still jacked up. Shaking his head in disbelief, he decided to lend the inept tire-changer a hand and was immediately glad he did. "The jack had fallen over and he'd been there the whole time, pinned between the tire and the fender well. He was waving frantically because he was pinned," says Swift. "It was not a busy road. He could have been there a long time."

In an incident near Deadman's Flats, while he was stationed at Canmore, Swift almost certainly altered the life trajectory of a young man who had been accused of raping a teenage girl in his truck at a gravel pit. While taking the woman's statement, Swift asked her to gauge how long the incident had taken. Her reply, "How long does it take to fill a gravel truck?" seemed like a strangely composed answer, so he carefully revisited other details. "Turns out it was totally false," he says. "He was her boyfriend, it was their first time and she thought she was going to be pregnant, so she told her parents she was raped."

Swift learned several foundational principles of good policing in Wainwright, AB, his first posting after "Depot." On his first day in the rural detachment, the Sergeant gave him "the best advice I ever had," says Swift. When making an arrest, "Ask, tell, then take," the Sergeant told him. "This simple little rule saved me a lot of grief throughout my career," says Swift. "You don't just grab ahold of someone and chuck them in the car. You ask them, 'Sir, would you mind getting in the car?' and if they didn't, then you told them, and after that, then you'd take them. No matter what you were dealing with, even with crowd control, it worked."

He also learned the importance of having a partner who shared his belief in the value of staying calm, by experiencing the liability of a frightened one. While on foot patrol one night, Swift discovered a store that had been broken into, and when his backup colleague arrived, he entered the dark building. "A few steps in, with only the illumination of my flashlight, I heard the distinct sound of a gun being cocked and when I turned around, I came about three inches from the barrel of his revolver being

poked in my nose. That was more frightening than what turned out to be an empty building."

Happily, Wainwright is also where he had the best experience of his life—meeting Donna, the woman who became his wife in 1968. Fittingly, since she was married to Swift for 50 years (until her death in 2018), from the outset Donna possessed sharp

Bob and Donna Swift, Cold Lake, Alberta, June 8, 1968.

instincts well suited to being part of the RCMP family. "This beauty worked in the jewelry store, so when I bought the engagement ring, I worked with the store owner after-hours, thinking it would be a big surprise," says Swift. "The next day, she noticed an engagement ring was missing from under the counter and confronted the owner. He must have stammered too much in his explanation, in that she figured it all out. So, no surprise. It was a valued lesson learned. It's not what you say, but the way you say it."

While in Wainwright, Swift also learned the compassionate art of when not to speak up as a law enforcement officer. His detachment was close to the Wainwright military base, where Canadian soldiers often train with soldiers from Britain. One night, they picked up a couple of drunken British soldiers, put them in cells and called their provost the next morning. The provost chewed them out for about half an hour, says Swift, and then suddenly took the big swagger stick he'd arrived with, "pulled it back and hit the guy square between the legs. I never saw anything so cruel. It was terrible. After that, we never called the provost again. We just held them [drunken soldiers] overnight and released them in the morning."

Providing whatever assistance is necessary to people in trouble is the core of policing anywhere, of course, but because he spent so much of his career in rural areas, Swift shouldered a high proportion of the type of calls that occur more frequently there. Providing backup to Fish and Wildlife officers to deal with poachers, or to capture and relocate nuisance bears was one busy category. When he was assigned to take a boating course in Cold Lake, Swift learned how to drag a lake and was subsequently in charge of all the drownings at whatever detachment he worked. "I dealt with a lot of deaths. Way more than 10," he says somberly, recalling the eerie, unnerving experience of a lake that suddenly stilled after he'd been searching in vain for some time, and how, as the birds appeared to quiet, it unexpectedly released to the water's surface a boot that was attached to a body.

Constable Bob Swift during a traffic stop, Banff Detachment, 1967.

Mercifully, Swift attended far fewer fatalities while on rural highway patrol. Yet the pain of the worst of those events always draws tears, he warns, before relating a story still seared into his psyche five decades later. "A dump truck had smashed into a station wagon, and when I arrived there we found the mother and father had been killed. The kid in the front seat was still alive, one in the back seat was dead and two others were alive. One, a young girl, 10 or 11 years old, had a broken femur, a compound break that had hit her main artery. There's no chance you could ever stop the bleeding. I could see that. But I was putting a pad on her anyway when she said to me, 'I'm going to be OK. You just take care of my family.'" Swift's composure breaks audibly. "I can picture it all the time. Her trying to be helpful ... if I could only tell her parents how brave she was ..."

The key to coping and thriving as a police officer in a small community is to become a strong thread in its fabric, says Swift. He coached sports, joined service clubs and volunteered. His efforts were greatly appreciated, although one attempt to be helpful created an amusing miscommunication. While coaching boxing, Swift was approached by one of the young boxers who was upset because his nose would often bleed when he practised. Swift explained that he probably had a vein in his nose that was susceptible to the slightest jolt, but that it could likely be fixed by being cauterized. He told the boy to suggest that to his parents. A few days later, the boy's father dropped in on Swift. He commended him for the coaching he was doing with the area's youth but then asked, "Why does my son say that in order to continue boxing he needs to be circumcised?"

Swift's other ideas to assist local youth had better outcomes. To combat the high incidence of damaging petty crime that usually befell Canmore each October 31, he helped organize a Halloween dance for children and youth, funding it with confiscated liquor bottles. The wildly successful venture, chaperoned by RCMP members and their wives, was an ongoing tradition for many years. To help reduce the ever-present risk of a mining disaster in that coal-mining community, he joined Canmore's Mine Rescue Team as an assistant training officer.

Knowing his neighbours and earning their trust in any of the smallish communities he served (which also included Drayton Valley, Wainwright and Fort Saskatchewan) often proved useful in gathering tips and information during investigations. One of his favourite characters was a travelling rural judge in northern Alberta, an unorthodox elderly man who boldly let the police know he carried a revolver under the seat of his car for protection. During one court case in which an accused faced half a dozen charges, each necessitating the presence of different arresting officer, Swift was the last member of law enforcement in line because he had simply arrested the man for illegal possession of liquor. The accused, representing himself, nonetheless crafted a preposterous defense that suggested Swift couldn't prove that the bottle he'd seen the accused drink from was the same one at the scene. The judge listened intently and then pronounced the man not guilty. Dumbfounded, Swift approached him afterward to ask what he could do to improve his testimony in the future.

"Nothing," said the judge. "You had him cold. But I convicted him on the four or five charges ahead of you, and by letting him off on that one, he's happy—he thinks he won." He paused. "And not only that, it was worthwhile just to see the look on your face."

However, the same dearth of witnesses that allowed a well-meaning judge to skirt rules in a frontier-like environment also created some situations in which Swift faced false accusations. These ranged from a claim of sexual assault in a cell that was easily disproven by an observant jail matron to other outrageous charges. In one case, after a drug-intoxicated driver who fled his car was arrested and jailed so he wouldn't cause an accident running through highway traffic, the man accused Swift and his partner of kidnapping and assault. He entered photos of his bruised and battered face as evidence. Although another prisoner eventually testified that the man had bragged about faking an injury and the officers were found not guilty, the event certainly caused Swift and his family trauma. "The hardest part was not knowing if it would cost me millions of dollars for a court case, and whether I'd get kicked off the Force if I couldn't prove the case."

Nor was Swift immune from the regular brand of danger that every police officer risks on every shift. While posted in Fort Saskatchewan, he was walking past a tire store parking lot in plain clothes when he saw a drunk smashing vehicles. Although he apprehended the man and hustled him inside the business to call for a police car, in the ensuing struggle he got tangled in a car hoist and landed hard on his back and head against the concrete floor, with the perpetrator atop him. The close call placed him in a turtle shell and neck collar for three months, and eventually the injury ended his ability to do active police work.

Swift spent his last eight years with the RCMP in Edmonton's Forensic Laboratory, and while it was interesting work, it was never as compelling as what he'd experienced already. Yet he never second-guessed his decision to serve with the RCMP. Not when he was working 300 to 400 hours a month without overtime, nor when he was being called back to work after a full day shift, first right after supper, then at 10:00 p.m., at midnight and at 2:00 a.m., all because he was the only one in his detachment who knew how to administer a breathalyser test.

His dedication is entirely believable since he proved his nerve on the very first morning at "K" Division barracks in Edmonton, when he was freshly arrived from "Depot." "To my surprise, two other members were wrapping up the bedding of the Constable I had met the night before and boxing up his belongings. He (23-year-old Constable Gordon D. Pearson) had been shot and killed at a restaurant near Stony Plain that evening. Welcome to the real world."

"Helping people was the most rewarding part," Swift says of his RCMP career. "I can tell you every ruddy time when people thanked me for things I did. I can't tell you all the times when people gave me shit, which happened much more often."

— *Helen Metella*

J.
(John)
TURNELL
Reg# 24848

C66/67 Troop
50th Year Reunion

TURNELL

YOU MIGHT THINK that when a federal police officer who stands almost 6′6″ in his boots pulls over drivers who are clearly speeding, the drivers would behave somewhat contritely. "Not always," says John Turnell, who spent 31 years with the RCMP, most of them on highway patrol. "People think we're out there to harass them, so you'd get people saying, 'Go chase some real criminals—don't pick on us, all we're doing is driving; go catch a drug-pusher or murderer, go do your job.' They used to whine that they were going to lose their driver's licence. Whenever I stopped a vehicle I usually knew what I was going to do—give them a warning or a ticket. But as soon as they started whining, they'd get a ticket."

Over and over again, says Turnell, highway patrol officers see and hear the same dumb driving behaviour; occasionally, they see the same dumb driver over and over. During the mid-1970s, Turnell worked Unit C Freeway Patrol, which encompassed the Trans-Canada Highway east of Vancouver from Abbotsford to Agassiz, BC, two lanes in either direction. "We were known as the horizontal yo-yos, going back and forth on 39.6 miles of highway. On a Friday there could be four of us working, covering four districts going in and out of Vancouver: Matsqui, Abbotsford, Chilliwack and Agassiz. This one night, I was working Matsqui and got this guy for speeding. I finished writing the ticket and he was gone like that, so I got on the

John Turnell, "Depot," Regina, September 1966.

radio and said, 'Hey guys, you got a hot one coming.' By the time he got to Agassiz, he had four speeding tickets. It was hilarious."

Nor do some drivers seem to appreciate how unaware they are of their surroundings, says Turnell. "There was an overpass in Matsqui where we would go sit for the graveyard shift, midnight to 8:00 a.m., in marked cars. You'd sit there under these lights shining down on you in plain view, and you'd be getting speeds of 120 MPH coming through, at least three or four cars in a couple of hours."

When accidents occurred, many drivers compounded the problem. "The freeway was bad. You always had to use Code 3, which means lights and siren, because if you didn't get there quickly, you could guarantee you'd have a couple more accidents with all the gawkers."

Turnell encountered the abrupt and grim results of a car colliding with a person during his very first traffic accident investigation while he was posted to Prince George City Traffic Section and General Duties, immediately after graduating from "Depot." A driver had hit a drunk pedestrian in a hit and run. While Turnell and his colleagues were at the site, dealing with body parts

305

strewn across the road, a routine highway patrol check stop elsewhere halted the car. That unfortunate police officer was confronted with a hole in the windshield and gruesome evidence that a human being had created the hole.

The likelihood of dealing with numerous tragedies probably wasn't foremost on Turnell's mind when he joined the RCMP at 21. He was simply after a steady job. Born in Britain, he was raised on Jersey, one of the Channel Islands, where his parents ran a hotel. During the summers, he returned to England and spent pleasant vacations at his grandparents' farm. So, when a family friend who had become the dean at Alberta's Olds Agricultural Vocational College (since renamed Olds College), arranged for him to study there, Turnell eagerly moved to Canada.

But his dream of being a rancher foundered after graduation, when he realized that buying enough land for a ranch was unaffordable. After a stint in the hotel industry in Edmonton, he signed up with the RCMP. The first posting, in Prince George, was a mix of city and rural traffic enforcement plus general duties, in a bustling service town with many logging trucks, a busy CN rail line and a regional correctional centre. Life was far less sophisticated in Fort Nelson, BC, where he and his wife, Jane, transferred next.

Cutting the cake at John and Jane Turnell's wedding, December 1968.

"We were on Mile 300 of the Alaska Highway and the gravel road started about Mile 48," says Jane. "It had a good hospital and a radio station, but we had four hours of canned TV that was a week old. We lived at the airport—that's where the government housing was—seven miles out of town. It was wartime housing, from when they built the Alaska Highway."

Jane became a desk clerk at the Fort Nelson Hotel, and while on duty one night she inadvertently gathered a tip for one of her husband's next investigations. A single man, to whom she'd assigned a room on the first floor, phoned her desk to complain that his room hadn't been cleaned. He wanted Jane to take a look. Jane called the manager, but when he and his wife refused to rouse themselves from their quarters, she reluctantly went. Still, she kept her guard up and was alert enough to flee when the man tried to grab her. He quickly disappeared out of the hotel, and Jane couldn't identify him from any police sketches. But she did remember that he'd had an unusual accent.

A couple of weeks later, when Turnell was working 36 hours straight trying to locate a man who had sexually assaulted another woman, he remembered what Jane had heard and how it seemed to corroborate the victim's description. "I sent a Telex to Fort St. John and to Dawson Creek about him, and put in that he had a weird accent. In a couple of hours, they had the guy, in Fort St. John. He had a Newfoundland accent."

While being married to a policeman probably gave Jane the street smarts to be alert to a dodgy developing situation, she also knew what to worry about several transfers later when Turnell was posted to the highway patrol at Williams Lake, a town located in the Chilcotin Cariboo of BC, about halfway between Prince George and Kamloops. "What I worried about was them losing track of where he was because the dispatcher sometimes wouldn't write down where they were. I was mostly concerned if he was run off the road or was frozen somewhere. That was my biggest concern, that he'd be run off the road and no one could find him."

That never happened, but an RCMP patrol officer's hours were certainly relentless, and being an RCMP spouse left home alone was nerve-racking in those pre–cell phone days. "In Williams Lake we would go to Bella Coola [further west on Highway 20] for two or three days, and when I was in town often we'd be late doing paperwork, or be called out to a bad accident. After midnight, the Williams Lake Detachment office was closed, so our radio went through Kamloops Telecoms, and our wives wouldn't know where we were or when we'd be home. One night in Fort Nelson, I was working the 5:00 p.m. to 1:00 a.m. shift, and I said, 'I'll see you about 2:00 a.m.'—it was 2:00 p.m. the following afternoon before I got in touch with her. I had ended up at Muncho Lake, 140 miles north of Fort Nelson, BC, dealing with an XKE Jaguar that was abandoned in a gravel pit. It was involved with a crime that had been committed in the States, so we were having it seized under the *Customs Act.*"

Even when the office was open, phoning the detachment was frowned upon. Jane did not want to seem to "be a nag or a Nervous-Nellie nuisance," so she developed a blackly humorous way of dealing with the question of when she might expect her husband home. "I would wait the three or four hours after the shift ended and then call and ask, 'Should I be counting my insurance money yet?'"

Turnell remembers Williams Lake as his favourite posting, in part because of how vast and varied the areas were that the detachment covered. It also provided insight into how precariously everyday life is lived by some Canadians. One day, he and a colleague were patrolling a reserve near Anahim Lake, when Turnell stopped a white Jeep and asked the driver for his licence. "He said, 'I don't have one; the government took it away in 1958.' This would have been the 1980s. I asked him why he didn't get another licence, and he said it was because he didn't want one. So, I asked him why he was driving this vehicle. He said, 'It's a school bus.' The first thing I did was check the brakes, and there weren't any, and there were numerous other defects. Needless to say, I had to condemn the school bus." For policing like that, "we almost got run out of town a couple of times," says Turnell.

His three-and-a-half-year posting in Fernie, BC, that preceded Williams Lake provided a less remote environment, but it was one of John's least happy stretches of work, due to several terrible tragedies he dealt with there. "I kind of put it out of my mind," says Turnell. "It really was one of the worst for me."

In February 1978, Pacific Western Airlines Flight 314, flying from Calgary to Cranbrook, BC, aborted its landing to avoid hitting a snowplow on the runway and crashed, killing 42 of the 49 people aboard. It was later determined that Calgary's air traffic control had miscalculated its arrival time after a flight delay, and the flight crew somehow missed reporting the plane's approach to the tiny airport, so the snowplow was on the runway at the wrong time. Rescue efforts were further hampered because there wasn't a firefighting vehicle capable of negotiating deep snow.

Turnell and two fellow members of the Highway Patrol from Fernie were called in to help three members of the Creston RCMP Highway Patrol guard the scene. "We were basically the security guarding the hangar and a little camper trailer set up on the opposite side of the runway where the plane was. We would work from 5:00 p.m. to 8:00 a.m., making sure nothing got onto the scene and that everything was OK for the next day when the investigators came back. It was winter, it was quite dark and there were only a couple of other people in the hangar and on the site. The worst part was, if you went to guard the crash site, you had to go through the hangar where all the bodies were on the floor. It took a lot out of you, but you survive. I can still see the pilot and co-pilot, sitting upright because of the impact of the crash. You see that and you do think about how fragile life is."

Just a couple of months later, in April 1978, a Montana Highway Patrol officer with whom Turnell had become good friends after meeting him at the border crossing in Roosville, BC, was shot and killed by a patient recently released from an institution for the mentally ill.

During the same posting, Turnell was called to the site of a head-on collision between a car and a tractor-trailer in which all four drunken adults in the car survived, but the three children who were also passengers all perished. "He had trouble sleeping for months," says Jane, "He would wake up in the middle of night and ask, 'Are the kids OK? Are the kids OK?'"

Without a doubt, says Turnell, he was suffering from post-traumatic stress disorder, but at the time the world was still a couple of decades away from naming the kind of emotional distress that is now widely recognized to be a by-product of experiencing a horrible event. "I just thought it was part of the job. You had to 'be a man,'" he says.

Nor would an RCMP member dare seek help for a problem dealing with their emotions, says Jane, "because that would go on your working record and you wouldn't get a promotion."

Turnell isn't inclined to dwell on how the accident affected him. His reflections seem reserved for the stupidity of drunk driving. "Rules and regulations are there for a reason. It's a lethal combination, a 2,000-pound vehicle and a drunk driver. And it's amazing how often an accident happens and the drunk driver doesn't get hurt. It's some sober person in the vehicle who does."

While his stints in Fernie and Williams Lake were followed by a 10-year stretch in the beautiful vacation and wine-making region of Penticton, BC, Turnell still managed to find himself in several gritty situations there, while carrying out a mixture of highway patrol, city traffic and rural general duties. "I've only been involved in four riots, and that's enough," he says. One was a Halloween night riot in Prince George, one was a prison riot in Matsqui and two others occurred while he was stationed in Penticton. Those latter two were the most unruly.

In 1987, during the August long weekend, the city of Kelowna hosted a three-day hydroplane regatta. Things got out of hand after the RCMP tried to ticket a youth for disorderly conduct. By the time it was over, RCMP riot police had subdued and dispersed about 1,000 people from the city's downtown.

"But Penticton in '91 was the most intense," said Turnell. "There were 10 or 12 of us marching on Main Street, with shields, toward a crowd of 2,500 or 3,000. We had every moron from Western Canada there for the BC long weekend and the Peach Festival. MC Hammer had just finished performing, too. A lot of people were blaming him, but he had nothing to do with it. There were just a lot of people who came from that, and from the beach, and something else was going on, too. They were all released at the same time. What they should have done was stagger the release."

Newspaper reports said the riot started when about 20 drunken teens started throwing rocks at RCMP officers who were directing traffic about midnight. It quickly escalated to beer bottles and garbage cans being tossed. Before the night was over, 37 storefront windows were smashed, a police vehicle vandalized, a tourist booth ransacked, decorative benches and streetlights wrecked, and a waterfront peach-shaped ice-cream stand rolled into Okanagan Lake.

Making matters worse, says Jane, the region's trained riot police crew was stationed not in Penticton, but 65 kilometres up the highway in Kelowna, so it took some time for reinforcements to arrive. A makeshift crew of RCMP members were roused from their homes, and ordered to throw on uniforms and deal with the crowd. They didn't have the proper equipment or correctly fitting helmets or masks. Turnell and his partner's helmets and masks were essentially useless. "We're marching north on Main Street, and someone threw tear gas canisters into the crowd, but the wind was blowing it back at us. We both were gassed three times," he says.

As a home base, Penticton provided more choice and opportunity for the Turnells' three children in terms of schools and activities. So, when the RCMP offered a transfer to Vancouver Island's Integrated Traffic Camera Unit in 1996, Jane and the family stayed put, while Turnell finished the last 11 months of his RCMP career on the West Coast.

The Integrated Unit conducted photo radar on behalf of three different police forces, covering all of Vancouver Island as well as Powell River on the mainland western shore of BC. "I was basically a single man, so I'd come into work, they'd ask if I wanted to go to Campbell River for three nights, then did I want to work in Nanaimo?"

While the work was enjoyable, it was time for Turnell to rejoin his family, so after 31 years and 23 days with the Force, he retired on July 2, 1997.

He has hardly stopped working, however. For a while, Turnell drove transit and school buses in the city of Penticton. Then he and Jane started a drug and alcohol testing service, also in Penticton, offering the then-new technology to the USA Department of Transportation (USA DOT) truck and bus drivers, and to companies in the oil patch or other industries who wanted to test employees. They also became USA DOT-certified breath alcohol technicians. The business is still thriving, now as a specimen collection service, with Jane doing the collections and Turnell handling the administration.

In addition to creating a second career for Turnell, the business liberated Jane from one of the less pleasant side effects of being an RCMP spouse in Turnell's era—unexpected financial hardship. When the RCMP transferred them out of Williams Lake to Penticton, their house in Williams Lake failed to sell. It was the late 1980s, and the Force did not have a policy for covering financial burdens brought on by transfers. In order to continue paying for that house and the one they purchased in Penticton, Jane took a job pumping gas. While the house eventually sold, the financial loss they took on it was considerable, so she kept working.

Launching their own business was an idea she embraced immediately. "I wanted to stop pumping gas. I had done it for 12 or 13 years, and whenever gas spilled on my hands I could taste it for hours, and after being robbed at knife-point, I was *done*."

While the difficult repercussions of leaving the Williams Lake post are now more than 30 years in the past, Turnell's reputation for fair and detailed policing in northern BC has apparently not dimmed. A few years ago, their adult daughter gratefully realized that a routine speeding ticket she'd been issued near Kamloops, east of Ashcroft on Highway 1, was for substantially less than the amount it could have been. As the officer walked away from her car he turned around, recalls Jane, and said, "'Oh, by the way, say hi to John.'"

— *Helen Metella*

IN MEMORIAM

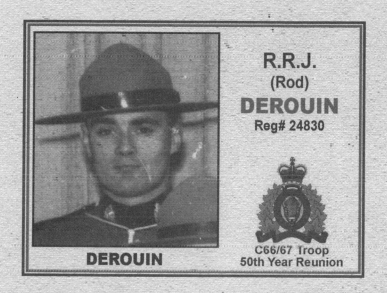

R.R.J.
(Rod)
DEROUIN
Reg# 24830

C66/67 Troop
50th Year Reunion

DEROUIN

THERE'S A PHOTO of RCMP Sergeant Rod Derouin in an October 1992 edition of the *Squamish Times* newspaper, inspecting an AK-47 rifle turned in during the roundup of such firearms required by the then new federal legislation. The photo sheds some light on what and where Derouin's duties were, a few years before he retired from the Force in 1995. But it's also confirmation of what his troop mates remember about Derouin when they first met him on the parade grounds of RCMP "Depot" Division, on the cool early morning of June 10, 1966.

"He had a thick mane of almost black hair that just about gave him that 'Elvis' look," wrote his friends recently, as they reviewed their memories for details that conveyed the spirit of Derouin, who died in July 2007. "His greatest shock during training may have come from the haircut we all had to endure. Mind you, even if the locks had to be shorn, Rod—who was ever resourceful— had gainfully employed a fellow troop mate to 'lower his ears' on

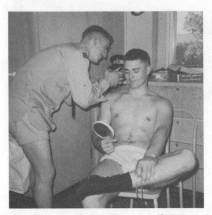

Ron Keeping saves Rod Derouin from paying the "Depot" barber for a haircut.

a frequent basis, thereby saving his hard-earned money for more important things."

In their mind's eye, Rodney Reginald James Derouin possessed great inner strength and compassion, equalled by formidable physical strength and fortitude. He was a natural athlete, they say, who displayed that on the running track and with his prowess during inter-troop field competitions. His athleticism was a prominent feature of his character before his life at "Depot," too. An online record of the 1962–63 sports results from Hemer High School in northern Germany, a school attended by children of four Canadian Infantry Group Brigade members, shows one Rod Derouin repeatedly placing in the top three during the Olympic shot-put event.

For Derouin, top physical conditioning and "a willingness to oppose criminals with greater size and/or strength" was essential to his surviving an encounter early in his career, according to troop mate and detachment colleague, Rick Saville. Saville and a co-worker had just finished their shift at Nanaimo Town Station and returned to the rented accommodation they shared with Derouin and another unmarried member. Before they could change out of their uniforms, they were called to a break-and-enter in progress at a warehouse where Derouin and his RCMP partner, Terry, had been dispatched earlier.

The two off-duty members responded and found Terry covered in blood, standing with his gun pointed at a prisoner on the floor. Derouin was fighting a larger man some distance away.

After Saville helped bring the larger man into custody, he learned that the larger man had tried to stab Terry in the head with a chisel but hit him in the back of the neck instead.

Although Terry was seriously injured, he was able to take the smaller man into custody while Derouin fought with the chisel-wielding perpetrator. Derouin could have easily been killed, says Saville. Instead, the violent criminal was held at bay and subsequently received 14 years for assault of a police officer. Derouin was always willing and able to take on the difficult arrests, says Saville. "He was a policeman through and through, devoted to law enforcement no matter the personal cost or exposure. He had your back—always."

Derouin also had a gentle and caring side. "When one of our troop mates, Dave Mate, had to leave the troop for medical reasons, Rod volunteered to express C Troop's profound regret at his leaving," write his friends. "It was especially sad in that Dave Mate only had three weeks until graduation. Rod gave him a rousing speech and reinforced to Dave that he would always be considered and remembered as a fully served member of our C Troop. He then gave Dave a memorial RCMP-crested plaque on his last day with the Force. Rod's tribute of fellowship brought tears to many of us who felt part of Dave's sadness. Others bravely smiled, although their hearts were shaken. Rod's humanity and caring showed, and he hoped that Dave would always feel that a part of him never left the RCMP."

As a young constable, Derouin was assigned to several detachments throughout British Columbia's Lower Mainland. In Vancouver, his duties included VIP protection, and so he provided security for Prime Minister Pierre Elliott Trudeau when he visited the city. Later, stationed at the University of British Columbia Detachment as a Corporal during the late 1970s, he

Rod Derouin (left) providing security for Prime Minister Pierre E. Trudeau, North Vancouver.

was involved in addressing campus thefts that, by some unofficial accounts, amounted to close to $100,000. He was then deployed to the detachment in Squamish, where his duties ran the gamut of expected and unexpected events in a small but bustling logging community and resort region—petty crime, sexual assaults, highway incidents, clashes between loggers and environmentalists, and murdered bodies discovered in nearby bush or provincial parks.

There were also small-town tussles that included the RCMP briefly pulling out of a high school graduation event in protest of a dry grad weekend that wasn't really dry, and a memorable break-in representative of all the dumbest criminals, everywhere. That one involved two young thieves who robbed the residence of an RCMP officer while the detachment's Christmas party was taking place. Not content to simply grab cash and electronics, they also stole the member's RCMP uniform, which they scattered in pieces along their getaway trail. Since those details were mentioned in Derouin's report to the press when the thieves were apprehended, it's safe to assume these "clues" played some role in tracking down the perpetrators.

Derouin was married twice. His second marriage to Lorraine and his deep affection for his three stepchildren was lovingly recounted by his stepdaughter, Danielle Linfitt, who eulogized him when she addressed the members of C Troop during its 50-year reunion at "Depot" in Regina, in June 2016. "If we are being technical, being my mother's husband made Rod my stepfather —although to me he was always so much more than that," she said. "I was a teenager when Rod entered my life. I already had a biological father who was very involved in my life, as well as a previous stepfather figure. Rod never tried to step in, in any way.

Rod Derouin and his wife, Lorraine.

He simply entered my life as someone who genuinely loved my mother and wanted to be a part of everything she loved and lived for—her children. He quickly became a loved, honoured and respected member of our family. Rod led by example; he gained my love by loving me and gained my respect by respecting me. Although I only knew him for a decade, Rod made an enormous impact on my life. Ironically, he taught me more than any other person, without ever once preaching or notably trying to teach me a thing. He taught me how to express emotions; he taught me how to communicate; he taught me how to forgive (but not necessarily forget); and, most of all, he taught me to be passionate. Rod showed me that true love is real and that it is always worth fighting for never, ever let it go. He was a very rational, intelligent man, but in the end, he let his heart guide him."

In 2006, Linfitt made her first trip to Regina for her brother Brian's graduation from the RCMP. "It was an emotional flight for me," she said. "On the one hand, I was really excited to see Brian since I hadn't seen him in several months; but then again, I was also heartbroken that Rod could not attend. He was far too sick by that time and only arose from bed every second day to go to the hospital for dialysis. Rod was enormously proud of Brian and would have done anything to have been there. He began many great stories with 'When I was a young Constable...' or 'When I was a Mountie...' and 'In the Force...' Back then, I never expected the RCMP to become such a huge part of my own life."

During Brian's graduation, she met her brother's troop mate and good friend, Mike Linfitt. The two hit it off and later married. "I think the majority of my family and friends thought I was pretty crazy for picking up and leaving my life in Vancouver, BC, to move to Onion Lake, Saskatchewan, to be with Mike just a few months after we met. Some probably even placed bets on how soon I'd be back, but not Rod. He knew me well and encouraged me to follow my heart. So here I am today, a part of the RCMP family for the past decade, several posts later, with many of my own stories to tell. I cannot even count how many times I have wanted to pick up the phone, call Rod, and be the storyteller."

In 1995, after 29 years with the RCMP, Derouin retired. Still in his early 50s, he wanted a new career. He began working in real estate and then delved into the management side of property management by starting Black Tusk Realty. In 2001, he and Lorraine opened Hometown Realty Property Management, which they ran together until 2005. He also pursued his other passions with endless energy and enthusiasm. He was an avid hunter and loved taking his fishing boat, *Lulu*, out for a day on the water with his son-in-law Andrew or best buddy Barry.

In 2005, Derouin started to feel "not OK." Hospital tests revealed he had severe kidney deterioration, which would never improve. He needed a kidney transplant and was put on a waiting list for a suitable donor. He started dialysis and tried to continue with his recreational pursuits. But his body finally gave out on July 24, 2007, at the age of 61.

Derouin was survived by his children from his first marriage, Christopher and Danica (Andrew); his second wife, Lorraine, his stepchildren Brian (Nicole), Danielle (Mike), and Mike. His grandchildren, Kailen, Dylan, and Riley, were very special to him. His sister Marlene (Eddie), and brothers David and Michael were also high on Derouin's I-like-you-a-lot list.

His troop mates write that they still tightly hold memories of his spirit, and especially his enthusiasm, dedication and compassion. "To us, he continues to 'have our back.'"

—*Helen Metella*

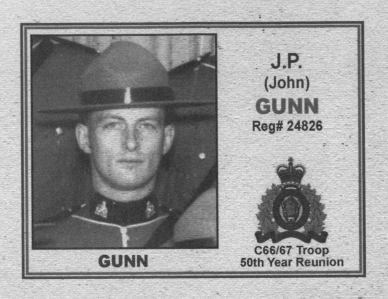

J.P.
(John)
GUNN
Reg# 24826

C66/67 Troop
50th Year Reunion

GUNN

JEAN (JOHN) GUNN joined the RCMP on June 8, 1966. He was born in 1942, and had two brothers and two sisters. His parents, Aline Barnabe and James Gunn, were very proud of him and of his career choice. He was affectionately called "Ti-Jean" ("Little John") by his mom, but was known to his troop mates as John. His desire to give back to his country was inspired by his deeply rooted pride and respect for his uncle, Corporal Bernard Barnabe, who was killed in action in Sicily during World War II. This led Gunn directly to "Depot" Division in Regina, Saskatchewan, which was a huge change from the forested region of Quebec where he grew up. Like the rest of his newly formed C Troop, Gunn was in awe of the regimentation of the RCMP—a paramilitary force created to enforce civilian laws and protect Canada's citizens from criminal activity.

Gunn was always a stylish and neat dresser. Spotless in his attention to his kit and dress, Gunn taught many troop mates the skill of tying a single or double Windsor knot for the uniform tie. One such pupil was Jerry Forst, who relates that Gunn had infinite patience and repeatedly mentored Jerry's attempts to master this art. As appearances were everything during training, it was imperative that ties were freshly tied every day—reusing the same knot repeatedly ensured wrinkles and over time led to a shortening of the visible part of the tie. This, of course, would attract attention from instructors and surely gain a verbal blast and extra duties or push-ups—if you were lucky. Shirts, pants, and gym shorts with pressed creases hung in precise order in his wardrobe closet, and he spent long hours polishing his high browns, holster, and belt. Everything had to be perfect, and this desire for perfection fit well with Gunn's personality of looking his best. But Gunn found a whole new meaning to the words "turned out."

The following story was related by Ernie Brydon, a former member of the RCMP who was stationed in Vancouver "E" Division in the Commercial Crime Unit. He had occasion to meet Gunn over a common file. At the time, Gunn was a member of the Commercial Crime Unit stationed in Montreal "C" Division.

To further the investigation, both Brydon and Gunn were sent to England to co-ordinate with Scotland Yard. It was Gunn's first trip to the United Kingdom, but Brydon had been born in England and had visited Scotland previously, so he became the designated guide for London sights and experiences. Brydon recalls relating the merits of Harrods, an internationally famous department store, well known for its high end merchandise and the famous line that you could buy anything there, including an elephant. It was lunch time and Brydon insisted that they dine in one of Harrods's many cafés. According to Brydon, dining at the café would permit them to enjoy an affordable portion of the "high-end life." The image was enhanced by the servers garbed in tuxedos and bearing themselves with a lofty air. "We felt like part of the elite for the moment. Servers were flying all over the place with trays etc., when suddenly one with a silver tray full of liquors in shot glasses, perhaps 20 plus, came whizzing past our table and tripped on the back of Jean's chair. All the shot glasses went flying ... all over Jean's hair, head, tweed sports jacket and pants. What a sight. I could not contain myself and let out a laugh ... Jean did not. He was in slight shock for a moment. The server was aghast!"

As previously noted, Gunn was a meticulous dresser. He was immediately swarmed by Harrods employees, including the manager, full of apologies. They ushered him into a private room with a washroom, where he disrobed while his clothing was taken away for cleaning. Meanwhile, Gunn was given a Harrods bathrobe to wear and was set up at a café table, provided with a menu and served lunch. "We had arrived, we were royalty!!" His freshly laundered clothing arrived within the hour, and the experience provided a few laughs but no bill. Harrods absorbed all the cleaning and lunch expenses. The one remaining mystery was the fate of the server.

Gunn was also a prankster. His sister Marguerite relates a story about how she and a cousin painted the kitchen in their parents' house while their parents were out. It was meant to be a pleasant surprise. For reasons which shall remain unknown, Gunn repainted the kitchen in a hideous colour sometime during the night. His sister and cousin were furious, and his parents were appalled. Gunn kept the rationale for his exploit completely to himself.

Marguerite reports that Gunn cared deeply for his parents and his siblings, providing unrestricted support during times of stress and need. This is the man we knew in training. He came from Quebec and spoke fluent French, but had a good command of

English and frequently helped his French-speaking troop mates. At the time, all RCMP instruction was conducted in English, and the French-speaking members were at a severe disadvantage. Gunn's skills were invaluable in helping the unilingual French-speaking members overcome this challenge. It is worth noting that two of the French-speaking members of C Troop climbed to officer ranks within the RCMP. Without Gunn's help during training, Canada may not have benefited from the skills and insight these members contributed.

Gunn was tasked with being in Red Serge during Canada's Expo 67. His presence there was recorded in a photo of him talking to a youngster that appeared in a French Catholic review entitled *Le Precurseur* in January 1968. Of course, he carried out all sorts of duties while in "C" Division, from ceremonial uniform presence to plainclothes investigations. Little is known

Jean Gunn (left, speaking to child) at Expo 67 in Montreal

about the details of his duties, however, as he kept to himself and was quiet and reserved. He preferred to focus on the job at hand without seeking fanfare or acknowledgment. In training, he saw his duty and did it well. Whether it was discomfort at expressing his feelings in English or whether he had nothing to say, we'll never know. He was quiet and did not share his experiences.

The *Ottawa Citizen* published the following obituary on May 25, 2002:

GUNN, Ti-Jean (John) 1942–2002. Died in Montreal, April 2002. Cherished son of the late Aline Barnabe and the late James Gunn. Dear brother of Jacques (Renée Gervais), Marguerite, Gerald and Patricia Lee. Uncle to Michael, Sylvie, Richard, Steven, Daniel, Louise, Kristin and Ryan. Also remembered by Francine Gunn. Family and friends may attend a Memorial Mass on Saturday, June 1st at 11:00 a.m. at Église St. Joseph, 245 St. Joseph Blvd., Hull in the presence of his ashes. Those desiring may make memorial donations to the Canadian Cancer Society.

We miss you, John. We will not forget you.

—*Members of* RCMP *C Troop* 66–67

MIKE HAMPEL WASN'T given to outbursts of emotion—not as a member of the RCMP and not as a youth before he joined the Force, either. His early life experiences trained him to be stoic.

Hampel grew up on a farm outside the small town of Cobden, ON, located on the Trans-Canada Highway about an hour's drive west of Ottawa and half an hour south of Pembroke. His father died young, leaving his mother with six children to raise, the youngest just a year old. "He was the eldest and left high school at 16 to help support his family," says his widow, Leona, who believes Hampel wasn't all that fond of working with farm animals, much preferring machinery. Instead, "he found work at a local feed mill and then moved on to work in the Inco nickel mine in Sudbury. This was not something he wanted to do for the rest of his life. However, at the time he felt family obligations came first."

By the end of his teenage years, Hampel had decided he wanted to go into policing and approached several forces. His first application to the RCMP ended in disappointment for the young man—the routine medical revealed that he was colour blind, something Hampel had been unaware was the case. However, luck—or perhaps a need for recruits—caused the RCMP to call him back and decide that his type of colour blindness would not impede him, so he became a member of C Troop.

Mike Hampel, "Depot," Regina, 1966.

At the RCMP Academy "Depot" Division in Regina, Hampel was known as a fine athlete, funny and fun-loving, but with a strong work ethic. As his C Troop pals remember, he wasn't willing to tolerate a lollygagger. "He insisted that things be done right, like the time he had a disagreement with a fellow troop mate who was not living up to expectations and had become a problem for the entire troop," recalls Hampel's friend, Jerry Forst. "He [the errant colleague] was always pushing the limits, just to tick us off. About three-quarters of the way through training, an Inspector was coming through our barracks. Now, if you don't pass inspection, the whole troop stays in for the weekend. So just as the doors opened, this guy said something to taunt Mike. Mike turned and abruptly knocked him to the floor, sending his bed into the walkway and knocking his holster and other equipment to the floor, too. The Inspector must have known this guy was a shit-disturber. As he walked past the upturned bed, he said, 'It looks like C Troop had a problem within its ranks, but it appears that the troop straightened the matter out themselves.' Then the officer continued to pass without missing a step. Those were the days," laughs Forst. "Today you'd be hauled in for assault."

While the athletic Hampel excelled at the physical requirements of police work and worked hard at the other required
studies, his nose wasn't always pressed to the grindstone. During
training, his friend Forst's parents visited Regina and stayed at
the Westward Inn. When Hampel and Forst visited them, Forst's
mother introduced them to two young ladies who were staying
at the hotel because they were on tour with the Ice Capades. The
two RCMP members had a final first aid exam scheduled for the
next morning, and had planned to go back to the barracks and
study. Instead, they took the two skaters on a date and returned to
barracks late. The next morning, they both failed the final exam.
They had to complete the work and earn their certificates when
they reported to their first detachment.

Hampel's sense of fun was recorded for posterity when another troop mate, John Turnell, asked him to be a member of his
wedding party. The policemen in the wedding party were dressed
formally in Red Serge, and when the wedding party was being

John and Jane Turnell's wedding party. Fellow C Troop member Mike Hampel
(far right) was honoured to be part of the Turnells' special day.

photographed, the bride's sister had a very serious look on her face. Hampel decided she needed to smile, however, and pinched her as the photo was snapped. All who've seen it agree that her smile is big.

After graduation, Hampel began work at "K" Division in Edmonton, where he met Leona, who was working in the administration department at the old RCMP Headquarters there. "We met while he was setting up tables and chairs for a function in the old gymnasium," she says. The two were married in 1970 and had two children together, Jason and Michelle. While they were dating, however, Hampel worked at several detachments, including St. Albert, a bedroom community outside of Edmonton.

"After training, buying a car was one of Mike's first priorities, and he purchased an old Volkswagen," says Leona, who was able to observe Hampel's particular mix of "goofball who was also a serious law enforcement officer" while he was behind the wheel of said vehicle. "He came to pick me up one day at my parents' home, and drove right up the sidewalk to the front door! My father was watching out the front window, looking none too pleased. Later that evening, he spotted a car going through a red light. Being a gung-ho, fairly new recruit, he decided to go after him and get the licence plate number. He reported the incident and the case went to court. We were called in as witnesses, and I went into panic mode when asked what direction the car was moving. Being nervous, I couldn't remember, but ultimately the driver was convicted."

Not all his early duties were discharged so smoothly. On patrol one night, Hampel spotted a heavily inebriated woman walking along a country road. Stopping to speak to her, he realized that she was on the verge of being sick. Like all new recruits, he'd been schooled to never put an intoxicated person into a warm car unless you wanted disastrous results. So he handcuffed her to the back door handle while he rolled the windows down and turned off the car's heat. Then he radioed the detachment, telling them he was bringing her in. Alas, when he went to unlock her from the door handle, he discovered that he had somehow lost his handcuff key. That required an embarrassing call to the detachment to send another member out to free the prisoner.

While the Hampels were raising their children, Leona stayed at home and did not return to work until 1989. However, she certainly contributed significant support to her RCMP spouse, who was transferred two separate times to Fort McMurray. "Living so far north was very different," she says. "Highway 63 was mainly a gravel road, no shoulders and with few pay phones along the way in case of an emergency. Cell phones didn't exist then. I was only able to visit my parents once or twice a year in those early days, and Mike did not often see his family. There were regular power outages that lasted for several hours. I remember on one occasion, in mid-winter, just after Mike left for work, the power went off for eight hours. Within a short period of time, the house was so cold that the kids and I spent the rest of the day huddled underneath piles of quilts and blankets. I read them lots of stories, sang songs and invented new games, as it was hard to keep them entertained. No TV in the bedroom in those days! Eventually power was hooked up to one of the plants and re-directed into town. Being very young, our children have no memory of this, but I do."

Just as Leona tolerated the decidedly unglamorous life without complaint, Hampel didn't confide much about the experiences he or fellow members encountered while on shift, says Leona. "If anything of interest happened to him or others, I might hear about it second-hand. Only rarely did he talk about situations that involved him. On his first posting to Fort McMurray, he did tell me that one of his first calls was to dispose of several wild dogs that were causing havoc for local residents. There were several children looking on and he was hard-pressed to distract them while doing this discreetly."

Other family members also had occasion to play a supporting role in this RCMP's officer's work. During his second transfer to Fort McMurray, Hampel had the opportunity to hire a temporary matron for several months. Matrons were civilian females who could be called upon to be present for propriety whenever officers were interacting with a female prisoner. Hampel asked his mother to apply, since she did not visit Alberta often and it would allow them to spend more time together. "Right after she accepted, we lost our home and contents to a fire," says Leona. "Friends took us in for several days, but it was a trying time having to reorganize our lives. Housing was almost non-existent for rent or purchase. In the end we managed to temporarily rent a small trailer that accommodated all of us, including his mom!"

Highway Patrol was a duty Hampel really enjoyed, says Leona. He appreciated the relative quiet of the shifts and the opportunity to ride a motorcycle on patrol. In Fort McMurray, Highway Patrol included the use of aircraft to monitor Highway 63. "He always liked anything to do with planes and enjoyed having the opportunity to be airborne with the pilot for several hours."

For many years, sports occupied much of Hampel's free time. He played, coached and refereed hockey and basketball, and umpired softball. He also coached in the minor leagues, and was particularly happy when his Junior "B" Men's softball team won the Alberta provincial championships. He also retained the physical evidence of having been a jock while still a young RCMP member. While stationed in St. Albert, Hampel played goalie on the detachment's hockey team against an aggressive team from the Edmonton City Police force. During one game, Hampel took a puck in the mouth that knocked out his four front teeth, requiring a series of bridges for the rest of his life.

Hampel resigned from the RCMP in 1976. One of his favourite post-policing positions was as a transport instructor for Keyano College in

Mike and Leona Hampel were married for 39 years. Mike passed away on January 20, 2009.

Fort McMurray. He also worked with Diversified Transport.

Hampel had quintuple bypass surgery in 2006, and died at age 62 in 2009. He was on his daily afternoon walk and had stopped to buy a cup of coffee when he had a heart attack just before heading home. At the time, he and Leona were making future plans to retire. Instead, she retired in 2011 from the provincial government and moved back to St. Albert where her daughter also lives. Their son resides in Calgary.

Forst's and Hampel's families kept in touch throughout the years. At one such meeting, about a year before Hampel died, Hampel broached the topic of Forst's battle with PTSD and asked if he could pray for him. "This deeply touched me," says Forst. "No other policemen or friend had ever prayed for me and my family, and Mike told me he had been praying for me and my family for a long while." Forst subsequently delivered the eulogy at Hampel's funeral in January 2009. "The church was packed and many shared stories about Mike's compassion, and of course, about his humour," says Forst. "He's missed but not forgotten."

—*Helen Metella*

D.J.
(Dave)
MATE
Reg# 24843

MATE

C66/67 Troop
50th Year Reunion

SOME OF C Troop's memories are so agonizingly sad that the police officers to whom they happened don't want to preserve them in print. But the troop emphatically does want to respect with a tribute the poignant story of Dave Mate, a bona fide Constable who was never an active member of the Force after training.

"Ever since he was a young child, his ambition was to become a Mountie," says his older brother Malcolm. In the eyes of C Troop, Mate achieved that goal.

Mate grew up in Burnaby, BC, the third of four brothers. After high school, he worked as a yard switchman with the Burlington Northern Railroad, based in New Westminster, a suburb of Vancouver. At the same time, he was also a member of the Seaforth Highlanders of Canada, a Primary Reserve of the Canadian Armed Forces, where he rose to the rank of Corporal. Primary Reserve members train to the level of their Regular Force counterparts and are interchangeable with them when called upon to serve. At one time, says Malcolm, all four brothers proudly served together in the Seaforth, and were known as Mate Mark 1, Mark 2, Mark 3 and Mark 4.

When Dave Mate was accepted into the RCMP, he resigned from the railroad and also received a discharge from the Seaforths. For more than five months, Mate toiled alongside his RCMP classmates, a sworn-in Constable from the moment he signed up for training, as were all trainees of that time. He was no doubt as bewildered and overwhelmed by some of the demands at RCMP Training Academy "Depot" as the others, but likely more familiar with a military-style program, given his experience in the Seaforths.

What Mate could not have expected, however, was the shock delivered to him by RCMP medical staff just three weeks before graduation. He was being discharged from the Force because he'd been diagnosed with fallen arches (flat feet). The condition had been so painful during physical training that Mate's troop mates observed him subtly lifting one foot and then the other when they were supposed to be standing at attention. RCMP administration considered it was a sufficiently debilitating ailment that Mate would not be able to carry out future policing duties. "Everybody was just sick about this," says troop mate Jerry Forst. "Everybody loved him."

Rod Derouin delivered a heartfelt farewell speech as the troop bid Mate goodbye, assuring him that he would always be remembered as a fully served member. Thirty years later, when C Troop members were filling out a pre-reunion questionnaire that asked about their toughest moments while in training, virtually everyone mentioned two things: Ron Keeping's mother dying in Newfoundland while he was at "Depot," too far away to return for the funeral, and Dave Mate being discharged so close to graduation.

Rod Derouin presents an RCMP plaque on behalf of C Troop to Dave Mate. Dave was told by his troop mates that he would always be a member of C Troop.

Helen and Dave, with sons Christopher and Michael.

Mate returned home to Burnaby, BC, where he was rehired as a switchman with Burlington Northern Railroad. While living with his brother Malcolm, he met Helen, the woman who soon became his wife. They became parents to Michael in 1975, and Christopher in 1977. Both Mate and Helen were active volunteers with their church, with Mate also coaching sports at the school. Mate progressed at his job, becoming a locomotive engineer in the Vancouver yard of the railroad.

In 1996, when active and former C Troop members began planning for their first reunion, Forst began searching for those with whom the troop had lost touch, including Mate. That's when a second shock thundered through their ranks. "I determined through record checks the story of Dave and his family visiting 'Depot,' and then being killed by an impaired driver about 10 years prior to our 30-year reunion," says Forst.

Still proud of his service at "Depot," some 20 years after leaving, Mate and his family had made a stop there during their summer vacation in June 1985. The family then continued its road trip, en route to his brother Malcolm's cottage near Winnipeg. "David and Helen had never taken a full four-week vacation before and were almost as excited as the boys were," wrote Malcolm in a tribute.

On June 29, 1985, three kilometres west of Brandon, MB, on Highway 1A, their car was involved in a head-on collision with a vehicle travelling approximately 120 KPH. Mate, 38, and Helen, 37, were killed instantly, as was a 16-year-old female passenger in the other vehicle. Mate's two boys, aged nine and seven, were transported to hospital, where they later died.

According to retired RCMP officer Gerry Poole, the accident reconstructionist for Brandon Subdivision who investigated the accident, the only survivor was a 25-year-old male. He had been drinking heavily for several hours and had picked up the teenage girl on the highway just outside of Brandon.

As that man's car was travelling westbound, its right wheel caught the gravel shoulder and he veered into oncoming traffic. The impact with the Mate family's car was so severe, it was pushed 17 metres back west, while the westbound car burst into flames. Adding more pain to the tragedy, the male survivor contended that the young girl had been driving. Investigators proved otherwise by examining the accelerator pedal and the right running shoe of the young man. "Under a microscope, striation marks of the accelerator could be seen on the bottom of the footwear that had been seized," says Poole. "This was evidence that placed him as the driver, and he was convicted of the Criminal Code offences using this evidence."

At his trial, the driver showed little remorse, and in 2020, Poole reported that it is greatly upsetting to recall the event himself.

The Mate family agreed to the publication of the accident photos in this book not only as a memorial to Dave, Helen, Christopher and Michael, but also to show the lifetime impact on both the families of the victims of drunk drivers and on the RCMP officers who investigate and respond to accident scenes. They want to emphasize the ongoing effects of impaired drivers on society.

In August 2018, Mothers Against Drunk Driving (MADD) added the names of the Mate family to a memorial that honours victims of drunk drivers in Manitoba, located in Glen Eden Funeral Home and Cemetery in West St. Paul, north of Winnipeg.

The MADD Memorial in Winnipeg, Manitoba.

"On behalf of Dave's brother Larry, and his family in Port Coquitlam, BC, I would like to thank you and all of the class members of RCMP C Troop for remembering David and his family," says Malcolm. "They are missed."

—*Helen Metella*

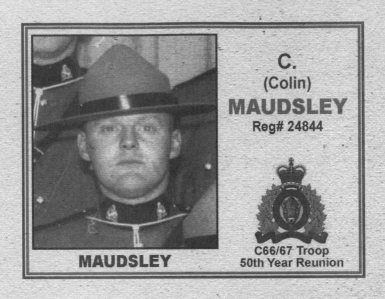

C.
(Colin)
MAUDSLEY
Reg# 24844

C66/67 Troop
50th Year Reunion

MAUDSLEY

COLIN MAUDSLEY'S ADULT life was brief, and he spent roughly a third of it as a member of the RCMP. He was born in Lancaster, England, in 1942, in the middle of World War II, the only child of Reginald and Joan Maudsley. Lancaster sits in the northwest corner of England, where the Lune River empties into Morecambe Bay of the North Atlantic. Even though the city had an airfield that was a target of the Luftwaffe and was close to the U-boat runs, it never experienced the Germans' Blitz bombing campaign of 1940 to 1941 that felled London and other British cities. Nonetheless, Maudsley's family immigrated to Canada in 1957. They settled first in Red Deer, AB, and then moved to nearby Stettler, 80 miles east in central Alberta. It must have been a culture shock to be living in a rather dry and rural setting after growing up by the ocean in a small city that boasted a castle built on Roman ruins, museums and coastal views.

The family had come to Canada because it was a land of opportunity and part of that dream was realized for them when

Maudsley's parents opened a bakery in Stettler. Joan ran the bakery while Reginald, a craftsman, did odd jobs around the community while assisting with the baking. They operated it until 1966, the year their son joined the RCMP.

Maudsley was 24 by the time he joined C Troop, making him about four years older than the average recruit. Between the ages of 18 and 23 he had returned to England, likely seeking the type of work he wanted to pursue as a lifelong career. "Remembering some of the stories he told brings you to a scene out of *Coronation Street*, where the darts and the pints were all part of a normal day's end," says troop mate Jack Snoeks.

As for Maudsley himself, "I remember an infectious grin, a cheery British accent, and a cigarette constantly in hand," says Ross Mortlock, another troop mate. "He was larger than life, both in stature and personality," says Snoeks. "He was about 6'1" and heavy-chested with carrot-red hair and rosy red cheeks to go with it all. He had a joyful personality with a quick wit, an even quicker, almost omnipresent, smile, and that thick British accent that almost cried for subtitles. His natural, unbound personality won over everyone he met." Maudsley was fond of beer and with the other, older trainees, spent time enjoying 25¢ pints at Regina's Red Lion when off duty, with members of the troop who were over 21.

He had driven to "Depot" in a 1965 Oldsmobile, a rather swanky ride in 1966, since its manufacturer's suggested list price was about four times that of a Volkswagen Beetle at the time. A Beetle did, however, accompany Maudsley. It was driven by Jerry Forst, who had joined the RCMP in Edmonton, as had Maudsley. A third new RCMP member, John Turnell, had also signed on to the RCMP there, and split his time riding with Maudsley and Forst.

Colin Maudsley and troop mates at the "Depot" parade square, October 1, 1966. Front row, left to right: Bill Pertson and Michel Laverdière. Back row, left to right: Peter Albertson, Bob Bossence, Ernie Otway and Colin Maudsley.

Arriving in Regina, Turnell recalls the trio heading to a restaurant before reporting to "Depot," and being greeted by shouts of "skinheads," which they would later learn was the derogatory nickname given to recruits by some of the local youth. It had long been hung on those training at "Depot," says Snoeks, because the recruits were new prospects for Regina's young female population and thus competition. The short haircuts they'd had before setting off to "Depot" made them standouts in the "hairy '60s." Shortly afterward, the three travellers also learned that it was hardly an accurate taunt. Skinhead was a much more apt description once they visited the RCMP barbers.

In training, Maudsley was always "one of the boys," says Snoeks. "He fit in well and pulled his weight. He felt at ease in both the gym and the pool. In his quiet hours, though, he was a rather private person and loved to read and do word games and crossword puzzles." Snoeks thinks that his worldliness, compared to the younger troop members, contributed to his impressive stature among them.

After training, Maudsley's RCMP service took him to locations throughout BC. His first posting was to Burnaby Detachment. Although it was new territory for him, he wasn't alone, as he had fellow C Troop member Derk Doornbos with him for the drive to the Lower Mainland. Patrolling the streets of Burnaby, Maudsley was both a well-liked and respected member, says Doornbos. "Colin had the ability, through not only his burly presence, but more importantly his huge smile and contagious laugh, to disarm anyone looking for a confrontation. That British accent often helped to confuse and set ruffians aback."

Fellow Burnaby RCMP member Wayne Symes also recalls Maudsley's considerate nature. A week before he was to be married, Symes was rocked to learn that he was being transferred immediately to Tahsis, a tiny and remote fly-in community west of Campbell River on Vancouver Island. Learning of his colleague's distress, Maudsley stepped in and said that because he was a single man, he would gladly go in Symes's place. Maudsley was transferred to Tahsis the

Colin Maudsley always had a smile on his face and a joke to tell.

345

next day. That team-spirited favour is one that Symes and his wife, Mimi, have never forgotten.

Years later, while visiting with Forst and his wife, Ruth, Maudsley regaled them with a misadventure he'd had shortly after arriving at Tahsis. Recalls Forst: "He had responded to a call about a party on an ocean beach, and when he arrived he decided to drive and park the police vehicle down at the party on the beach. All went well in reaching the party. However, when he was leaving, the tide had worked its way up the shore and he got the police vehicle stuck in the wet sand. Once it was stuck and with all possible help closed for the night, Colin said that was the last time anyone drove that police vehicle."

After 10 years and multiple transfers, Maudsley decided to leave the Force. In 1976, he chose Burnaby as his new home base and went into the trucking industry. His RCMP friends lost touch with him. None of them knew that he had been diagnosed with cancer in his early 40s. He returned to Stettler to be comforted by his parents until he died in August 1988. Just 46, he predeceased both of his parents. A funeral service for Maudsley was held at St. George's Anglican Church in Stettler.

After C Troop learned of his death, the members proudly included him in a memorial service held during their 30-year reunion in 1996, at the RCMP Chapel in Regina. He was remembered again at their 50-year reunion, also in Regina, and if there is another reunion in the future, his name will be invoked once more. "He will always be part of those 32 'skinheads' who fast-marched through the streets of 'Depot,'" says Snoeks. "Those who are left behind salute you and your memory."

—*Helen Metella*

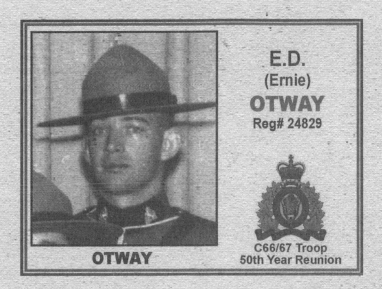

E.D.
(Ernie)
OTWAY
Reg# 24829

C66/67 Troop
50th Year Reunion

OTWAY

IT MADE SENSE that Ernie Otway wanted to join the RCMP at age 21. By then, he already held many of the high-calibre qualities needed to be a man of the uniform. The youngest of six brothers, he had been an atypically disciplined teenager growing up in Port Coquitlam, BC, where his family moved from Thunder Bay, ON, when he was three years old. Keen to show his integrity, he enrolled in a seminary school at age 14, and for a time considered joining the priesthood.

"He was such a precious soul," says his daughter, Samantha, who enjoyed a close bond with her father. "His patience and kindness always shone through whatever he did."

At 16, Otway joined the Royal Canadian Navy Reserve to expand his dedication to discipline, and said he thoroughly enjoyed the experience. However, long influenced by a neighbour who was the Sergeant in Charge of the Port Coquitlam Detachment, he chose the RCMP as a profession, instead.

Ernie Otway, "Depot," Regina, 1966.

"Training was an enjoyable experience," he wrote in 1996, prior to C Troop's thirtieth reunion. "I was used to barrack life and regimentation. The friendships that were made were great and will last ... a lifetime. The worst part was having to say goodbye to Constable Dave Mate and him not being able to be part of the Passout."

At the time Otway graduated, RCMP policy dictated that a new officer could not be posted within his home province, so he chose to go to detachments in Alberta so he could remain as geographically close to his brothers and parents as possible. His first deployment was to Mayerthorpe, followed by a move to Fort McMurray

Georgia, Samantha, and Ernie Otway.

Town Detail in 1968, and Fort McMurray Detachment in 1970. In Fort McMurray, he met the love of his life, Georgia Martin. They married in December 1970, and she joined him in his new detachment in Edson. Their first child, daughter Samantha, was born the following September.

By then, Otway was working in Edmonton for "K" Division, General Investigation Section. He completed several undercover operations while there, including two that took him to Kamloops and Whitehorse. The travel attached to his policing job meant that when his son, Douglas, was born, Otway was actually several provinces away from the Sundre Detachment where he'd been put in charge in 1976. "I was in Toronto, attending a robbery trial," he wrote. "They guaranteed me I would only be there a couple of days. One week and one addition to the family later, I was allowed to come home."

Yet Otway enjoyed and excelled at his work, becoming a leader and mentor to many. "He always said he worked *with* people, not that they worked *for* him," says Samantha. His friend and fellow RCMP member Bill Larocque remembers visiting him and noting, "It was obvious he was sure respected by not only the staff but the citizens of Sundre."

Doug discovered just how revered his father was when he moved back to Fort McMurray in 1999, looking for work in the oil patch and temporarily dealing cards at a casino. Striking up a conversation with one of the casino volunteers, Doug mentioned that his father had been with the RCMP in Fort McMurray. "The volunteer—I forget his name and that's the big difference between me and Ernie; even now, I am sure Dad would have remembered his name—tells me he used to be an auxiliary member. He asks me what my father's name was. I tell him. The man's face changed. An instant look of respect and reverence."

The casino volunteer said he had been an auxiliary member of the RCMP for years, both before and after Otway arrived. He'd worked alongside and had respected many RCMP members. But Otway stood out, because he never distinguished between volunteer auxiliary and actual members of the Force, the way virtually everyone else did. "Didn't matter how or why you put that uniform on, if you put it on, you were one of his guys and he treated you as such," the man said. "He was just such a great leader and great man ... Your dad made doing the job, even as a volunteer, that much more rewarding."

Says Doug: "Parents always like to tell the stories when they are sitting somewhere and their children do that one thing that makes them beam with pride. On that day, as a child, I experienced that feeling in regards to my father. It just confirmed in my mind what I had always known ... how lucky I was to have him as a father, and how lucky the RCMP were to have had him within their ranks."

During Otway's posting in Sundre from 1976 to 1978, he was a 30-year-old Constable in Charge of four very young rookies. One of them, now-retired RCMP member Brent Sanderson, vividly recalls how Otway taught him that the job demands both gentleness and toughness. The first lesson occurred during the rookie's very first call to a sudden death.

"The man had been in a trailer for more than three weeks, with the furnace blasting full heat. Your dad was on the scene and radioed in to wake me up and come out to assist. He told me to pick up some of his Colts cigars and Vicks VapoRub. I went to the scene, and Ernie prepared me for the worst, assuring me it was OK for me to refuse. But he needed me to go in and lift the body to the front door so we could body-bag the victim. The scene was horrific, the smell was overwhelming, and the body was partially decomposed. Job got done, we zippered the bag, and Ernie put his hand on my shoulder and said, 'You handled this well, good job.' I felt proud to have pleased a man I totally respected and as my career advanced, I thought back many times on what a positive influence he was on a young, naïve teenager."

Meanwhile, Otway taught by example when displaying the grit being an RCMP member also requires, says Sanderson. The case involved a speeding ticket and open liquor in a vehicle. "Two rig workers in the car I stopped wouldn't give me ID," he says. "I was writing the ticket, and they took off. I had their licence number and which rig they were on. But instead of chasing them, I went back to the office and wrote a long account of what happened on a night report. Ernie woke me a few hours later, as he couldn't sleep that night and had read the report. We drove to the rig and served the appearance notice in a very 'firm manner.' Ernie said to the accused, while kneeling on his chest, 'Don't ever disrespect one of my people, or I will visit again.' I was a bystander for this process, but learned that we had a duty to fulfill and that not every client was going to appreciate us."

In 1979, Otway was transferred back to Edmonton, where he became part of the Edmonton Integrated Intelligence Unit (EIIU), a joint city police and RCMP unit. In 1981, the EIIU investigated the first kidnapping of a child for ransom in the city's history. It became a three-day ordeal that was resolved without the public knowing that the youngster, the son of a CBC employee, had been snatched from the bathroom of a suburban elementary school. The kidnappers were low-level criminals who wanted $100,000 in ransom money to launch their own crew of drug dealers. "The boy, Kevin Alarie, was only six, and Ernie was a pivotal part of saving him, as he entered the house after much surveillance and saw the boy under the table, terrified," says Otway's EIIU colleague, Bert Goodrich, an Edmonton Police Service

Ernie Otway, operating undercover, Edmonton, Alberta.

detective. "Ernie bent down and said to the scared little boy, 'It's OK, we are the police, you are safe now,' and extended his arms as the boy ran into them. Ernie carried the boy out of the house and handed him over to the gentleman who worked for the EPS (Edmonton Police Service) as the EIIU had to remain a secret."

One of Otway's less glorious moments as an RCMP officer also occurred in Edmonton, and is described in cringe-worthy detail in retired RCMP member Chuck Tweedy's memoir, *Stories I Never Told My Mother*. During the fall of 1978, Tweedy writes, there was an epidemic of copper wire thefts from telecommunications storage facilities located in rural areas surrounding Edmonton. Thieves would unravel the valuable copper wire from the large wooden spools and sell it to scrap-metal dealers.

Tweedy and Otway were both members of the Edmonton GIS unit that had identified probable suspects. Late one afternoon, a source told them that the suspects were headed to an Alberta Government Telephone compound near Barrhead, northwest of the city. The team decided that two other members would hide in the bush with night-vision binoculars, observe the crime in progress, and radio Otway and Tweedy, waiting out of sight in a car, to apprehend the crooks once the job was completed. Writes Tweedy: "With our magnetic fireball light on the roof, we would pull out onto the highway in front of them and do the 'take down' with the others close by for backup."

As evening fell and the waiting dragged on, Otway and Tweedy consumed junk food in their car. Suddenly, their stakeout team members radioed that three male suspects had arrived in a pick-up truck. However it was not until midnight that the suspects made their way out. "Ernie was driving our unmarked car. I was in the passenger seat," writes Tweedy. "At just the right moment, Ernie snapped on the headlights and accelerated forward into the middle of the two-lane highway. At the same time, I jammed the fireball plug into the cigarette lighter. Then—damn! The fireball was still sitting on the dash in front of our face. During the long boring hours waiting for the excitement to begin, we had forgotten to put it on the roof. Well, they don't call those things a fireball for nothing! We were blinded by the dazzling red rotating beacon in our faces. Ernie grabbed it in a panic, and through his open window reached out and slapped it up onto the roof. With our eyeballs still seeing a red blur and potato chip crumbs falling from our shirts, we leaped out onto the road, drawing our side arms. Unfortunately, the fireball cord had been wrapped around Ernie's ankle. When he jumped out, the light was jerked off the roof and landed on the pavement with a clatter. At the same time, when he pulled out his snub-nose revolver, its clip-on belt holster came with it. When I jumped out, a partly full can of Coke that had been forgotten on the seat between my legs dumped its sticky contents all over the seat and my crotch. The now empty can rattled out onto the pavement.

"So try to picture this from the approaching suspect's perspective as he jammed on his brakes to avoid collision. Here is this car from out of nowhere blocking their way with a red flashing light on the dash. Then the rotating red beacon appears on the car's roof, and then falls sideways on the pavement shooting beams of red erratically in every direction. Now picture Ernie hopping around, trying to free himself of the cord around his foot while pointing a revolver still in its holster in the general direction of the suspects, and both of us staring into the truck's headlights, blinking madly, trying to restore our night vision. And an empty can of Coke spinning around on the road. This could have been a scene out of Leslie Nielsen's *Naked Gun* movie."

Fortunately the thieves didn't resist arrest, even though they were armed with a .22 calibre rifle. "They were probably in a total state of shock at the goofy display vividly illuminated in their headlights on the highway in front of them," says Tweedy. "I'm sure our comedy act was something they shared with fellow inmates for a long time."

Ernie Otway providing security for Prime Minister Pierre E. Trudeau, Edmonton, Alberta.

Edmonton was Otway's longest posting, from the late 1970s to the late 1980s, and it included several special security projects for visiting dignitaries. He helped guard the Queen Mother, many prime ministers, and the Pope. To blend in on the latter detail, he was dressed as a priest. "That was very touching for him, since he was Catholic and had once considered going into the priesthood," says troop mate Pete Albertson.

In 1987, he was transferred again to Fort McMurray City Detail, and then to Lethbridge in 1991. There, after 29 years of service, Otway retired from the RCMP as a Staff Sergeant, in January 1996. He continued to work part-time as a private investigator, for the Blood Tribe in Standoff, AB, for Parole Services, and even for a funeral home.

He also continued volunteering avidly with the Royal Canadian Legion, a commitment he'd begun early in his RCMP career. In 2003, the Legion posthumously presented Otway with the Legionnaire of the Year Award, noting that his background in

Ernie Otway (dark blazer) was a tireless worker for the Legion, and he was posthumously honoured with the Legion's Volunteer of the Year award in 2003.

the RCMP meant that he solved problems and persistently tracked down answers to questions so that they made sense.

The Legion also highlighted that the celebrations for the Queen Elizabeth II Golden Jubilee, which Otway chaired, was the largest, most outstanding tribute to the Queen in Alberta. Kimberly Lyall, a 26-year-old who worked with him on the committee, voiced special gratitude to Otway at the award ceremony. "He was a true leader, in that he sought out the talents and potential of the people around him, and inspired them to climb beyond their reach."

As a father and husband, Otway is remembered exactly as his RCMP and Legion colleagues recall him. "He was loving and affectionate," says Doug. "He always had time for anyone who called, and he helped so many that reached out for his help. You could not pull the wool over his eyes, as he was sharp and intuitive."

After surviving his first heart attack at age 44, Otway was, in his daughter Samantha's words, "a walking miracle for 13 more years." He was on a waiting list for a transplant when he died of a heart attack on September 13, 2002. In his honour, a scholarship was established at the Lethbridge Community College for students interested in pursuing a career in the criminal justice system, and a golf tournament was held for almost a decade to support it.

"Sadly, the world only got to have Ernie for 57 years," says his wife, Georgia. "He would be so proud of this book and so pleased to participate. His fellow C Troop comrades were very special to him."

—Helen Metella, Georgia, Samantha and Doug Otway

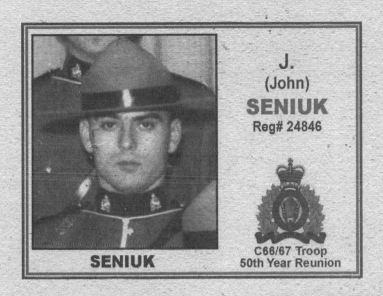

J.
(John)
SENIUK
Reg# 24846

C66/67 Troop
50th Year Reunion

SENIUK

WHEN HIS FUTURE wife, Elsie, met John Seniuk as a teenager, she believed him to be a fairly shy, quietly serious guy—possibly because it was hard to compete as the baby brother of an overtly gregarious male sibling who was six years older. After joining his fellow C Troop colleagues at the RCMP "Depot" Training Centre in Regina, however, "he just blossomed," says Elsie. "Getting to know so many personalities, there was something about when he spent that six months in training ... his personality just blossomed. It was just a different lifestyle to be with 31 other guys. It was such hard work, and sometimes gruelling, but it was fun."

Seniuk, who died in 2002 at age 56, is remembered by his wife as a fun-loving husband and RCMP member with a quirky sense of humour, especially if he could put an amusing spin on the sometimes preposterous incidents a rural police officer was called upon to investigate. While stationed in Moosomin, SK, for instance, he and another officer dutifully drove out to a farm one evening because a farmer had complained of there being "a

357

large number of owls around," remembers Elsie. "John, ever the joker, got down beneath a window and started hooting. Someone from the house called out, 'Who's there?' to which John replied, 'It's the owl,' creating a scene so ludicrous it caused his partner, Bryan Cafferata, to crack up at the memory for years."

Despite his lightheartedness, Seniuk focused on his goals with determination, even when it felt risky. In the first week of his RCMP training "We were all marched in at the edge of the pool filled with approximately eight or nine feet of water," wrote Seniuk years later, in notes he made in a questionnaire prior to C Troop's thirtieth reunion. "I was asked, 'Swimmer or *non*-swimmer?' I said, 'Non-swimmer.' I stood there for what felt like forever and they *made* me jump in. I knew I was dead."

A farm kid from northern Manitoba who was needed as an extra hand during the seeding, growing, and harvesting seasons, Seniuk rarely had the opportunity to go swimming, says Elsie, who also grew up on a farm outside the same small town. "We got to go to the lake two, maybe three times a summer, and there was no such thing as swimming lessons." Yet within three months, Seniuk had become a strong swimmer with Bronze Medallion level skills by fitting in extra lessons and practice. One night,

John Seniuk taking a rest between shining his boots, "Depot," August 1966.

that meant he was still in the pool at 8:00 p.m. when he was scheduled to be mucking out the RCMP stables. His pit partner, Ken Scheske, covered by answering "present" when Seniuk's name was hollered out at roll call, earning both a visit to the Command Sergeant Major to explain the deception.

Seniuk was equally single-minded about joining the RCMP in the first place, over the strenuous objections of his parents. The farm Seniuk grew up on was just outside of Ethelbert, MB, a service town of approximately 1,500 people, located 360 kilometres northwest of Winnipeg and 60 kilometres north of Dauphin. Every Saturday night it filled up with area farmers eager to catch the latest Elvis Presley movie at its theatre (which is where Elsie and John's first dates took place). Both of Seniuk's parents were immigrants who operated a mixed farm and they were utterly dismayed when their youngest son, who had never travelled more than 120 kilometres from home, announced he was joining the RCMP. At the time, Seniuk thought it was because they wanted him to stay and take over the running of the farm, but with hindsight Elsie wonders if there were other, more complicated reasons. "They came from 'the old country,' as we called it and, there, having anything to do with police was not a good thing. I think that was in the back of their minds. People did not have a high opinion of the police. They didn't accept it until they came to his graduation [and that took a bit of convincing]. They were unhappy when he left, and they were starting to feel the aging part. He was extremely helpful. He'd been working on the farm since he was 10 years old."

Although Seniuk had toiled hard for his parents, had been athletic all his life, excelling as a runner, and had already held a full-time job as a lineman for Manitoba Hydro for two years before joining the RCMP, "I think the whole time he was at 'Depot,' he was concerned he wouldn't make the grade," Elsie says. "He didn't have an easy time going through school. You had to spend so much of your time on the farm working; you didn't have extra time for the books." Yet his strengths were evident while training. In the summer of 1966, Seniuk was instrumental, along with

John Seniuk, "Depot," Regina, 1966.

troop mates Bob Swift, Jack Snoeks, David LeBlanc, Ernie Stagg and Carter MacDonald, in winning C Troop the coveted RCMP "Depot" trophy and medals for the best athletic troop.

Despite his dedication to becoming an RCMP member, Seniuk was none too pleased with the dramatic drop in income that his newly chosen career demanded. Remembering his first few days at "Depot," his notes say that he had been thinking, "What am I doing here, why did I do this? I left my last job making $1,400 a month, clear, and here, $245? My mom told me there'd be days like this!"

"That was a shocker," confirms Elsie. "And it took many years after he graduated before he caught up. But he never regretted it."

In fact, while Seniuk was concerned he would fail training, he was more afraid of having to face friends and family if he fell short of his lofty goal. So, graduation day was a huge triumph, not the least because his parents had overcome their displeasure and attended. "I was very proud. All my family was present. I felt I was on top of the world. I could not believe that I had actually become a police officer. To this day, it still seems like a dream," he wrote.

His first day of work, in the two-man detachment of Langenburg, SK, east of Regina, started with considerably less fanfare. Seniuk drove himself there in full uniform but experienced gas filter problems en route. He drove slowly into town and headed

John and Elsie were married in 1968. John's best man was Ken Scheske, another member of C Troop.

for the local garage first, then walked to the RCMP office located above the old post office—but while it was just 11:30 a.m., it was locked up tight. The lone Corporal/NCO was on patrol and didn't appear for another two hours.

Seniuk's living conditions were just as barren: an 8′ × 10′ room with a bathroom in the same building next door. During his posting, he ate at the town's Chinese restaurant most days, until he was befriended by a local family who shared their dinner table with him.

Eager to make a great impression on his first day patrolling with the official RCMP vehicle, a black, 1965 two-door Dodge, Seniuk was pleased to write his first two traffic tickets, for separate stop-sign violations. Unfortunately, while one recipient was a travelling salesman, the other was the town's mayor. Seniuk's NCO was slightly upset. "They both pleaded not guilty," wrote Seniuk, adding with a palpable tinge of pride: "It was my first time in court. But we convicted both."

However, his other enduring memory of that posting was so tragic he didn't even address it in those pre-thirtieth-reunion notes. "A call came into the detachment that there was a young man who appeared suicidal," says Elsie. "So, they went up to the house. They were already in the home, talking to the parents, when they heard the shot. It was a very difficult experience. The young fellow was in the bedroom, and at first they didn't know where the shot came from. I don't remember John being depressed or anxious or anything like that," she says. "It was just a matter of him and his Corporal talking about it. The thoughts didn't last."

After Langenburg, Seniuk spent most of his career being transferred to small detachments around Saskatchewan, never staying more than two years in any one spot. In Punnichy, north of Regina, Seniuk was a newly married man, and although Elsie was a teacher with her own job, occasionally she was drawn into RCMP activities, too. "Some prisoners had escaped from the cell block, and John was at work on patrol," she says. "I got a phone

John Seniuk spent much of his career at postings in small towns throughout Saskatchewan.

call at home from one of the prisoners, and I couldn't figure out what was going on. I have no idea how he got our phone number. Maybe it was posted on the wall. This prisoner was trying to get help because he didn't want to escape. Whatever he was in for was minor, and he didn't want to get into more trouble. In those days, the guards were retired people who got paid to do the job. Anyway, they rounded them up, and they all got caught."

A posting to Regina Highway Patrol meant that Seniuk's assignments took him outside the city, predominantly running radar, or working general duties on rotating shifts. "For a while, the powers that be decided to run shifts for one month at a time, so you could be on nights from 11:00 p.m. to 7:00 a.m. for a month, and vice versa," says Elsie. "That was difficult for our family because by that time we had a two-year-old and a baby."

One unusual break in routine occurred when the Queen visited Regina and stayed for several days. While the RCMP provided security, the members' wives supplied important additional and unpaid support. "All these guys were assigned areas of the hotel, or floors, but *we* still had to bring them lunch," says Elsie. "There was no arrangement made so they could spot each other off and go get lunch!"

Postings to the towns of Glaslyn, Moosomin, Hafford and Morse followed. Glaslyn was a small, quiet village north of North Battleford, where Seniuk started working on converting an old school bus to a camper in his spare time, a project that allowed Elsie and their two girls to travel frequently over the next few years, often back home to Ethelbert. Those trips meant she never felt isolated in their rural Saskatchewan postings, says Elsie.

In Moosomin, Seniuk ramped up his athletic pursuits, joining the 1,000 Kilometre Club for tracking his running distances and coaching the new men's recreational hockey team.

Hafford was another tiny, two-man detachment in northern Saskatchewan, where Seniuk was given his first post as NCO. His lone staff member was Corporal Lincoln Keough, and though they each shouldered many one-man patrols, during their three years working in the same office the two "became like brothers," wrote Seniuk. Keough was transferred away about eight months before Seniuk received his own transfer. But before that happened, Seniuk received a terrible phone call one evening, telling him that Keough had been killed in a car accident. "I thought this was a joke," wrote Seniuk. "I nearly hung up." In his notes, Seniuk cited that moment as the saddest one he could recall as a policeman.

Aside from that sombre period, Elsie doesn't remember the work in the rural towns being especially stressful for Seniuk, who seemed to take great pride in integrating himself into the farming communities that shared many of the same issues that had been familiar to him growing up on a farm.

"In Morse, a small farming village off the Trans-Canada Highway, John became the rep for Crime Stoppers for farmers in the southwest corner of Saskatchewan," she said. "He did many presentations in surrounding small towns, discussing ways to prevent thefts of farm machinery, and a TV interview in Regina. Moving there was an adventure. Our rental had been sold and we ended up on a farm, five miles out of town. Of course, John loved it. Pretty soon we had two Angus steers, lots of chickens, bunnies, cats and our dog, Sam."

However, both regular and extracurricular RCMP responsibilities were always accompanied by an expectation of all-in commitment. "It didn't matter what number of people were in the detachment, you were often assigned to be far away if roadblocks were needed somewhere," Elsie says, recalling how an Easter

Sergeant John Seniuk always had a prank up his sleeve.

weekend with visiting family was derailed when another prisoner escape occurred nearby. "There was no overtime. Nothing was made of the fact that you'd just done an eight-hour shift and had to get up again at five. You had to put the uniform on again."

By the time Seniuk was transferred to his last detachment, in Watrous, SK, he had been promoted to Sergeant, with less shift work and fewer patrol duties. However, when he was offered a transfer to Meadow Lake at age 45, he decided that his RCMP adventures had satisfied him sufficiently. "I think he'd had enough of small-town issues, of neighbours complaining about neighbours," says Elsie. "In small towns you could make a difference without actually being strict. You had guidelines to follow but you didn't have to be rigid. You could ease off. The difficult part would come when there were issues of whether you were friends with a person. Can you let him go? Sometimes you just can't. And some people didn't take it well. Those things used to bother him, I think."

In retirement, John and Elsie continued to move around often, with Seniuk building new homes at each location. First it was to Yorkton, where he worked in a machine shop, rebuilding motors with skills he'd first acquired while repairing machinery on his family's farm. When their grown daughters settled in Vancouver, the couple moved to Grand Forks, BC, where Seniuk worked as a mechanic at a car dealership. Then it was on to Airdrie, AB, where Elsie worked in special education, and John enjoyed himself immensely with the parks department, looking after trees and greens, and conducting warehouse duties.

In January 2002, John Seniuk died of esophageal cancer. "When he was diagnosed, we wondered if all the time he spent on highway patrol might have been a contributing factor," says Elsie. "In recent years, there's been a number of articles written about why cancer has started in police officers who worked with radar guns in their laps. John was on highway patrol, using a radar gun for two years. The doctors didn't have a possible explanation for his cancer. I often wonder if that could have had anything to do with it."

Although Seniuk attended the thirtieth reunion of his RCMP troop in June 1996, Elsie wasn't able to get away from her end-of-school-year duties to accompany him and meet his friends. At the fiftieth reunion, however, a memorial service was held at the RCMP Chapel at "Depot." The service was conducted by RCMP-GRC Chaplain Jean Morisset and honoured John Seniuk and the other members of the troop who had passed away since leaving training in November 1966. Elsie attended the service, along with Danielle Linfitt, step-daughter of Rod Derouin. "I was very glad I did. Although there were few members or their wives that I recognized, the event was so very enjoyable. Many members

C Troop held its first memorial on the Troop's thirtieth anniversary in the RCMP Chapel at "Depot," Regina, June 10, 1996. On the fiftieth anniversary, it was important to again recognize and remember those who had died. The memorial service was conducted by RCMP Rev. Gene Morrisett and the Chapel was filled with C Troop members, their families, and the families of those whose lives were honoured.

Front row, left to right: Rev. Morrisett, Jerry Forst, Danielle Linfitt, Derk Doornbos, Carter MacDonald, Elsie Seniuk and Michel Laverdière. Middle row: Peter Albertson, David Leblanc, Bob Dolhy, Rick Saville and John Turnell. Back row: Ken Scheske, Bob Swift, Jack Snoeks, Ron Beaucaire, Ron Keeping and Ross Mortlock.

expressed their feelings about John, and I was happy to hear them. I think C Troop was an amazing group."

As for Seniuk himself, the notes he prepared before the thirtieth anniversary in answer to the question, "Can you share some of your most memorable moments as a policeman?" are a permanent record of how much he valued his RCMP experience: "Really, during my entire 25 years, all was very memorable to me. I always felt very proud to be able to wear an RCMP uniform."

—Helen Metella

AFTERWORD

WORK ON THIS BOOK by our troop members and professional writers took approximately two and a half years, and as the editing work was being completed the COVID-19 pandemic crisis became a global reality, as did demonstrations, riots, and protests against racism and inequality across the world.

For many members of our troop, this has recalled the emotions of the 1960s and 1970s, when similar demonstrations surrounding the Vietnam War, the recognition of visible minorities and the rights of individuals took place. During that era, many of our troop members were called to prisons where inmates had rioted over living conditions. On inspection, we too challenged those conditions.

As young policemen, the majority of our troop had little life experience or background as to many of the demonstrations being held; our primary purpose during this tumultuous time was to keep the peace. Our intervention in many of the organized marches and activities was not appreciated, and occasionally riotous activities occurred spontaneously. Many were instigated by peripheral hooligans who had nothing to do with the protests themselves, but used the crowds to blind the police to their activities. The similarities to present-day protests do not go unnoted!

In the 1970s, a number of workshops dealing with First Nations rights and obligations were held. Indigenous people took the opportunity to speak to RCMP members about their traditions and expectations. These sessions were the beginning of an ongoing dialogue and better understanding of values that make up the basic interests and needs of Indigenous people across Canada.

This book is a snapshot in time. During the start of many of our careers, Indigenous people were referred to as "Indians" and the laws we studied were called *The Indian Act*. In time we have come to know that change was needed, and while some progress has been made, there is undoubtedly more to come.

Police work, police/community relations and use of modern crime-solving methods have all changed dramatically since our policing days, and they continue to evolve. It is extremely important for both the policing community and the community as a whole to fully understand the history and historical changes that can divide us, and instead to create situations that encourage progress and positive change.

It is also important that the dream of many police recruits to make the world a better place, to keep the peace and maintain the right, not be forgotten as new recruits embark on their careers. As in our time and the time before us, if this quest for "right" is not balanced with education and improved understanding and support from the community, it can destroy the trust that must be fostered between the police and the community they serve.

Although the police are paid through government funds, that pay comes from the people the police serve, and therefore the police represent the needs of the people rather than the government—a truism that is often lost in public translation. We knew it and we lived it, and we thank you.

We are proud to support the Mounted Police Heritage Centre in its goal of sharing the RCMP's history: the adventures and adversity, the mistakes, mishaps and successes, the tragedies and triumphs—the lives of everyday officers that make up the story of the Force.

—*C Troop*

About the Authors

HELEN METELLA is a former journalist who has written extensively for major Canadian newspapers, the CBC, magazines, and television, on subjects ranging from music to military families, and weight loss to Olympic hockey. She lives in Edmonton, Alberta.

PAMELA COWAN enjoyed reporting at the *Leader-Post* for more than two decades, and her stories appeared frequently in papers across the Postmedia chain. While studying at the University of Regina's School of Journalism, Pamela received numerous awards and scholarships, and she was the recipient of four provincial and national awards for health reporting during her career. She is the author of three books and currently resides in Regina, Saskatchewan, home to the RCMP "Depot" Division.